THE SACRED VAGINA

The
SACRED VAGINA

My Portal into the Soul

F. SAM GLEASON

Library of Congress Control Number: 2020902087
ISBN: 978-0-578-71512-4

BIOGRAPHY AND AUTOBIOGRAPHY / Personal Memoir
RELIGION / Spirituality

Cover Design: Nita K. Alvarez, Alvarez Group
Interior Design: Michelle M. White, MMW Books
Illustrations: Edward L. Rubin, ed@edwardlrubin.com
Editors: Barbara DeSantis, Los Angeles Editors & Writers Group,
    Elana Golden and Roberta Forem
Publishing and Marketing: Susie Schaefer, Finish the Book Publishing

Published by Your Sacred Heart Books

Author Websites: thesacredvagina.com & fsamgleason.com

I dedicate this book to the five women partners
mentioned in these pages, each of whom
has made a weighty and unique contribution
to the evolution of my soul.

*The Sacred Vagina is
the opening in a man's heart,
through which he enters into the life of God
and out of which God is born again
into the world.*

F. Sam Gleason

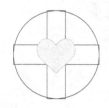

CONTENTS

PART THREE
A SOUL AWAKENS
The Fruits of the Feminine

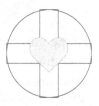

INTRODUCTORY REMARKS

I never dreamed that the breakup of my sixteen-year marriage would be not only the most horrendously painful single event of my life—but also the incident which would shepherd me into the most alive, enriching and meaningful years of my life. From the chaos and tragedy of a failed marriage, a magnificent new order emerged over the next ten years. *The Sacred Vagina* is about "life after death": a journey into the life of my soul, after the death of my marriage. Yes, a phoenix would arise from these ashes.

At the time of the final separation, I had a weak faith, a faint hope, that I would somehow survive this traumatic midlife upheaval. In fact, my suffering did *gradually* steer me into an array of new experiences, both external and internal, resulting in an exciting and entirely new life. I became a very different, indeed a re-created man.

During a four-year celibacy after my wife and I separated, my aching heart drew me inward for answers. Rather than fleeing my suffering, I faced my pain and entered into it, hoping to find the source of my suffering and the purpose of my pain. In the process, I inadvertently uncovered innumerable treasures buried within my soul and my deeper Self.

After my celibacy, I entered into a brief, ten-week liaison with Diana. A month after she broke up with me, I sculpted my heart in clay. Filled with pain and grief, I made a wound-like incision into the moist clay. As I sculpted, this wound was suddenly and mysteriously transformed into a vagina. In an instant, this dazzling, life-affirming symbol of a vagina—indeed a sacred vagina—was imparted to me.

Through that vaginal opening into my heart, a midlife, psycho-spiritual journey into an extraordinary interior kingdom was inaugurated. I began an inner mythic quest to become conscious of who I am. This odyssey into myself was launched when I was forty-three years old.

This sacred vagina became the key symbol for the radical opening of my heart. Through that vaginal orifice, I would be able to more readily give and receive love. Moreover, with this womanly orifice in my heart, I could have frequent intercourse, indeed dialogue, with the mysteries of my soul. Consequently, out of that vagina, some of the abundant "fruits of the feminine" would be birthed into my consciousness.

Over the next five years, a miraculous recovery gradually took place. From the loss of my wife, my home and daily contact with my children, a rebirth of my consciousness and the awakening of my soul transpired. Ultimately, my awakened soul would give birth to my authentic Self: "the birth of God in the soul." Looking back, this was a midlife miracle in slow motion.

This is the story of my soul. Yes, a soul in a book. *The Sacred Vagina* is the saga of my challenging midlife transition and transformation. My purpose in writing this memoir is to share the metamorphosis of my soul with my men and women readers, with the hope they will unearth some of the unimaginable gifts buried within their souls. And I hope they will accept even the darker aspects of their souls, and perhaps discover a divine purpose for everything.

My Dependency Problem

Sigmund Freud believed that men have a dependent (*anaclitic*) style of loving, although their dependency needs are usually unconscious. Even so, men frequently pride themselves on being independent and self-reliant. Yet to the astute observer, a man's need for a woman in his life is often quite strong and most telling. In both my personal life and clinical practice, I have been acutely aware of the significance of this dependency issue in a man's psychology.

In the nine chapters of this book, the symbol of an umbilical cord is used to illustrate my attachments to five women during my adult years. This umbilical cord is a metaphor for my pathological dependency on my first wife and Diana—and later for my healthy, interdependent attachments to Cara, Patricia, and my present wife, Marigrace.

Hence, the thread that runs through this book is dependency, beginning with my symbiotic attachment to my childhood family. After leaving home for college, I began to search, *unconsciously*, for a woman upon whom I might become dependent. I found that woman in college and married her. During our marriage, as might be expected, my childhood dependency problem was activated and transferred onto her. This issue created enormous conflict between my wife and me, and it was fatal for our marriage.

<hr />

After my wife and broke up, I began my midlife quest to find "the one" who would complete me and make me whole. Throughout *The Sacred Vagina*, I use the phrase "the one" to refer to the four distinct "realities," which I came to depend upon.

- Initially, "the one" refers to the one special woman I was seeking.
- Later, "the One" refers to my dependence on my soul.
- After that, "the ONE" refers to my dependence on the Self.
- Finally, "THE ONE" refers to my dependence on the Infinite Mystery, or God.

During my midlife celibacy, I began to dream about "the one" special woman with whom I might fall in love with again. Then, four years after the separation from my wife, I took the first actual steps to find "the one" with whom I might fall in love.

When I met Diana. I quickly became convinced she was "the one" for me. But when she broke off our brief liaison, I realized she was not "the one" for whom I was searching.

A month after that, while sculpting the wound in my heart from the breakup, the wound was transfigured into a vagina. And ten days later, a *Woman-with-No-Head* came to me in a dream. This sacred vagina and the headless dream woman were both images—symbolic manifestations—of my soul. Having encountered these two images, I realized that my soul was "the One" for whom I was actually searching. Thereafter, instead of my wife or Diana, my soul became "the One" I would become dependent upon.

Furthermore, while sculpting the sacred vagina in my heart, I experienced the death and rebirth of my ego-identity. Over a period of many years, my new, conscious self-identity became rooted in the transcendent Self (see Glossary). So then, the Self became "the ONE" that I would depend upon. Indeed, the Self was "the ONE" who would complete me.

The Five Women

In my adult life, five women partners have contributed to the evolution of my soul and the consequent transformation of my life. With three of them, I had a relationship as lovers. The other two, I married: my first wife and my present wife.

Regarding my first wife, my impressions of our marriage presented in this book are, of course, only half the story. My focus is on myself in our marriage, not on her. I describe the struggle to forge my identity not only when still living together but also during the four-year celibacy following our final separation.

After four years of celibacy, I became involved with two women, each of whom played a critical role in my transformation. To protect their privacy, I name the first woman "Cara" and the second "Diana." I selected these names since these convey the core meaning each woman had for my life. Cara was my "beloved friend." Her warm, feminine love played a major role in the resuscitation of my broken heart after my marriage had failed.

A few months after breaking up with Cara, I entered into a liaison with Diana, whose name means "goddess." She was "the one" who provoked the madly romantic projection of my soul onto her. For the first time, I saw my soul outside of myself, in Diana. But with her sudden departure ten weeks later, I was painfully forced to retrieve my soul-projection. Once returned to myself, then my soul could gradually awaken as a goddess-like presence within me.

Five years later, I began an eight-year relationship with Patricia who was, and still is, a significant part of my life, now a best friend. After retrieving my soul projection from Diana, I was able to love Pat for who she *actually* was, not as a figment of my romantic imagination.

Five years after Pat and I broke up, I met and married Marigrace, my second wife, about whom I speak in the Epilogue. With her as my wife, I have now been graced with "the one" who was meant to be my final, human life partner.

Christianity, Carl Jung and Me

In *The Sacred Vagina*, memoir, myth and meaning are deeply intertwined. My memoir is personal, yet it becomes everyone's story because of its archetypal, mythic components. Through the intermingling of memoir and myth, I have found meaning for my life. Now, I realize I am a part of a larger story.

References to the Christian myth and the psychology of Carl Jung appear throughout this book. These two frameworks are the skeleton upon which the flesh of my saga is hung.

As a child, I was taught that the Christian God is all-perfect and masculine. And I believed the Christian story literally. Yet as an adult, I began to see the limitations of this concept of God. By midlife, evil and the feminine had become a part of my experience and understanding of God, as an imperfect and androgynous deity.

In this book, I describe my struggle to accept and integrate my personal shadow—and Christianity's long-repressed, very dark shadow—as an individual who harbors both personal and archetypal evil in the distant corners of his soul. Within my soul, I find an imperfect "gray God," who is neither purely good (white) nor purely evil (black), but both.

Furthermore, with the arrival of the inner feminine into my consciousness at midlife, my father's patriarchal God gradually becomes feminized within me and evolves into an "androgynous God." As a result of this metamorphosis, my spiritual life has been greatly enriched by the experience of the feminine side of God.

I am thankful my parents bequeathed me their faith, although they believed it literally. In contrast, the Christian myth eventually *happened* to me symbolically, as I was struggling to find the purpose of my life. Over many years of interior experience and reflection, the

Christian myth has unfolded within me, vastly expanding my inner life; to be sure, it has given meaning to my life. (See Glossary for more information about my understanding of the Christian myth and myth in general.)

The Christian myth has been the central orienting framework within my psyche; and it is the story that has shaped my spiritual quest. For me, the Christian story is primarily one of *internal* transformation, although frequently not recognized as such—especially by those who believe it literally. This book describes how my personal narrative and this archetypal myth intermingle within me, thereby giving direction and purpose to my life.

In a non-literal fashion, four Christian symbols have become especially meaningful to me. Each represents a part of me:

- The Virgin Mary = the heart, the inner feminine, the soul, the *anima* (Latin), and Anima which refers to my soul as if she were a person
- The Christ = the Self (the archetype of wholeness within a person)
- The Incarnation = individuation (becoming conscious of the inner Christ/Self)
- The Crucifixion, or sacrifice, of one's ego-identity and its resurrection into a greater, conscious wholeness (the archetype of death and rebirth)

As will become clear, these four symbols are the cornerstone of my self-understanding. They are embedded in my life experience, rooted in my soul, anchored in the earth.

When I use the word "God," I am not referring to my childhood understanding of God as a loving parent, "a loving consciousness in the sky." And I do not use this word in the usual Christian or even necessarily non-Christian sense. Instead, I am referring to the Infinite Mystery that permeates Everything: a mysterious Indwelling Presence, and the mystery of the Infinite Universe surrounding us. (For more information about my notion of God, the soul and other terms used in this book, see the Glossary at the end of the book.)

In addition to the Christianity of my childhood, the psychology of Carl Jung has been the second most important orienting framework, during my adult years, especially by helping me discover the spiritual value of the Christian myth. Although I was first exposed to Jung while in seminary in my mid-twenties, I did not read his *Collected Works* until I was thirty-eight years old, after my wife and I had separated. However, in *The Sacred Vagina*, I do not attempt to present Jung's understanding of Christianity. Rather, I present a description of my experience of this faith, as a result of having read about some of Jung's unique ideas regarding the Christian myth.

Jung's radical reinterpretation of various Christian symbols has greatly assisted me in perceiving and naming some of these realities within my soul. His ideas on particular Christian symbols, which had become meaningless to me, have guided me to re-experience these as meaningful and life-enhancing. Regarding the Virgin, the Christ, the Incarnation, and the death and rebirth of one's ego-identity, and God, Jung has helped me experience these as expansive and life-giving.

In addition, Jung's map of the soul has been extraordinarily useful in helping me experience and understand the shadow, the *anima* and the Self as parts of myself. Through these concepts, he has furthered my self-understanding.

For Jung, the unconscious Self contains the totality of everything innate within a human being. The Self is the *image of God* within each person. As such, the Self is the archetype of God's wholeness and the source of the individual's wholeness.

For Jung, the central task of human life is individuation: the task of becoming conscious of unconscious facets of the Self. This psycho-spiritual process is about becoming the unique individual, the distinct self, each of us is destined to become.

Personal Source Materials

Throughout my adult life and career, thankfully I have taken time to journal my struggles and sorrows, seeking to explore and know myself more deeply. In that process, I have written down many of the most important details of both my inner and outer life. Through journaling, I have given expression to my feelings, thoughts and night-time dreams, in an effort to better understand the deeper aspects of myself. And as a consequence, I have become more conscious in my interpersonal relationships. As a form of self-therapy, this kind of journaling has been profoundly healing.

While writing this book, my journals have been extremely useful in recalling the details of many events or numerous ideas which occurred or were thought decades earlier. At times, I quote a sentence from my journal, which conveys my feeling or thought at the time.

But other parts of the book are from memory since I failed to journal some external events, even a few very important ones. Of course, my memory of these incidents three decades ago is *incomplete* at best. Additionally, *selective* memory is always a factor in telling one's story, even if an event occurred just yesterday. In spite of these limitations, I have attempted to convey my memories accurately and truthfully. In sum, I have written this book with the intent of portraying events in my outer life and describing my internal experiences, using both my journals and my memory.

Background of This Book

For thirty years, I have wanted to write this book. For several reasons, I chose not to pen this midlife memoir until I retired. For one thing, while working full-time, I did not have the time or the energy to craft my memories and journal materials into a book.

Furthermore, as a mental health professional working in a large public institution, I felt I could not truthfully disclose my inner experiences and honestly reveal some of the events in my outer life, for fear of damaging my career. But now retired, I am no longer fearful of divulging the intimate details of my life. My hope is that my transparency about my private life will be useful to others who are struggling with similar issues.

Finally, I am old enough not to care very much about what others think of me. So, I write with no particular concern for my professional reputation or personal ego. Now, I write about my flawed humanity, perhaps imperfections shared by many of my readers. This book is about allowing my mask, my persona, to crumble, fall away and decay. I dig up forsaken aspects of myself, yet in the process, I unearth much inner gold. My most prized treasures have always been found within the dark depths of my soul.

My Use of Quotations

Throughout this book, I incorporate quotations that are personally meaningful to me. I use these brief quotes to exemplify what was happening in my heart: to echo events within my soul, at the time. I have been deeply touched by these expressions since the truth of each has reverberated in the remote corners of my soul.

Most frequently, I quote Jung and the Bible. Most of Jung's quotes can be found in his *Collected Works* (Princeton University Press, 1953-1979), *The Red Book* (W. W. Norton & Company, 2009), and in his *Answer to Job* (1952).

Throughout this book and in the Glossary, I present *my* understanding of Jung's terminology. This is a memoir, not an academic book intended to precisely convey Jung's concepts.

When quoting biblical verses, I quote passages relevant to my life experiences, which express profound, psycho-spiritual truths. I have chosen different versions of the Bible for specific verses. With every passage, my personal preference has guided my selection of the translation, which renders a given verse most simply and meaningfully to me.

Most of the other quotes, I have retrieved from my quotations file. Some of these have inspired me for many years, whereas others I recalled while writing this book. In addition, I searched the Internet when I needed a remark fitting for the subject I was writing about.

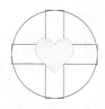

PROLOGUE

My Childhood Family Womb:
The Uncut Umbilical Cord

Like every human being, my life began in my mother's womb. As a young man, I frequently joked that I was conceived on Easter Sunday afternoon in 1944, after my father, a minister, had preached his sermon that April 9th morning.

By the sixth week, my heartbeat was likely detectable: now two hearts beating, not just one. Totally dependent upon my mother via the umbilical cord, I received all the nutrients and oxygen necessary for life. In the warmth of her womb, I developed into a normal, almost full-term baby.

I was delivered from my mother's womb thirty-seven weeks later in late December, 1944. I took my first breath, no longer dependent upon her for oxygen. I nursed at her breast. The umbilical cord was cut and the placenta discharged.

Looking back, although I matured and slowly separated from my mother, I remained overly attached to her *and* to my family throughout childhood and adolescence. When I married in my early twenties, this unconscious, dependent attachment was transferred from my childhood family onto my wife. Into my marriage, I unknowingly brought a dependent boy, although I thought myself a mature and independent man. This *psychological* umbilical cord would remain uncut until my sixteen-year dependency on my wife was broken by our final separation.

Growing Up

As I was growing up, my parents endeavored to foster independence within me. My mother required my three sisters and me—second born—to do chores, so that we would become responsible. Our parents punished us for our misbehaviors, holding us accountable for our actions. As we became older, my mother sent us to overnight summer camps for increasingly longer periods of time. Yet in spite of my parents' best efforts to promote autonomy, I failed to become emotionally self-reliant.

Since my parents had married for the first time in their late thirties—coupled with the fact theirs was not the closest of marriages—perhaps they became overly invested in the lives of their children, thereby stunting our growth and development.

Or maybe my unresolved dependency problem was the result of their love for me. Even though hugs and declarations of "I love you" were not frequent, I never doubted my parents' love. Even when they disapproved of my misbehaviors, their love was unshaken.

I now believe I was overprotected as a child: spoiled by my parents' constant attention and kindness. Living in this womb of unconditional love, I became a dependent child. Even though my parents were not especially critical or rejecting of me as a child, as a dependent adult, I would experience deep feelings of rejection with my first wife. Feeling rejected would play the major role in the demise of our marriage.

Maybe if more differences of opinion and overt friction between family members had been tolerated by my parents, during my teenage years, I could have more easily fought my way out of that nurturing womb. But anger was "not Christian." Consequently, I could not use anger as a tool for emotionally separating myself from my parents.

When I was sixteen and upset, the closest I ever came to being angry at my parents was the time when I loudly threatened to join the Marine Corps. Looking back, had I joined, I would have been chewed up and spit out by the Marines.

My childhood family, a warm and nurturing womb, smothered the development of an independent identity. The umbilical cord tying me to them—and later attaching me to my wife—would remain uncut until my wife and I separated when I was thirty-eight years old.

Likewise, I was deeply entangled in, and became totally dependent upon, my parents' Christian beliefs and practices. Their religious faith played the dominant role in our home. For us, family and Christianity were synonymous, seemingly identical.

Later, in college and seminary, I would dissect, piece by piece, their traditional Christian belief in a transcendent God. Yet eventually, I would discover an immanent—a "here and now"—God, with whom I could intimately relate. And I would unearth some of Christianity's profound mythic meaning and salvific value for my life.

My parents were not particularly psychologically evolved or savvy, although extremely well-intentioned. Their Christian faith, especially my father's, was the sole solution to life's many problems. As a child, I imagined my father's God to be a loving parent, a loving consciousness in the sky, who could remedy anything and everything.

Growing up, I strongly identified with my father, a Presbyterian minister, and his Christianity. He repeatedly and endearingly reminded me of the Hebrew meaning of my name Samuel: "called by God," from the Old Testament story. We were taught that God loved us. Never once were the words "hellfire and damnation" spoken by my parents.

Yet as a Christian minister, my father had great difficulty accepting his humanness and owning his earthly nature. Consequently, in college and seminary, I began the lengthy search for my identity, which included embracing my animal nature—the biological ground of my humanity—and other aspects of my humanness neglected by my father.

Furthermore, I began the arduous task of differentiating myself from my father and his *patriarchal* God "in the sky." While in college, instead of reactively arguing with him about the Christian concept of God and trying to convince him of my point of view, I gradually learned to calmly assert my ideas by saying, "Dad, I see it differently."

While in seminary searching for God, I looked inward hoping to find God within my soul. In this endeavor, I became dangerously introverted and almost drowned in an interior abyss—a dark nothingness. Yet because of this dark journey into the depths of my soul as a young man, at midlife I was able to experience a mysterious, Indwelling Presence whose essence was *matriarchal*.

Until I became more aware of my dependency problem later in my marriage, I thought my mother and I had a healthy relationship. I saw no issues. When I was sixteen, I briefly dis-identified with my father and regressed into an interior maternal womb. A few months later, this regression resolved itself. However, looking back, I realize that I had an unhealthy, unconscious dependence on my mother, suggestive of a "mother complex."

Living with a mother and three sisters—and having a father whose primary focus was on family and our religious life—my childhood was flooded with feminine energy. Unlike my friends' dads, my father had no interest in sports or the stock market. With so little focus on masculine interests, I would have difficulty forging my identity as a man.

———— •♥• ————

Our family's many enjoyable recreational—and at the time, meaningful religious—activities also promoted dependency. For recreation, every Monday, my father's day off, we hiked or sledded in one of Louisville's (Kentucky) many large public parks or had other fun activities in the community. We ended the afternoon by having supper at a diner, a special event in the 1950s. Each summer, the six of us took a three-week family vacation.

Religious activities included my father saying a blessing at every meal, including breakfast, as we four children were rushing off to school with books in hand. Each morning, my parents prayed together in the privacy of their bedroom. Every night, we had dinner together, followed by "family prayers": reading from a children's Bible storybook and praying aloud. Each Sunday, we all went to Sunday school and church. Every summer, we attended Vacation Bible School. Our family identity was that of a "loving Christian family."

These Christian practices and beliefs inhibited the development of strong, independent identities. My sisters and I were not trailblazing individuals. Instead, we were members of the Christian flock. I was *not* encouraged to think for myself: to explore my unique ideas and formulate my own religious beliefs. Furthermore, our biological natures and negative emotions were mostly ignored. After all, we were "Christians." As a member of the Christian flock, I became profoundly dependent upon my parents' unquestioned belief in a transcendent Christian God.

My parents' inadvertent promotion of reliance on the family, and on their Christian beliefs and practices, fostered unhealthy dependencies within me. I was not only dependent on my childhood family but I was also dependent upon the collective view of the all-perfect, male Christian God, as a loving consciousness in the sky.

———•♥•———

Growing up, I did not acquire from my family the psychological awareness and skills necessary for developing a secure, masculine identity. My primary tool for establishing my identity was by trying to hide or suppress everything that did not fit into my parents' Christian framework. I attempted to paste on the facade of a good Christian boy.

This approach left me with what I would later call my "Christianized ego," my persona of goodness and love. My ego-identity was sanitized: evil and the darker aspects of life were "other" than I. Devilish traits were not qualities I possessed.

But not surprisingly, I began to act out in elementary school. My misdeeds were a reaction to the demands that I behave like a proper preacher's son. I lit several small fires in dry weed fields, skinned an old woman's sapling with my new pocketknife, and shot a neighbor girl in the neck with a rubber band-fired paperclip.

With Jerry, my best friend, I threw a water balloon into the open window of a passing car, which hit the pregnant passenger. Her husband chased me home. As would be my luck, she and her husband had just joined my father's church. My father spanked me with a belt: one of only two occasions in my life. Most definitely "a little devil" lived within me, in spite—or perhaps because—of my Christian upbringing. Acting out was my forte. My parents were frequently aghast.

———•♥•———

Yet during my teenage years, I became deeply introverted. I turned inward into massive confusion and deep feelings of inadequacy. The neglected and disowned aspects of my psyche from childhood resulted in an abysmal teenage inferiority complex.

Now, my aggression was no longer "acted out" in the neighborhood. Instead, my anger was "acted in" toward myself, in the form of self-hatred and low self-esteem. I faced my inner darkness alone, without parental or professional help. Sadly, in the late 1950s and early 1960s, therapy was not a commonly sought-out resource, especially for a minister's family.

Additionally, my anger was expressed as hostility toward my two younger sisters. I teased them mercilessly, giving them "frogs" (a knuckle to the upper arm), among a myriad of other immature, mean behaviors. I was desperately trying to compensate for my feelings of inferiority. For some reason, I hassled my oldest sister the least.

In my twenties, I apologized to my middle sister since I felt especially guilty for the way I had treated her. Then by midlife, I realized that I had teased her because she was an extremely sensitive child. As a teenager, I did not want to be like her: delicate and vulnerable, more feminine qualities. In my attempt to be *tough like a man*, I was cruel to her, unconsciously trying to fight off and suppress my own very sensitive nature.

For most of my adult life, I thought my youngest sister and I were quite close. She always laughed with me when we joked about my adolescent teasing of her. Yet in recent years, I learned that she had been deeply wounded by my periodic bullying. Now, she revealed the depth of her pain. Her laughter had been a disguise.

I knew my teasing was "not Christian." And my parents firmly reprimanded me. Fortunately, I had outgrown most of this behavior by my late teenage years.

On my own, I struggled to embrace and integrate not only my aggression but also my sexuality. In the privacy of my bedroom, I masturbated and felt good about it. Only in private did my sexuality became a healthy part of me, without guilt. But to express my sexuality openly was "not Christian." Even though I had prolific masturbatory fantasies about attractive females, I was too shy to become sexual with a girl.

Early in my college years, I realized that a loving God would not have created me with a sex drive, if He had not intended for me to enjoy sex. Only a cruel God would create me as an inherently sexual being and then expect me to feel guilty about my sexuality.

I dealt with my "unchristian" sexuality and aggression in the only ways I knew how. Yet inwardly, I was a confused and troubled adolescent. I felt profoundly insecure and deficient. Given my dependent nature, I felt inferior to most of my more masculine peers.

———•♥•———

As a part of my quest for my adolescent identity, I attempted to understand the partial truth in every person's point of view. But in college, I thought this openness to different viewpoints made me "wishy-washy," or "spineless, like a jellyfish." Yet through my inner exploration, and partially from the differing perspectives of others, I eventually synthesized a fragile sense of self.

Growing up, my overt identity was that of a Christian, not as a man or a person. This hollow sense of self—which had *not* openly and fully integrated my aggressive and sexual instincts, unpleasant emotions and other "negative" aspects of my humanness—resulted in a weak ego. Underneath this frail façade remained a highly fragmented and dependent young man.

I was socially awkward in groups, although I had one good friend next door. Two years of rigorous weightlifting helped me feel better but only about my body. Furthermore, I was flunking out of a large public high school. So, for the last two years before college, my parents placed me in a private day school for boys. By the end of the first semester in this prep school, I was third in my class of thirty. Now, I felt good about my body and my intellect. In spite of that, I still felt inwardly inferior—as a person, as a man.

With a weak ego-identity, I was not equipped to deal with life's normal challenges, especially that of leaving home and becoming independent. The umbilical cord of dependency firmly yoked me to my childhood family and its faith. I was slow to separate from the warm and nurturing womb of this Christian home. Growing up in this uncommonly protected family womb delivered me into adulthood immature and emotionally crippled. Going off to college would be a colossal challenge for me.

Somehow, on my own, I would have to forge an identity as a self-confident man. My identity was yet to be hammered out from the disparate components of my family, their Christianity, my instinctual nature and my innate and unique humanness.

Leaving Home: College and Seminary

Unlike many others, my childhood was not the rough portion of my life. The tough part was leaving that warm family nest. After leaving home, I discovered that the rest of the world was not nearly as kind to and supportive of me, as my parents had been. At times, I found the extra-familial world to be cold, intimidating and frightening—even cruel.

I had always regarded my childhood family as "close and warm." But in fact, my childhood home was a maternal womb from which it was difficult to expel myself. When I left for college, I was delivered only halfway from that family womb. I had not psychologically separated sufficiently from my family and established my identity as a man, so I could stand confidently on my own two feet.

Fortunately, my only college acceptance letter came from a small liberal arts school, although I had applied to two larger universities. In this church-related, supportive college family in small-town Ohio, I gradually began to feel at home.

At The College of Wooster, I started dating my wife-to-be when I was a junior and she was a freshman. Eighteen months later, we became engaged.

After obtaining my B.A. degree, I felt anxious and frightened, as I thought about moving into the larger world. I wanted to marry before starting graduate school in New York City. Even though I very much wanted to attend Union Theological Seminary, I definitely did not want to move to NYC alone. The thought of living in that large, impersonal city by myself frightened me. Clearly, I lacked self-confidence.

So, as a young man not yet conscious of his dependency problem, what did I do? After graduating from college in June, I had managed to marry by summer's end. I was twenty-two years old; my wife was nineteen, three days shy of twenty. I loved my wife and was filled with excitement as we embarked upon our marital journey—an adventure I believed would last a lifetime.

When I married, I thought I was a man. And physically, I looked like a man. But unconsciously, I harbored a dependent boy within me, still bound to his childhood family by that uncut umbilical cord. After a two-week honeymoon on Nantucket Island, my wife and I moved into the seminary dorm for married couples. Thankfully, I would not have to live by myself in that daunting metropolis.

As a married man, I consciously believed I had married for the comforts of a close relationship. Yet unbeknownst to me, I had transferred my unresolved dependency needs onto my wife. Retrospectively, this meant marriage was a place where I could hide out, at least for a while, from my dependency problem. I had left behind the womb of my childhood family; but now, my marriage became a replacement.

Unconsciously, I wanted to be enmeshed in another "close and warm" womb. Apparently, I preferred the regressive safety of a marriage that would replicate the womb of my childhood family. Intimacy with a woman was my focus, not my independent identity. Although unaware at the time, I did not want to grow up and become a self-reliant man.

I did bring my warmth into our marriage. Along with my warmth, I dragged that dependent boy. Yes, I was warm, but I was also weak. "Warm but weak" described who I was. At midlife, looking back on myself as a young man, I was able to see my extreme weakness and neediness: my lack of a strong masculine identity. Yes, when I married, that umbilical cord was still uncut. My self-diagnosis: a dependent personality.

PART ONE

THE DEATH OF A MARRIAGE

＊♥＊

Midway along the journey of my life,
I awoke to find myself in a dark wood,
for I had lost my way.

OPENING LINE,
THE DIVINE COMEDY,
DANTE

CHAPTER 1

MY MARRIAGE

A Crucible for Self-Discovery

For even as love crowns you
so shall he crucify you.
Even as he is for your growth
so is he for your pruning....
All these things shall love do unto you
that you may know the secrets of your heart.

GIBRAN

My wife and I separated for the last time in March 1983, when I was thirty-eight years old. At the time, I was enrolled in the PhD program in marriage and family counseling at the University of Southern California. A month after separating, I was registered for a required, early-morning class. One typical Tuesday, I drove the usual thirty miles from my rented room into downtown Los Angeles for this twice-a-week, 8 a.m. lecture.

As a graduate student, I had an on-campus parking permit. On this overcast Southern California morning, I drove my 1972 Corolla into my assigned parking structure. The lot was almost full, but I found a spot in the center of the roofless top floor.

With books and notebook in hand, I got out of my car and locked the door. Since I was in the middle of the rooftop area, I walked toward the corner where the elevator was located. As I strolled, I felt the damp morning air brush across my face.

As I neared the elevator and was within an arm's length of the waist-high safety wall around the edge, I suddenly felt an impulse to jump off this five-story building! Seemingly out of nowhere, I felt a strong urge to leap to my death.

But simultaneously, one of my legs resisted the impulse to jump. My left leg tightened, as if it wanted to stop me from climbing over the edge and jumping. The manifestation of this suicidal impulse—and then the protective cramping of my left leg—were both entirely unexpected and involuntary.

I hesitated and was suddenly aware of two things: apparently, I wanted to die—but something was blocking the impulse to jump. For some reason, my leg had stiffened, causing me to think twice and step back from the waist-high wall. In that instant, my body chose not to die. Shaken and confused, I took the elevator down to the ground floor and walked to class.

Even though quite depressed about the separation from my wife, I had absolutely no idea that I was feeling suicidal. I had no conscious desire to kill myself. Yet in the unconscious, the thought, "I want to die," was indisputably present.

———•♥•———

As the day passed, the inflexibility of my left leg worsened. Over the next several days, this progressed into a semi-paralysis. By the weekend, my leg was severely incapacitated: most of my leg's usual strength had evaporated. I was acutely aware of every step, as I began to walk with an obvious limp.

Fortuitously, that same Tuesday evening, I had my weekly "psycho-motor" therapy group. The therapist, Dick, was highly skilled in this healing modality. During the last two years before our final separation, he had counseled both my wife and me individually. This group approach to healing entailed working with the body as a method for dealing with intensely painful emotions rooted deep within the psyche, within the body.

This group was the perfect place for the treatment of my depression and for my now-partially paralyzed leg. At that time in my life, being in a bodywork group was truly providential.

But what was the meaning of this paralysis?

That morning, I became acutely aware of an internal struggle between my suicidal depression and this life-saving paralysis in my left leg. Inwardly, a fierce battle was being fought between death and life. That evening, after working with me for a while, Dick suggested my paralyzed leg was the part of me that wanted to live. In fact, it had stopped me from jumping. Instantly, I knew this was true. I broke into tears. I was relieved.

This partial crippling of my left leg got my full attention. Loud and clear, it had screamed out an opposing point of view: "Do not kill yourself!" Psyche had blessed me by bringing this internal conflict abruptly into my awareness—through this dramatic kinesthetic reaction, with this convincing metaphoric symptom. That involuntary paralysis saved my life.

On that rooftop, my body had boldly declared "Life!" I could *not* have argued with my left leg. The instant my leg stiffened, the part of me that wanted to kill myself lost the battle. The survival instinct triumphed over an unconscious death wish, hence averting a suicide.

Being in the mental health field, I soon realized this was a hysterical paralysis, a conversion reaction. Excruciating emotional pain had been converted into a protective physical symptom. Thankfully, psyche interceded by producing a symptom contrary to the impulse to kill myself.

My psyche not only grabbed but also held my attention for an extended time. For more than two years, the disabled condition of my left leg was a constant physical reminder that I wanted to live. Even though my leg gradually strengthened, three years would pass before it would be totally free of weakness and feel entirely normal.

That deadly impulse—and the simultaneous life-saving paralysis of my left leg—startled me into a state of hyper-awareness. From that moment forward, the Life Force pointed me in an altogether new direction—toward a growing optimism.

———•♥•———

Five years later, I would discover how to kill myself *symbolically*, instead of literally. My life as I knew it, my marriage, was ending. I was hurting and in great pain. Like all persons who feel suicidal, at some level I wanted to be put out of my misery, freed from the agony.

My impulse to jump was a *literal* approach to bringing an end to my anguish, which most likely would have been fatal. Instead, on that Tuesday morning, I was prompted to endure my suffering, then hoping I could survive the pain.

At the time of the impulse to jump, I was unaware that a death of some type would still be required. Five years after that gloomy Tuesday morning, I would sculpt my broken heart in clay with a wound-like incision into the center. In that process, I would inadvertently experience a symbolic death. This sculpting experience would mark the beginning of a radically new life for me. The psyche required another kind of dying from which I could be reborn.

MARITAL RETROSPECTIVE

Nine years before that suicidal impulse, my wife and I had moved from Illinois to California with our two young children: our not-quite three-year-old son, and our three-month-old daughter. Within two months of our arrival, we were able to purchase our first small house. Although a severe national recession was in progress, we personally experienced none of it.

Previously, on the East Coast and in Illinois, I had worked as a student chaplain at the South Carolina State Hospital, and later at the Brooklyn Methodist Hospital in New York City. In Illinois, I interned for a year as a pastoral counselor at a community mental health center.

We came to California, so I could attend the California Family Study Center for an MA degree in counseling. Throughout the work week, I eagerly anticipated my Saturday classes. The classes were quite stimulating, both academically and interpersonally. At the end of the day, I returned home, inundated with exciting new ideas and insights.

At thirty, I was eager to learn about the dynamics of couple conflicts; and I wanted to understand my own internal struggles. With more insight into our marriage and myself, I became aware of how my internal issues contributed to the conflict in our marriage. During my entire career, I never lost sight of how intrapsychic problems contribute to interpersonal conflict.

Three years after coming to California, I had finally arrived! I had a wife and two small children, a wonderful family. We owned our home. I had a job I liked, now with the appropriate graduate degree. I had created a family and established my career. And I had new friends from my graduate program. As a young man, I had everything I wanted.

At thirty-three, I felt completely content. Everything was seemingly perfect. In California, I had found my West Coast paradise. I truly believed no earthshaking challenges would ever erupt in the future. I had reached life's pinnacle.

Yet I soon discovered I had not been on the mountaintop. Little did I know, this was but a plateau of contentment, situated on frightfully shaky ground. Over the next six years, the earth-shattering events in our marriage would leave my life in shambles. Thereafter, I would regard every period of tranquility in my life as simply another plateau on a challenging journey to a peak, which I would never reach.

Our Marriage

Even though our marriage worked fairly well, and I was mostly satisfied, periodic conflicts would erupt. Even so, after a few days, things would get resolved and return to normal.

Fortunately, my wife and I had common values and interests, and similar ideas about money. Even though we had different roles in our marriage, I believe ours was egalitarian. And each was faithful to the other.

When our children were quite young, my wife and I got on the same page—as a parenting team—in our limit-setting. And during the evenings, we shared childrearing responsibilities: feeding, bathing and putting the children to bed. On the weekends, we had many fun family activities, both at home and in the community.

My wife *seemed* fairly content. About 1977, she started teaching part time at our children's preschool, which got her out of the house and back into her profession.

The Decline of the Marriage

After ten years of marriage, my wife started therapy with "Helen," a therapist at our church counseling center. As an adult, this was her first individual therapy. At first, I was thankful for this since I thought counseling would help her deal with unresolved childhood issues. And privately, I wished she would address some of *her* behaviors in our marriage that were problematic *from my point of view.*

About a year later, my wife woke up one Monday morning, having undergone a profound psychological change. My extremely conscientious wife told me in an almost inaudible voice, "I can't get out of bed. . . . I can't go to work." Clearly, something was terribly wrong. She was physically weak, lethargic and spoke very little. I did not go to work that week.

For a month, I did most of the cooking and dishwashing after I got home from work. She stayed in her robe for several weeks. I escorted her from our bedroom to the dinner table. I took charge of putting the children to bed, with her help, and got them ready for school the next day.

I had not foreseen my wife's seemingly sudden onset of a major depression, even though I was a mental health professional. Immediately, she began brief phone therapy with Helen. No medication was required or prescribed.

Over the next several months, my wife regained her footing. She resumed her daily routines and returned to her part-time teaching job. She continued her therapy with Helen. She made progress working through some of her childhood unhappiness. Her old self returned, but was undoubtedly deepened by this depressive episode.

———— •♥• ————

Soon, I learned that my wife was starting to address her dissatisfaction with our marriage. I was frustrated with some of our interactions, but I did not realize the extent of her unhappiness. I became aware that her major disappointment was not from childhood, but was now with our relationship. Suddenly, she was questioning the viability of our marriage.

After a year of therapy, my wife asked me to move out of the house. At her request, I saw her therapist once. But I refused a second session. And I declined Helen's referral to another counselor. After all, I had been in a year of individual therapy and a year of group therapy when we lived in New York City. In truth, I was angrily denying the fact that my wife no longer wanted the marital status quo.

Several phone calls from her therapist, and a visit to our home by our minister, focused on whether or not we should separate. But at this time, we remained together.

————•♥•————

A year later, my wife entered the same graduate program in marriage and family therapy from which I had graduated three years earlier. Before long, there would be two therapists in the marriage, not just one.

Even though she taught elementary school in Illinois and preschool in California, my wife was gradually drawn into the mental health field. From the California Family Study Center, she received her MA in 1981. After licensure, she combined her educational and therapeutic skills for the rest of her career, teaching troubled high school students in various residential treatment facilities.

In all probability, my wife seeking therapy—and entering a graduate program for therapists—reflected her search for solutions to our marital problems. She was the one who had the courage to take the first step by seeking professional help.

Marriage Counseling

At the graduate school, my wife sought out additional therapy with one of the faculty. Several months later, her therapist, Dick (the same "Dick" referred to earlier), requested that I participate in counseling with her. By this time, I was no longer in denial. I readily consented.

Initially, Dick saw us jointly for a few sessions. But he quickly decided to see us separately, I suspect because of the high level of conflict between us. For the two years before our final separation, both my wife and I had individual, weekly sessions with him.

Having the same impartial therapist made me hopeful that our marriage might be salvaged. I received support and gained insight into myself, as I struggled to understand our marriage. We both made progress as we began to better comprehend the repetitive, conflicted dynamics in our relationship.

But at home, the conflict intensified. And for me, chaos reigned internally. I was struggling to fathom my troubled emotions and was attempting to change myself, so our marriage might work. After a while, I no longer knew who I was.

We did have two brief separations before the final one. For two weeks, I lived at a Motel 6. A year later, I rented an apartment for two months, a few miles from our home.

My Part of the Problem

During my individual therapy sessions, Dick would ask, "What's your part of the problem?" He must have asked that question in a hundred different ways. He was trying to help me become aware of my role in the marital conflict. I replied, "I grew up in a happy home," unbroken by divorce. Furthermore, twelve years into our marriage, I now felt more mature, self-confident and independent. I saw myself as mostly problem-free.

In contrast, my wife had come from a "broken" home: her parents had separated when she was three years old. I thought my wife's childhood problems—coupled with the fact she wanted me to move out of the house—made *her* the problem partner.

Yet even as a young therapist, I knew couples' theory asserted that *each* partner always plays an *equal* part in a conflicted relationship. In other words, it takes two to tango. But in our case, I was blind to my part in our pathological dance, not yet aware of my deficiencies.

On the positive side, my wife's childhood, single-parent family situation had forced her to become independent. Her mother worked full time while rearing four small children by herself. So, as a child, my wife learned to be self-sufficient and survive on her own.

———————

Through lengthy therapy with Dick, I gradually came to realize—to truly believe—that half the marital problem was mine. I was as much a part of the disharmony in our marriage as my wife, if not more so. With his help, I became aware of a significant deficit in my childhood home. I discovered that my idealized childhood family was also "broken," but not by divorce.

My family was "broken" because it had rendered me dependent and ill-equipped for adulthood. In contrast to my wife's family—which prematurely forced self-sufficiency—my parents had failed to breed independence within me. In opposite ways, our childhood homes were equally deficient.

The deficiencies of our childhood homes were complementary: my enmeshed family retarded the development of independence, whereas my wife's disengaged family did not provide enough time for her to be dependent. From my point of view, she was excessively independent and I was unacceptably dependent. For us, psychological opposites had attracted.

As such, ours was a symbiotic marriage. We each lacked an important character trait which the other possessed. I was deficient in the ability to be independent; and my wife was deficient in the capacity to be dependent. In effect, we each compensated for the quality absent in our partner. In other words, two half people—united in marriage—made for one whole person.

As a dependent male with an independent wife, our gender roles were reversed. During my teenage and college years, I had disidentified with my father, resulting in a weak masculine identity. So perhaps, I took on more of my mother's feminine role. Often, women are seen as the more dependent of the two sexes. But in our marriage, I was decidedly the more dependent partner.

My love for my wife was pathologically dependent and regressive. With therapy, I slowly became acutely aware of this problem, and even more so after our final separation.

My primary deficiency was an unresolved dependency problem. I thought I was independent. But in fact, I lacked a strong masculine identity: emotional strength and self-sufficiency. Yes, I suffered a "mother complex," although it felt more like a "family complex"—overly-dependent on my childhood family, not just my mother.

Marital Dynamics

At such a young age and after a lengthy courtship, partner selection is almost never an accident. The psyche of each partner has an unconscious agenda that seeks to remedy individual deficiencies. Each partner is unknowingly guided to find his/her missing half; each is drawn toward a quality in the other which compensates for a weakness within oneself.

In our case, my wife and I—while we were dating—were unconsciously attracted to each other for yet-to-be-discovered reasons. The then-unknown plot of our marital drama was still to unfold, was yet to be enacted.

As we were dating, I became attracted to my wife's "regal" nature. I saw her as stately and strong, at least in contrast to myself. As a man unaware of his dependency problem, I had unconsciously selected a very independent woman. Dependent women, who were more like myself, were not the least bit appealing to me.

Yet shortly after we married, I began to resent my wife's independence—the very quality which had initially attracted me to her. I came to perceive my regal wife as not simply independent, but also as "royally" distant and aloof. I was angered by her independent nature since I felt weak and needy simply by being around her. Throughout our marriage, I became increasingly aware of my unresolved dependency problem.

Some observers may conclude that we were a poor match. Be that as it may, probably a dozen years into our marriage, I realized my independent wife was the perfect match for me. If I needed to become more self-sufficient, what better partner model—or example—could I have chosen for developing greater independence within myself?

——◦♥◦——

As a result of this combination of traits, the central conflict in our marriage was between my craving for closeness and my wife's appetite for distance: my dependence versus her independence. At the core of our disharmony were our opposing characterological needs: my longing for intimacy versus her clinging to her identity. From our marriage, I needed togetherness, whereas she required separateness.

Early in my career, I had read an article by the family therapist Gus Napier, PhD,* on *interpersonal distance regulation*: that is, the dance of togetherness and separateness between intimate partners. His article was pivotal for both my personal life and my professional career. This challenging dance of closeness and distance is perhaps the major conflict in most relationships, yet to differing degrees for each couple. (**The Rejection-Intrusion Pattern*, Journal of Marital and Family Therapy, 1978.)

Our marital tango was especially conflicted and emotional. With respect to "distance regulation" in our marriage, I wanted emotional intimacy, whereas my wife was focused on maintaining her identity as a separate person. I spent several decades trying to grasp the psyche's madness, and extrapolate her wisdom in bringing us together.

—————•♥•—————

Like most couples, we soon fell into a vicious cycle of trying to change our partner, as we grappled with these differences. Like two-year-old's, we pointed our fingers at each other, placing blame outside ourselves.

We were both hoping that our partner might change, and thereby become more like ourselves. This would result in more similarity, and thus greater harmony. I wanted her to become more dependent like me and seek togetherness. And I imagine she wanted me to become a more separate individual like herself.

When each was focused, almost exclusively, on trying to change our spouse, *neither of us changed ourselves*. Since we were trying to change our partner, instead of ourselves, the marriage did not improve. We became entrapped in a self-defeating cycle of escalating conflict, blaming behavior and entrenched positions. Blaming and trying to change our partner created *not* harmony but resulted in greater disharmony.

—————•♥•—————

As a dependent type, I was fighting for intimacy, whereas my wife was struggling to hang on to her identity. With our conflicting emotional needs, I constantly felt rejected and deeply hurt by her more distant nature. I suspect she felt smothered by my neediness, my need for closeness.

Although I saw myself as "warm," the underbelly of my warmth was anger. My warmth could become inflamed, fiery hot, when I felt hurt or rejected. I would overreact by raising my voice, but with self-restraint, so the children would not overhear. I never damaged property, struck my wife or threatened to hurt her. Yet at times, my furious tone and irate words were definitely abusive.

Frustrated by the absence of closeness in our marriage, I would start an argument with my wife. After discharging my anger, I usually felt considerably better. But of course, my wife felt totally miserable. Gradually, I became aware that my angry behavior was causing her to become even more distant, cold and unresponsive to me.

My anger originated in my unresolved dependency problem. As a needy individual, I was angry and demanding because I could not get from my wife the closeness and attention which my parents had provided for me—and which I thought I needed to mature. So, when frustrated, I would regress into childish temper tantrums. Initially, I always tried to control my anger. But finally, I would fail and blame my wife, instead of scrutinizing myself.

The Hidden Agenda

A few years before separating, I was given a life-changing insight. One day, while sitting alone in our bedroom, I suddenly became aware of the unconscious plot of our marriage. I had *not* married for the comforts of intimacy, as I consciously believed. Rather, I had married because I was unconsciously seeking my independent identity. My role in our conflicted drama was finally exposed. I became aware of the covert plot, the hidden agenda: the quest for my own identity.

This life-altering awareness—this critical turning point—came as I began to realize that my anger was actually *driving my wife away* from me, and was *not bringing her closer*. I was causing her to throw up more barriers and build walls to protect herself from my verbal assaults. Why on earth would my wife want closeness with such an angry man!

Consciously, I was seeking closeness. But my angry words resulted in exactly the opposite—distance. Through my anger, I was pushing my wife away, frustrating my own *conscious* desire for intimacy. What on earth was I doing! Why was I engaging in such self-defeating behavior?

———•♥•———

With Dick's assistance, I carefully began to examine the effect of my anger on my wife, instead of my anger's intent. His chief strategy was to help me see this *discrepancy*: my anger's *intent* was closeness, whereas the *effect* of my anger was distance. My anger made closeness impossible, thus creating distance. Driving a wedge between my wife and myself suggested that my *unconscious* objective was a struggle for my independent identity. Now at last, my angry behavior was explained, but certainly not excused.

My *fight for intimacy* was actually a *fight for my identity* as a man. By unconsciously creating distance, I was establishing myself as a person separate from my wife. Like a dependent boy, I was angrily pushing away from a strong mother figure. By doing this, I would be less dependent on her; therefore, I would become more independent

I did not need to be gratified with the closeness that my parents had provided, and which I believed was necessary for me to mature. Instead, I needed to be frustrated, so that I could develop into a man. Only if my dependent child was painfully frustrated by my wife, instead of being gratified, would I find my identity as an independent man.

Through my self-defeating, angry behavior, I was unconsciously frustrating myself into independence. As I became more conscious of this hidden agenda—my quest for an independent identity—then I was able to focus my energies on the resolution of my dependency problem and the development of my identity as a man, instead of seeking intimacy with my wife.

⸻ •❤• ⸻

As a therapist, I knew that the path to marital improvement entailed the arduous task of changing oneself. And I knew it was a waste of my time trying to revamp my wife. Rather, I needed to change myself, *even if my wife did not change herself.*

Consequently, with every misunderstanding, I began to focus on my role in a given conflict since I knew I had a better chance of changing myself, than changing my wife. So, after every argument, I began to take responsibility for my words and actions, by identifying for myself—*and then acknowledging to my wife*—what I saw as my part in each dispute. If I initiated an argument, or overreacted to something she did first, I would own my piece without blaming her. Focusing on my contribution to a conflict and then changing myself was a far more worthwhile endeavor than another pointless apology for my repetitive, angry outbursts. Changing myself became my focus: working on me, instead of my wife.

By taking responsibility for my words and actions, I was doing what a "man" should do, not what an angry-dependent boy would do. I was learning, "Marriage is not so much a matter of who you marry, but of who you are" (author unknown). Instead of behaving like a dependent boy, I was choosing and struggling to become an independent man.

With two years of therapy with Dick and my own intensive introspection, I learned a great deal about myself, both before and after our final separation. From that awareness, and through great effort, I was changing myself and becoming a man. Professionally, I called this "the principle of self-change," instead of trying to change one's partner.

With maturation, I eventually realized that my wife was not the aloof, independent villain who I thought she was. If I developed more independence within myself—but *not* to the extent of my wife's more distant nature—then I no longer needed to attack that quality in her. In retrospect, she was my model for independence. In my quest for wholeness, she was the blueprint for my missing half: my independent identity as a man.

REFLECTION

Wholeness: Interdependence

Without a doubt, a great wisdom had been at work within me when I unconsciously selected an independent wife. Even though I was unaware of the psyche's objective at that time, in fact, I had "chosen" and was "given" in my wife, *exactly* what was required for my growth and maturation into manhood. Through my marriage, I inadvertently unearthed and then intentionally began to develop my independent, masculine identity.

By selecting an independent woman to marry, I was unconsciously attempting to heal my incomplete, dependent self. By gradually becoming conscious of my dependency issue—both before and after our final separation—I began to intentionally develop my "other half," independence. Eventually, I was able to possess both of these qualities in equal proportion: a balance of dependence and independence. Indeed, "self-completion"—as I referred to it professionally—had been the psyche's objective all along, not primarily the comforts of an emotionally close relationship. With this awareness and through challenging psychological work, a wholeness began to evolve within me as an internal state of being.

Neither dependence nor independence was the answer. I would be complete and whole only if I became *inter*dependent: simultaneously dependent and independent. Then, I could be emotionally close with a partner while maintaining a sense of myself as a separate person.

Most importantly, when my desire for closeness was frustrated, I would know how to manage my pain constructively: I could disclose my feelings of hurt or rejection to my mate. And instead of venting my frustration inappropriately onto a partner, I could lovingly attend to my internal hurt and manage my anger more appropriately.

Had I never unearthed the unconscious "identity agenda," I would have continued in this cycle of angry, self-defeating behavior, either with my wife or a future partner. If I had not become conscious of the wisdom buried within my marriage, its purposeful agenda would have remained in the unconscious, resulting in no change, no growth for me.

I regret I did not develop more of my masculine identity in my childhood home. As a teenager, my anger should have been directed, more age-appropriately, toward my parents as a tool for emotionally separating from them and becoming a man. Then, my marriage would have been spared some of the burden of my formidable dependency and anger problems.

Even though my wife and I were both therapists, and each of us had two years of individual counseling with Dick, we were not able to resuscitate our marriage. Many of our friends were surprised when we separated. Thankfully, at least I had started to change and remake aspects of myself.

Further Reflection

Through my anger, I had expelled myself from the womb of my marriage, initially being unaware that this was my agenda. But in fact—and *in effect*—my anger contributed to the demise of our marriage. By asking me to move out of our home, my wife inadvertently forced the resolution of my dependency and anger problems. She pushed me out of the marital womb, thereby forcing me to become self-dependent. In this manner, she made an unintended contribution to the development of my independent identity as a man.

Even though I had grown and changed myself considerably during my marriage, I still had much unfinished business. After separating, a four-year celibacy would finally force me to become more independent. In retrospect, I realize that only by living without a woman could my dependency problem be significantly outgrown and mostly resolved.

My marriage was a crucible for self-discovery. It was the vessel wherein I began to explore my troubled soul and the crucible in which I began to forge my identity. I became painfully aware of my dependency issue; and I realized my anger was a monumental problem for me. Indeed, I had uncovered the hidden agenda: the quest for my identity. As Gibran wrote, "All these things shall love do unto you, that you may know the secrets of your heart."

Eventually, out of the womb of my marriage, I would be led into the *interior* womb of my heart, my soul. My heart was not only a place of great suffering, but also the womb of my rebirth (Chapter 2).

THE FINAL SEPARATION

Telling the Children

When it was time to tell the children, my wife and I sat down in the living room with our son and daughter. The sofa bed was pulled out, which was typical at our house on the weekend. On Friday and Saturday nights, the children were allowed to watch TV and sleep in the living room.

The next morning, still in their pajamas, they were sitting on the sofa bed as we sat in nearby chairs. Calmly, we got right to the point. "Your mom and I have decided to live separately for a while. I will move out of the house and live in an apartment." My daughter burst into tears. Initially, my son was silent; he appeared stunned. Then, each of them asked a few questions.

I quickly reassured them, "I will visit you two or three times during the week and every other weekend. Your mother will stay in the house with you."

We told them, "We can't get along with each other," but gave them no details. Yet we made clear that our problems were "not just Mom's fault" and "not just Dad's fault." We said, "We can't figure out how to fix *our* problems. So, we have decided to live in different houses."

Separation Day

Several days later—Tuesday, March 15, 1983—I moved out of our home. Although my wife and I had "jointly" agreed to separate, she was the one who wanted me out. She was the partner most dissatisfied with our marriage, ready to act.

I knew marital unhappiness was always a joint venture. If my wife was unhappy, how could I possibly be happy as her spouse? I could try to overcome my disappointment. But I was powerless to alter her despondent condition.

Since I was moving into an already-furnished room, we sorted through a few linens for me to take. I took my clothes and toiletries, along with a few personal possessions.

Loss and Struggle

Separating from my wife was the end of my life as I knew it. Even though we were "just separating," I felt my marriage was coming to an end. In breaking my attachment to my wife, I was being forced to live by myself; I was reluctantly transitioning into independence. In my journal, I wrote, "Too painful, too great a task for me."

Suddenly, everything I had achieved was lost. I no longer had a wife. I no longer had a house. And I no longer had *daily* contact with my children. What I wanted out of life, and valued most, had gone up in smoke.

A month after moving out—severely depressed and unconsciously suicidal—I had experienced that impulse to jump to my death.

What remained was my job, visitation with my children, a few friends at work and others in my PhD program, and a small rented room in another person's home.

But I did have a purpose: to contribute financially to my family, and to provide as much good fathering to my children as possible. For the nine years before my youngest went off to college, I lived only a few miles from my children. Gratefully, my wife allowed generous visitation. My pain was significantly reduced by these frequent visits.

In time, I adjusted to not having my own house. At first, I rented a room in someone else's home. Next, I transitioned into three increasingly larger apartments. Nine years after the final separation—when my youngest graduated from high school—I was able to purchase my own home.

———— •♥• ————

With the separation, the umbilical cord anchoring my wife in my heart was cut. She was uprooted from my soul, my symbiotic dependence on her severed. I was astounded by the severity of my pain. I did not realize I had become so deeply attached to her during our eighteen-year relationship. The extreme depth of my suffering was a precise barometer of my unresolved dependency issue, my pathological attachment to her.

At thirty-eight, I was single again. Now, I was brutally confronted with my deficiencies as a man. Never in my life had I lived alone. First, I had lived with my childhood family. Then, I had college roommates. After college, I was married to my wife for sixteen years. Being so profoundly dependent, how could I now possibly live alone and survive?

Given my total inexperience with living alone—coupled with the trauma of the breakup—I was unable to sleep for more than two or three hours a night due to intense pain. I was riddled with anxiety, depression and anger. My general practitioner prescribed Ativan for a few months, so I was able to sleep at least four or five hours a night.

With the separation, I moved into uncharted waters. At this time, the resolution of my dependency problem would become the greatest challenge of my life. I had no idea how to live on my own and emotionally survive by myself, at least happily.

Sister Mary

A year after my wife and I separated, I was on the USC campus again for another early morning lecture. After class, I strolled with Sister Mary—a member of the Sisters of the Holy Cross—toward our cars, parked in the same structure from which I had experienced that impulse to jump.

At USC, Mary and I began programs in sociology the same year. She was working toward a PhD in gerontology, whereas mine was in marriage and family counseling. Since we shared required sociology classes, we were frequently together and became good friends. She was perhaps ten years my senior.

Mary was a brilliant, outspoken and unconventional nun who did not wear a habit. She had taught math, biology and chemistry in several large Catholic high schools. Routinely, she read the *New England Journal of Medicine*, in addition to the *Wall Street Journal*. After obtaining her PhD, she worked for a major HMO for a few years. After that, she managed her order's portfolio of financial assets until she retired.

———◆♥◆———

Sister Mary was cognizant of my marital difficulties. She knew I was separated. She was aware that I had felt that impulse to jump to my death. She understood I was still depressed. And my still-unresolved dependency problem must have been obvious to her.

She also understood that I now wanted to live; I was not going to kill myself. She saw me working through a major depression and developing a renewed enjoyment of life. I was still in pain, but I had a definite desire to go on living.

And she knew I had a network of friends at work and at USC.

She was aware that I wanted to finish my doctoral dissertation on "self-completion," as the unconscious motivation for selecting a partner with complementary personality traits. In this process, a partner unknowingly seeks to compensate for traits deficient in oneself. Moreover, Sister Mary was aware I had chosen this topic not only for professional reasons, but also because I was trying to understand my own marriage, and myself.

———◆♥◆———

While walking toward our cars—parked in the *same* five-story parking structure—she suddenly said to me, "We're praying for you." I burst into unexplained tears. Sister Mary and the nuns in her convent at St. Catherine by the Sea were including me in their prayers.

I quickly realized, if my father had been alive, that was exactly what he would have said to me. And physically, Sister Mary reminded me of my deceased mother—also large-framed and big-busted, with short reddish-brown hair and a ruddy complexion. She looked like my mother and spoke like my father.

After I regained my composure, I told her what those words and her person had meant to me. In that instant, I felt the loving presence of both of my deceased parents, at this very sorrowful time in my life. Upon learning that her community of nuns were praying for me, I felt surrounded by a circle of genuine compassion.

A FOUR-YEAR CELIBACY
The Suffering I Experienced

———◆♥◆———

The heart itself is only a small vessel.
Yet dragons are there, and lions.
There are poisonous beasts,
and all the treasures of evil.
There are rough and uneven roads,
there are precipices.
But there too are God and the angels.
Life is there, and the Kingdom.
There too is light,
and there the apostles
and heavenly cities,
and the treasures of grace.
All things lie within that little space.

MAKARIOS
CHRISTIAN MONK
FOURTH CENTURY

When my wife and I separated for the last time, I rented a room in another person's home. I thought living with a family would be less lonely than living in an apartment by myself. At least, I would know the names of the household members. At times, our paths might cross when I left my room to fix a meal or use the bathroom.

A Jewish woman owned the house and had become its sole owner after her divorce. The house was located in a modern, upscale neighborhood on a tree-lined street. This two-story home must have been at least 3,500 square feet.

In this spacious Mediterranean home, the woman lived with her two children and her boyfriend. Her daughter attended a local college, her son a nearby high school. For the most part, her children stayed in their upstairs bedrooms. The owner and her older, retired-Navy boyfriend had the master bedroom on the first floor.

I did not want to live in a crowded home since I wanted plenty of privacy. Yet I did not want to reside in a small apartment by myself. With this housing arrangement, I would have ample solitude, yet not feel completely isolated. This home was the perfect place for what was to be the commencement of my midlife transition and transformation.

Even though I had hoped some meaningful conversation or friendship might develop with some of the household members, I soon realized that I had little in common with any of them. After all, the two young people were about twenty years younger than me, and the retired boyfriend was probably twenty years my senior.

But at least I was not entirely alone; this family was always nearby. We cordially greeted each other when passing in the hallways. They engaged me in kindly conversation in the kitchen while I prepared food. For many years afterward, I felt a deep gratitude toward this family, who had shielded me from total isolation during this terribly painful period in my life.

———— •♥• ————

My small, second-story bedroom was in a remote back corner of the house. When not at work or with my children or friends, I stayed in my room most of the time, except to use the bathroom or the kitchen. For the most part, I chose to eat alone in my room since I was not inclined toward small talk.

My room was about ten by nine feet. The owner had used it for storage but now needed rental income. Unpainted for many years, the walls were a dull gray with scuff marks. No pictures were on the walls, nor did I hang any during the two and a half years I lived there. I hoped this would be a temporary home until my wife and I might reunite.

When I entered my bedroom through the corner door, I was greeted by an old wooden twin bed, situated diagonally across the room. A dull-yellow, medium-size dresser, with my small TV on top, was squeezed between the foot of the bed and the wall.

Next to the TV hung a small wall mirror. Here, I could see my face clearly reflected, although I was now uncertain who I was. The dismal, rainy days at the end of my marriage had left a puddle of muddied waters within me. My soul was in turmoil and drenched in confusion, now a murky pool of tears.

In front of the only window was a lamp on a small desk with a mismatched wooden chair. That was the only place to sit for eating meals, watching TV, journaling and reading. These meager furnishings took up two-thirds of the floor space.

A small closet held my clothing and linens which I brought in two suitcases. To save money, the owner rarely turned on the AC in the summer or heat in the winter.

In this dreary room, I had stumbled upon a place that mirrored my dejected soul.

My Cloistered Cell

In completing the practical task of renting a room, little did I know that this place would become the sacred space wherein my midlife transformation would begin. Freed from the stormy conflicts of my marriage, this port became my safe harbor. Even so, I was still immersed in the internal muck and mire of my midlife crisis: the misery of a failed marriage. In this small room, the mud in the waters of my soul would have ample time to settle to the bottom. Then, I would be able to behold myself more clearly and reflect upon who I am.

I brought other baggage too: my unresolved internal issues, notably my dependency and anger problems. Although free of marital conflict, I was still the same person, carrying with me all the same psychological baggage. Transported internally, I brought my dependent boy and his rageful soul.

Separating from my wife and children left me living alone. Now, I had only myself. No one else around to blame for my unhappiness. In this quiet place, I had plenty of time to scrutinize my anguished soul: to face myself and search for the internal root of my suffering. Here, I began a lengthy process of introspection, indeed, a journey into the depths of my soul. Only through such a solitary and arduous process would I be able to resolve my problems and unearth my essence: what I am, my authentic self.

Like a monk, I lived in this cloistered cell for more than two years. This solitary abode was my retreat from the world, my private sanctuary. In this small room, I was gladly sequestered with ample time for self-examination. I was by myself, yet not alone. As Makarios wrote, I brought with me "poisonous beasts": my rage and my dependency problems, indeed, my "dragon" of dependency. Now, I had to confront these devilish aspects of myself. Only much later (Part Three) would I find "God and the angels" within my soul, as also described by Makarios.

MY TORMENTED SOUL

My four-year celibacy was my "dark night of the soul," brought on by the collapse of my marriage. My marriage had failed, leaving me in a pit of despair. Now alone, I felt deeply hurt and extremely angry, along with experiencing severe anxiety and depression. A month after separating, I had experienced that suicidal impulse to jump to my death.

Midway through my life, I found myself wandering "in a dark wood for I had lost my way," as Dante wrote. I walked into an interior dark forest of chaos and confusion. Externally, the foundation of my life, my family, had collapsed. Internally, I was experiencing massive turmoil. But within this dark, yet potentially fertile *massa confusa* (massive confusion), I hoped to find a solution to my dependency-anger problem and forge an identity.

A Wounded Boy: Dependent and Angry

When I married my wife, I was not conscious of the fact that a needy, dependent boy lived within me. By the time my wife and I separated sixteen years later, I had become painfully aware of this problem. I still harbored that dependent boy: a hurt and angry child. But by age thirty-eight, my masculine identity had become better established. Now, my task was to *persist* in the further healing of this wounded boy, so he could grow into a self-confident man.

The most painful emotion in my marriage had been an acute, yet chronic, feeling of rejection. I felt cast aside by my wife, like a neglected child. She did not intentionally ignore or reject me. Yet because of my dependent nature, I constantly felt hurt as if she had. The *very fact* of her independent and more distant nature felt like rejection to me.

Inwardly, I was still trapped in a maternal womb, ensnared by an infantile dependency. In my late thirties, the failure of my marriage was forcing me to grow up. Now, it was finally time for me to escape from the marital womb—the one which had replaced the womb of my childhood family.

"Pray without Ceasing"

As a child, I frequently noticed my father praying in his home office, as he struggled with family life and his career as a minister. When I saw this, he would remind me of the biblical verse, "Pray without ceasing" (I Thessalonians 5:17). Although I now prayed to a very different God than my father, he was the perfect model of a man who was humble enough to ask for help when troubled.

Furthermore, early in my career, I had read the prayer of a little boy who was angry at God because of a tragedy in his life. To God, he confidently prayed, stating he believed God was "big enough" to handle his anger. Like this little boy, I trusted that God could accept all my negative emotions—no matter how "unchristian"—even my anger at Him.

During these four difficult years, my practice of prayer was crucial for my survival, and ultimately for my healing and rebirth. I prayed into my journal, giving words to my pain. I directed my prayers to God, to the "Universe," to the "Universe-God," to the Unseen Presence within me. "Oh God, help me," was the mantra I prayed.

As I prayed, I surrendered my pride in my ability to solve my own problems. I asked for assistance from some unknown source other than my ego, my "I" (ego, Latin for "I"). Somehow, I had the faith that the Universe surrounding me, and the one within, contained all the assistance I would ever need. I believed that the outer and inner worlds were both divine and infinitely greater than my tiny ego. Prayer became an act of humility and trust that *Something* would support me in my struggle.

My prayers were addressed to and somehow heard by "another." Talking to the Unseen Presence within, I did not feel as lonely afterward. I felt my words were "heard," although I was unsure how or by whom. I was alone. Yet after praying, I felt less lonely.

Instead of remaining passive and inwardly lost in my troubled emotions, I prayed out loud or into my journal, putting my feelings into words. I prayed my pain onto paper. With spoken or written words, I externalized my hurt. Everything I wrote on those pages was a prayer, even when swearing at God for my suffering. Through journaling, my mind gradually became more lucid; I was given some clarity amidst all the chaos and confusion.

Praying onto those blank, receptive pages was curiously healing for me. I began to feel a redemptive presence within me. In my suffering, I sensed some unseen God was near. I did not imagine God as a loving consciousness—a loving parent in the sky—as my father had believed. Yet on the other side of my suffering, I intuitively felt I would encounter a deity. As Jung reminded me, "God enters through the wound." Within my wounded heart, I believed some sort of God would be waiting for me with understanding and compassion.

Attempting to discover who I am, I journaled profusely, seeking to comprehend my powerful and varied emotions. I prayed mainly when I felt ferocious rage, excruciating pain or massive confusion. I doubt I would have survived had I not journaled and prayed, prayed into my journal. To stay alive, I had to "pray without ceasing."

At times, I was unable to distinguish between my words and the utterances of the God to whom I was praying. Was it I who was praying? Or was God crying inside me? My deepest prayers seemed to be those of *God praying within me*, giving expression to my pained heart—to His/Her suffering soul.

In my agony, I felt God suffered with me. My pained heart and God's suffering soul, both inside me, seemed to be indistinguishable. As Mignon McLaughlin wrote, "When suffering comes, we yearn for some sign from God, forgetting we have just had one," in the suffering itself. Indeed, God was near—yes, suffering with me, suffering within my soul.

SUFFERING: JOURNEY INTO MY BODY

While still living with my wife, I was often terribly angry since I constantly felt hurt; I felt rejected by her, simply by being around her more distant nature. Yet after I moved out of the house, I became quite anxious since I was then alone. As a dependent, middle-aged man separating from his wife, I was not only saturated with anger, but I was also riddled with anxiety.

I was profoundly attached to my wife, almost like a fetus *in utero*. The feeling of being separated from her was unbearable. Cutting the umbilical cord, the one attaching me to her, resulted in intense feelings of both rage and anxiety. I felt the energy of these agonizing emotions in every part of my body. By focusing on my body and my actual heart, I was able to more easily detect what I was experiencing and feeling.

Before the separation, slaying my "dragon of dependency" (separation rage)—and *after the breakup*, my "heart bleeding" (separation anxiety)—were steps toward the resolution of my pathological rage and dependency. Allowing myself to feel separation rage and experience separation anxiety were both stages in the transformation of these troubling aspects of myself.

Yet unexpectedly, my healing would ultimately come through the experience of "a snake in my spine."

Although the first of these visceral images may be troubling to some of my readers, I regard my rage as a part of my yet-to-be-redeemed soul. I knew my rage was not to be acted upon. But I had to admit it into my consciousness and completely accept this unacceptable part of myself.

Slaying My Dragon of Dependency: Separation Rage

A year before my wife and I separated, I began to feel a boiling rage within me, the only time I ever felt a homicidal rage toward someone I loved. Out of my frustration and pain, a murderous rage began to swell within my body. I wanted to kill my wife!

Yet I was absolutely certain that I would never do such a violent thing since I loved my wife deeply. Besides, I cherished our children and valued myself. When feeling this murderous rage, I never once threatened to kill my wife. Although inwardly enraged, the thought of actually physically hurting her was abhorrent to me.

As a therapist, I knew the critical distinction between being fully conscious of such a brutal impulse, yet firmly choosing not to act it out. Internally, I allowed this fierce rage into my consciousness, but I knew I would never act on it.

Yes, I had to suffer, to bear my rage. For my growth and maturation, I knew I had to be strong enough to contain my anger internally. Yet for my healing, I was also aware that I had to completely feel this murderous rage throughout my body until the anger was totally discharged. Consequently, I accepted homicidal feelings and images into my consciousness.

By killing my wife *in my imagination*, these vicious emotions could be gradually expelled from my body. The massive energy within such a savage image needed to be discharged in fantasy—or enacted symbolically—but certainly *not* literally acted upon. In so doing, I might gain relief from the hatred, and over time, learn how to better manage and master my anger.

Furthermore, a murderous fantasy would help me grieve and relinquish my wife. With such a fantasy, my dependent inner child—now in the body of a rageful man—was pushing away from his mother, by killing her in his imagination. Internally feeling my rage was an indispensable step in the painful process of letting go of my wife. My dependent boy needed the rage—the separation rage—to establish himself as a man separate from his mother.

Through this process, I could liberate myself from my symbiotic need for my wife. If I fantasized her being dead, she would no longer be available for me to be dependent upon. Imagining her death precipitated tears of grief, prompting me to further release her.

I had a staunch conscience and a strong ego, so I knew I would be able to contain my murderous rage. Even when in excruciating pain, I could control these lethal feelings.

Yet I still had to accept myself "just as I am," as professed in the nineteenth-century hymn, "Just As I Am." Never in my life had I been asked to espouse such a horrendous aspect of myself: a homicidal rage toward my wife. As Jung remarked, "The most terrifying thing is to accept oneself completely." Acknowledging a murderer within me was "the most terrifying thing" for me to accept.

———— ·♥· ————

Throughout the first half of my life, I had various types of "hero" fantasies in my quest for my identity as a man. As a boy, and as a man, I had imagined killing for heroic purposes. For example, as an adult, I imagined myself in a dark alley ferociously fighting off and killing an assailant, who was attempting to hurt my wife and children. But I had never permitted myself to have murderous fantasies, which were *not the least bit heroic.*

Yet now, I felt a homicidal rage toward my wife. No longer "a little devil" as in childhood. Now, a dangerous devil lived within me. Yes, this was an aspect of who I was. But ultimately, this murderous rage did not make me an evil person. Rather, the rage was a still-unredeemed facet of my reptilian heritage, although surely not part of a heroic self-image.

Most importantly, I knew that my homicidal rage had essentially *nothing* to do with my wife. My rage was rooted in my dependency problem. My rage had *everything* to do with my neediness, my pathological attachment to her. I did not need to kill her. I needed to kill *my need* for my wife.

I realized my rage should be redirected toward defeating my dependency problem: slaying this dragon of dependency within me, instead of killing my wife. A fantasy of murdering her was definitely unheroic. But in my imagination, enacting the slaughter of this fiery, interior dragon, this "poisonous beast," would be truly heroic.

----- •♥• -----

Yes, I had to slay my dragon of dependency on a woman. I needed to destroy my unhealthy dependence on my wife, or on any future woman in my life. This dragon was my "devil," my true adversary. I had to become stronger, so that I would not be devoured by my neediness. I needed to symbolically enact the slaughter of that formidable beast within me, that dragon of dependency, before it consumed me.

A year before our final separation, I went out into our backyard one Tuesday night when my wife worked late and the children were asleep in the house. On my knees, with a baseball bat in my hands, I began to angrily beat on a log. I wanted to relieve my body and my psyche of this murderous energy. I violently bashed that tree limb with all my strength, thereby releasing a ferocious rage. I bludgeoned that eucalyptus log until it began to disintegrate.

That night, I began to slay that beast symbolically. I had to destroy my regressive desire to stay in the marital womb; my infantile bond to my wife had to die! Most certainly, I needed to "cut off" that fiery dragon's head, a task usually accomplished by most men as teenagers or young adults. But now at midlife, I had to be finally victorious over my dependency.

In the process of conquering my dependency, discharging the rage that killed that dragon was pivotal. Only by killing that dragon could I establish my strength as a man. Only then, could I establish my independent identity. That night, I annihilated that eucalyptus log, which lay upon Mother Earth's breast. I knew I could not hurt the Earth. Most importantly, I did not hurt my wife in any way.

Exhausted, I fell face down on the ground and wept. My arms were outstretched, as if I had been crucified. I collapsed into the arms of Mother Earth—my rage released, at least for now. At that moment, I wanted to be held. With my body flat upon the Earth and my cheek against her grassy breast, I embraced Mother Earth. She was the only one to whom I could turn. In those tearful moments, she was all that I had left.

That night, Mother Earth was the only "woman" upon whom I could depend. My wife no longer wanted me. So, I grabbed onto Mother Earth to ground me. As I did this, I felt as if my alliance with the Earth, my *external mother*, was being reestablished. I was recovering my primordial kinship with the Earth, my dependency on her.

In time, I would discover an *internal mother* upon whom I could also depend.

A year after feeling this murderous rage, I experienced that impulse to jump to my death. After we separated, perhaps the homicidal rage toward her was being unconsciously redirected toward myself as that suicidal impulse. But with both the homicidal and suicidal impulses, I chose not to act out the rage of my pain. Thankfully, I decided to endure and struggle with these lethal emotions without harming either my wife or myself. A year later, I journaled, "Now, my anger is turned neither outward nor inward, but gives me spine."

So, what role might my anger, my wrath, play in my redemption? I wanted to discover the divine purpose within such a rage.

The Crucifixion of My "Innocence"

With these murderous fantasies, who or what was I actually killing? In my imagination, was I killing my wife? Was I slaying my dragon of dependency? Or was I also enacting the murder of some other part of myself? Who or what was I crucifying?

In retrospect, I realize my self-image, my identity as a Christian, was crucified when I allowed that murderous rage into my consciousness. My rage drove a nail into my innocence. Now, my virtuous persona—my self-image as a loving and good man—could no longer be my mask. This disguise was not an honest self-image, which I could present to others, nor one that I could still believe was me. As I assimilated this homicidal rage into my conscious identity, I crucified my belief that I was innocent, like the one on the cross.

My innocence had to be crucified, so that my rage could be experienced and converted into something useful. To become whole, I had to consciously embrace this rageful part of my shadow as an aspect of myself. Previously, love and hate had been mostly segregated within me. Love was my persona. Yet rage had been hiding within my shadow, still unredeemed.

Indeed, I was becoming a very different man. My virtuous "Christianized ego" was being asked to integrate a murderous rage into the person that I was becoming. Not just love but also hate was an aspect of who I am. I had always tried to be loving with my wife. Yet in spite of my best efforts, my anger would eventually surface. So now, I needed to embrace both emotions as parts of myself. A larger, more complex—yet integrated and unified—self-image was now emerging, wherein both love and anger could cohabitate.

Do not love and anger intermingle within us all? As Rumi wrote, "God turns you from one feeling to another, and teaches by means of opposites, so you will have two wings to fly, not one." As for me, I now had one wing of love and another of anger. My rage was no longer hiding in the shadows. Now, my task was to find its divine purpose.

By enacting my wife's "murder," I had crucified my innocence, my "Christianized ego." And over time, I slew my dragon of dependency. Yet I was not only a murderer, the villain; I also felt like a victim, the one slain. With the impending death of my marriage—the sacrifice of my dependent attachment to my wife—I felt like I was being crucified.

So, who was I? A guilty villain? An innocent victim? Or both?

Do we not all alternate between villain and victim: at times, an angry perpetrator—or at other times, a wounded victim? Do we not feel like the crucifier and, at other times, like the one on the cross? Are we not all both guilty and innocent?

As the one crucified, I would now experience "a heart bleeding." The heat of my fiery rage slowly smoldered into tepid tears, as I continued to mourn and release my wife. I moved from hatred into hurt. Yes, I was a rageful crucifier. Nevertheless, I was also the one crucified, now wounded and bleeding myself.

A Heart Bleeding: Separation Anxiety

As is the case with all deep loves, my heart was the organ within which my wife had become affixed. Cutting the umbilical cord resulted in incredible anger boiling up within me. But this rage had been a protective defense: a mask disguising the deep hurt and heartache underneath. By the time we separated, much of that rage had been discharged. So then, I was able to feel the pain of my wife's absence. Now alone, my heart was flooded with anxiety—yes, separation anxiety—from no longer living with her.

During the day, my wounded heart seemed to ache without end. But after the activities of the day, the daytime ache mutated into nighttime anxiety. When I climbed into bed at night, the anguish began. The intense pain and anxiety within my heart were excruciating, the wound itself commanding 100 percent of my attention. In the night, I rarely thought about my wife; she was not present in my awareness. Instead, the hole in my heart from the breakup, the bleeding wound itself was agonizingly omnipresent, as I suffered loneliness.

For more than two years, I lay in that twin bed at night, feeling a constant stream of painful energy flowing out of my heart. Lying motionless on my back, I could feel an intense anxiety burning within me. From the inside, it felt like acid was burning a hole in my heart. The anxiety of being alone was eating me alive: consuming my flesh, devouring my heart.

The experience was entirely visceral, although not literal. From the outside, it felt like thousands of needles were being stuck into the center of my chest, causing a tingly-prickly sensation, an awful distress within my heart. With arms outstretched as if dying on a cross, seemingly inexhaustible pain flowed out of my heart.

Was this a wound that would never heal? I had not expected my suffering to manifest so physically. I was utterly powerless to stop what was happening within me.

------•♥•------

Before long, I felt blood flowing from my heart. The flow of this painful energy from my heart had to be blood. So, intentionally and beneficially, I began to imagine blood pouring from my chest. My heart was wounded, bleeding pain profusely. I journaled, "I feel raw inside, like raw bleeding meat with tears."

Separating from my wife, I was expelled from the marital womb within which I had hoped to be safe. The umbilical cord attaching me to her had been cut. Now, entirely alone, I was left holding the bleeding cord. Five years would pass before that bloody placenta would be fully discharged from my heart.

Now, my task was to allow my heart to bleed. And while bleeding, I could bear witness to my suffering. I felt like the one crucified; yet my task was to witness my own crucifixion, my own dying. Lying in bed on my back, I would relax my body. I focused my attention on that painful energy flowing out of my heart, the bleeding from the wound. Indeed, "a heart bleeding."

As long as I was bleeding pain, I knew I was not dead. If I was still suffering, I must be alive. But if the pain stopped, I might be dead. I was afraid my heart would turn into stone: my pain might morph into bitterness, making my heart cold and hard. I did not want to have a dead, stone-like heart while still in a warm body.

I knew I should not try to stop the bleeding by ignoring my suffering or by anesthetizing my pain with alcohol. I sensed that I should just let it bleed. For some reason, I believed that if it bled long enough,

I would not die. Rather, I would somehow be restored to life. The pain could not last forever; I trusted there had to be an end to my suffering. Someday, the pain would be completely gone. Then, my heart would be fully healed.

And I trusted that my suffering was not in vain. Maybe a reason for the sacrifice of my marriage. Perhaps a divine purpose for the pain, a meaning in the suffering. Did I need to endure the pain, so that I would be drawn into my soul and therein find God? Yes, as Rumi wrote, "The wailing of broken hearts is the doorway to God."

This was my prayer, my nightly ritual: to feel what was happening within my heart and to surrender to the painful bleeding from my chest. At times, I was able to cry, which usually helped me sleep better. With that painful anxiety still flowing from my heart, I would eventually drift off into sleep. When I awoke at dawn, the anxiety in my chest had dissipated for that night. But the daytime ache in my heart began anew.

I knew my separation rage and my separation anxiety both came from my unresolved dependency issue, my neediness. Very gradually, and entirely unexpectedly, the rage of the perpetrator (the crucifier) and the anxiety and pain of the victim (the crucified) would merge and manifest as a single electrifying energy slithering through my spine—the energy of "a snake in my spine." Yes, my spine would take the form of a snake.

The Transformation of My Rage and Anxiety: A Snake in My Spine

For me, having a spine and being strong were synonymous. During my marriage, I was aware I was weak, "warm but weak." So, at times I felt "spineless, like a jellyfish." However, I was aware my weak warmth could burst into a fiery rage.

During my marriage, when angry and driving alone, I would fantasize a blowtorch blazing upward from the bottom of my spine and out the top of my head, burning a hole in the metal roof of my Corolla. I knew such a fantasy was a way of releasing intense feelings of frustration and anger, which I did not know how to handle otherwise.

And at times, with the car windows rolled up, I would scream profanities at the top of my lungs—with the full force of my entire body. While doing this, I could feel rageful energy move up the total length of my backbone and be discharged through my vocal cords. After yelling, my voice was always hoarse. Yet invariably, I felt better: relieved and less angry. Those were my first experiences of *anger in my spine.*

Furthermore, I had read Herbert Benson's *The Relaxation Response* (1975) when I was married. So, at that time, I began a daily practice of his relaxation technique during my lunch break, in my parked car. With the driver's seat reclined, I would lie back and close my eyes, relax and focus on any tension or anxiety within my body. Then, I could feel tension moving from the tips of my toes, up through my legs and spine. The energy would slowly progress upward and flow out the top of my head. Those were my first experiences of *anxiety in my spine.*

For a decade, I used these techniques beneficially so anger and anxiety could move up my spine and be drained out of my body. Evidently, these were precursors to my experience of a snake in my spine.

———— ·❦· ————

One night while living in my rented room, I came home, went upstairs and walked toward my room. Suddenly, I was terrified when I saw the four-foot pet python of my landlord's son, calmly coiled around the decorative wrought iron grate next to my bedroom door. I quickly entered my room and slammed the door! I was not pleased by the arrival of that snake at my door, so close to home.

But shortly thereafter, even closer to home—*in my body*—a snake came alive within my spine.

Usually, I slept on my stomach with no pillow, with my cheek pressed flat against the mattress and my mouth slightly open. Occasionally, as I was waking up, my teeth would be chattering as if shivering from the cold. When this would happen, I could feel an invigorating energy flowing up the entire length of my spine, causing my jaw to quiver. Deliberately, I would lie motionless, so my teeth could continue to vibrate. This animating energy felt like that of a snake.

This vital energy moving within my spine felt wonderful. Surging up my backbone, I experienced the energies of my anger and anxiety being discharged. With the flow of this cleansing energy, I felt emotional blockages were being flushed out of my body. Connecting to this healing, reptilian force within me was rejuvenating. For as long as I could, I would lie motionless because I did not want the flow of this vitalizing energy to stop.

Furthermore, over the next several years, I had three significant snake dreams, the first two about rattlesnakes. In the first dream, I try to kill a rattlesnake by dropping books on it from the top of a tall building where I am standing. With my bookish intellect, was I trying to kill my instinctual rage—that same murderous rage which I had used to bludgeon the eucalyptus log? Yes, I wanted to annihilate my rage and get rid of it. But if I had killed that rattlesnake, tragically, part of my primordial nature would have been eradicated. Thankfully, I failed to slay that poisonous serpent.

Reptilian rage was not something I had learned about in church as a child, except that anger was "sinful." Clearly, I was still struggling with this rattlesnake of rage. I had not yet fully assimilated this poisonous aspect of myself into who I was becoming.

In the second dream, a woman cradles a rattlesnake in her lap, without fear, while sitting in a rocking chair. Was this inner woman seeking to tame that venomous serpent, my rattlesnake of rage? Indeed, she was embracing that rageful, reptilian part of me. Instead of trying to kill the rattlesnake, she was rocking and befriending that poisonous snake.

Third, I had a dream of a black snake with a white skull—human-like—emerging from a dark hole in the earth. Was my reptilian rage now becoming humanized? Yes, no longer a rattlesnake that I am trying to kill, nor one being cradled in a woman's lap. This serpent was human-like and harmless.

I surmised that these three dream serpents were an aspect of the same snake-energy that had flowed up my spine and vibrated my teeth when waking up in the morning.

Indeed, the wisdom of the earth—the wisdom within the psyche and my body—had transformed my rattlesnake of rage into this harmless black serpent. Out of the soil of my soul, this snake with a humanoid skull was emerging into the light of my consciousness, aspiring to become a part of me. As Jung wrote (1913–1916) in *The Red Book,* "The serpent is the earthly essence of man of which he is not conscious.... It is the mystery that flows to him from the nourishing earth-mother" (page 247). By gifting me these three snake dreams and causing my teeth to vibrate in the morning, the earth-mother was mysteriously moving within me, refashioning me with her snake-like essence.

———— •♥• ————

Why was this harmless serpent arriving into my life, into my consciousness? No longer frightening, this black dream-snake had a human skull: it was akin to me. At first, my evil adversary, a rattlesnake; but now, a friendly, non-poisonous ally. Instead of a rattlesnake that could harm me, this black serpent seemed to want to help me.

Through these three snake dreams, my rageful reptilian instincts were gradually being tamed and humanized into something harmless. Yes, to remedy my rage and anxiety, Asclepius, the Greek god of healing, had sent his benevolent serpent to remake me.

A mutually beneficial alliance was being established between the snake and me. For one thing, the woman in my dream was embracing the rattlesnake, my rage, suggesting I should befriend my rage as somehow a part of me. Her loving attitude toward this poisonous serpent was encouraging me to milk the venomous rage out of my psyche, so that my anger would not be so deadly. By actively working to resolve my rage, I could perhaps transform it into something beneficial and life-supporting.

In a similar fashion, this black serpent was transforming me by energizing and strengthening my spine. Indeed, my rage was *not* a stone to be "rejected." In fact, it became the "cornerstone" upon which my strength was built. With rage, I had slain the dragon of dependency. And now, that same angry energy was being transformed into an emotionally strong backbone.

I journaled, "When I am filled with rage and anger, God is giving me more spine." My psychologically very real dragon of dependency and the black snake in my spine were both reptiles. But the dragon was dependent and rageful, whereas the snake in my spine was independent and strong. Indeed, my previously slain dragon of dependency was now being resurrected as this snake in my spine: my strength and my independence.

In this manner, my rage was redeemed. The anger within my heart and my body was salvaged and transmuted into a spine, my strength. My rage was not senseless; I had found its divine purpose. God was not only "big enough" to handle my anger, but also used my rage to remake me into a stronger man. Hence, *the resolution of my anger problem.*

No longer "spineless, like a jellyfish," I now had the spine of a snake, a backbone. I was becoming self-dependent. A spineless dependent boy was becoming an independent man with a spine to support him. Hence, *the resolution of my dependency issue.*

Thank God, I did not act out that homicidal rage. If I had, I would have spent my life in prison. Instead, my dependency and my murderous rage were refashioned into a calm strength. From the painful and rageful chaos within me, a new order had emerged. As Jung wrote, "In all chaos, there is a cosmos; in all disorder, a secret order."

In the "small vessel" of my heart had lived "poisonous beasts and all the treasures of evil": my dragon of dependency and my rattlesnake of rage. But, as Makarios also wrote, one of "the treasures of grace" had manifested as that black snake in my spine. I was graced with a quiet strength, an independent masculine identity. The healing serpent-power of Asclepius had awakened within my spine, indeed within the temple of my body.

BECOMING A MAN

Gutting out Celibacy

For the first four years after separating, I was celibate. By requiring myself to live without a woman, I was addressing my dependency problem. Like a monk, I forced myself to live a truly celibate life: no sexual relationship with a woman.

As a highly dependent individual, experiencing the pain and anxiety of living alone was critical for my maturation into manhood. Living by myself, the suffering I experienced was absolutely required, so that I could overcome my internal neediness.

I knew of no better method for breaking my over-attachment to a female, except to be celibate. I needed to conquer my addiction to a sexual relationship with a flesh-and-blood woman. I could still fantasize and masturbate as a coping mechanism. However, that was small consolation for a woman in the flesh.

I had not planned for my celibacy to last so long. In fact, four years passed before I renounced my vow of chastity and became sexually involved with a woman again. Looking back, for my psychological maturation and spiritual growth, *my four-year celibacy was the most consequential decision I made,* for the second half of my life.

This period of celibacy prepared me for everything that was to follow. Jumping into a new relationship might have temporarily and superficially eased my pain. But I realized that I had to suffer my aloneness, so I could mature and become a man.

Had I not been celibate, I believe my life would have turned out quite differently. I would have continued to believe I could find happiness outside myself—with a woman. And then undoubtedly, I would have found myself unhappy.

Most importantly, I may never have discovered the womb of the internal woman—the inner feminine—in such an amazing and astonishing fashion (Part Two and Part Three).

Self-Love

During my celibacy, I became stronger. I discovered that I had the ability to live alone. I did not need to kill myself because I had no woman in my life. Living without a female, I was forced to address my inner weakness and attend to my neediness. By compassionately focusing on the needs of my inner child, reparenting myself, I was developing into a more self-sufficient man.

While gutting out celibacy, I gradually developed the capacity for self-love. I had no other choice but to cherish and soothe myself. I realized I could give myself the love and care, which earlier I had hoped to receive from my wife. I took warm baths, listened to meditative music, and burned candles and incense, thereby nurturing and comforting myself.

Be that as it may, journaling was by far my most important act of self-love. Through writing, I nursed my injured heart. I expressed my sorrow and attended to the needs of my "little boy" on paper. In so doing, I was providing my inner child with a nurturing love.

I focused on loving the angry-dependent boy within me. If I paid enough attention to this little boy's needs, I knew his anger would eventually melt away. I wrote in my journal, "I must embrace my hurt and angry boy and smother him with love and affection. My inner child requires my loving attention, if he is to grow into a man." While gutting out celibacy, I nurtured this young boy, as he grew toward maturity.

At first, I resisted believing that self-love could compete with, or replace, the love of a woman. But I decided self-love was better than no love at all. At least, I could cherish myself, instead of having absolutely *no* love in my life. Indeed, when I provided myself with loving attention, I felt less needy and deprived. By loving myself, I was feeding my own hunger instead of expecting a woman to gratify my craving and fill my internal emptiness.

I concluded I could give myself much of the love that I had wanted from my wife. And then one day, a light suddenly went on! "No other human being could ever give such care-full attention to me as I can. Not a woman, but *I can best love myself.*"

———— •❤• ————

Through this long process of introspection and self-love, I began to grasp who I was. I became focused on forging an identity, instead of seeking intimacy with a woman. I accepted all aspects of myself, even if these parts were "not Christian." As a young man, I had embraced my sexuality. And now at midlife, I had consciously assimilated my rage into who I was becoming. Instead of relying on my fragile Christian persona, I began to depend on my identity as a man who was rooted in his true, earthly nature. By knowing and loving myself more deeply, I was further establishing my identity as a man.

I decided none of my thoughts or feelings were unacceptable. In the inner world, I need not apologize for anything, including my rage.

For my growth, I had to embrace and embody the unacceptable aspects of myself, without acting these out against anyone. I needed to value every previously rejected part of me. I trusted that every dark facet of myself had a divine purpose.

I knew Jesus' second commandment, "You shall love your neighbor as yourself" (Mark 12:31). Yet at this time in my life, I began to focus on the "as yourself" part of this verse. In other words, "You shall love . . . yourself." First, I had to love and accept myself before I could love others.

Self-love meant accepting myself in all my primal humanness, "just as I am"—with all my weaknesses and imperfections "without one plea," as the hymn describes. Because my parents had loved me and taught that God loved me, then surely, I could love myself. The *amazing grace* of my parents' love, and of God's love for me, helped me to love myself unconditionally.

During this four-year celibacy, I forged my masculine identity. As my strength increased, I evolved a spine. And being an attentive and nurturing parent to my inner child, I gradually matured. By gutting out celibacy, coupled with self-love, I was finally becoming a man.

———•♥•———

I grew more comfortable living alone, although I never totally mastered that challenge. My dependency issue slowly but steadily moved toward resolution. During these celibate years, I was building emotional muscle. Consequently, I was no longer cripplingly weak.

By gaining my strength as a man, I would be ready to restart the relationship with my wife, or prepared to begin a new partnership with another woman. Now that I was less needy, I could function as a psychologically healthier partner. With my identity better established, I was ready for mature intimacy with a woman. Or as Erik Erikson wrote, "It is only after a reasonable sense of identity has been established that real intimacy with others can be possible."

As I became more self-dependent, I learned better how to live by myself. But I also knew that I did not want to live alone for the rest of my life. In my marriage, I had been unhealthily dependent. Now, I was becoming more independent. Yet I did not want to go to the extreme of a fierce independence. I accepted my need for a woman in my life. I did not want to be overly-dependent or become too independent. My aim was interdependence in a relationship with a woman.

However, had I become too independent, too staunchly self-reliant? As a celibate man for four years, had I amassed too much masculine strength? Had my newly grown spine replaced my need for the umbilical cord? With that snake in my spine, did I need to depend on a woman again? For four years, I did not attach to a woman. Had I arrived at a point where I no longer needed—or even wanted—a woman in my life?

MY SUPPORTIVE COMMUNITIES

My Friends at School, Work and Elsewhere

In my self-designated cloister, I had no spiritual community with whom to live. Unlike a monk, I had no brothers with whom to work, worship and break bread.

My supportive community was outside my cloistered cell. My friends were in my doctoral program at USC, at my job and elsewhere. During those four difficult years, my soul was socially nourished and emotionally replenished by these friendships.

Thankfully, two and a half years before separating, I had started the PhD program. So, after the separation, I still had a cohort of fellow doctoral students as a built-in network of friends. For more than a decade, we gathered once a month on weekends for in-home parties.

Furthermore, a month after separating from my wife, I started a new job in the outpatient clinic of a psychiatric hospital headquartered in Bakersfield, California. The clinic was in a small town not far from Bakersfield. So, in Taft, I rented a small room in a couple's home on Monday and Thursday nights.

Since I lived a hundred miles away from my rented room in Los Angeles, this employer allowed me to work four ten-hour days. My day off was Wednesday. So, I traveled back to Los Angeles on Tuesday evening to spend time with my children.

This satellite clinic had one other therapist and two secretaries: all three women. One day, the female therapist pointed out that I had grown up in a family with three sisters. Suddenly, I realized I felt so at home at the clinic because I was surrounded by familiar feminine energy. I was truly blessed to have these three women as my surrogate family during the four years that I worked there.

Thankfully, I also had Pete and his wife, Mary, back in Los Angeles. I had known Pete for only four years. But I felt comfortable enough to drop by their home unannounced on many Friday, Saturday or Sunday evenings. When I knocked on the door, they always warmly welcomed me, offering me food, drink and friendship. Being with them, especially on a Friday night, took the edge off the start of yet another lonely weekend.

Frequently on Sunday mornings, I attended various churches in the Los Angeles area, each for a year or two: Bel Air Presbyterian, All Saints Episcopal in Pasadena and Agape in Culver City.

Even though I was with people some Friday nights and most Sunday mornings—and with my children for daytime visits—I was alone for much of the weekend and on Wednesday during the day. So, on Saturday and Wednesday mornings, I went to a fast-food restaurant for breakfast, where I would read and journal for three or four hours. I wanted to get out of my solitary abode; I needed to be around other human beings.

My Children

After the final separation, my son and daughter continued to give my life purpose. I delighted in being their father, not only before but also after the breakup. As a therapist, I wanted my son and daughter to have not only fatherly love but also appropriate limits. I felt a deep purpose and great satisfaction in nurturing and guiding them into adulthood. And I admired the unique individuals they were each becoming. Their presence in my life prompted me to become the best human being I could be, as an example for them.

I routinely saw my children three or four times a week. On Tuesdays, I saw them at their mother's home for dinner and to help with their homework, while their mother worked until 9 p.m. On Wednesdays, we got together at local restaurants for dinner and homework. On weekends for two years, we had various daytime activities and restaurant meals since I had no place for them to sleep in my small, rented room.

After the separation, I continued to drive our son to his soccer practices and games, and our daughter to her theater and musical rehearsals and events. My son and I worked out at my gym. My daughter and I were involved in the YMCA's Indian Princess program. I transported both children to and from their orthodontia appointments. I attended all their open houses and parent-teacher conferences. One day a week, I carpooled my daughter to her school. Even during my darkest hours, I still had a family—my children.

A Temporary Reunification

Two years after our separation—attempting to see if we could live together again—I visited my wife and children in their home on weekends for about six months. But instead of being happy, I soon felt miserable. Although my wife and I were both trying to make it work, our marriage was dead—beyond resuscitation.

The next year, my wife filed for divorce. We both realized the marriage needed to end. By this time, I had lived alone for two years, having resolved much of my dependency problem. I knew I could survive, maybe even happily, without my wife. Initially, I had not wanted to separate and was suicidal. Now, I did not want to get back together.

Even though we were in court only once for the initial hearing, our divorce was not finalized until seven years after our final separation. Since we worked well together regarding the children and money, apparently neither of us felt the need to finalize it more quickly.

REFLECTION

A Sanctuary Within: The Interior Womb

While living in my rented room, my solitary cell, I began to find a home within myself. As I gradually worked through my anger and anxiety problems, the mud settled to the bottom of my soul. The resolution of these internal issues cleansed my soul and opened my heart. Now, my soul was becoming a place, a sanctuary, wherein I wanted to dwell. No longer "lost in a dark wood," I was now being encircled by the dark womb of my soul.

In this sanctuary, I had discovered a sacred space, a safe and fertile womb, wherein I could abide. I had found a womb to replace not only the womb of my childhood family but also the marital womb. As a stronger man, I was becoming more dependent upon this interior womb for emotional and spiritual sustenance.

This sanctuary within me was replacing the cloistered cell in which I had lived for two years. With the passage of time, the womb of my soul would become the only sanctuary I would ever need. In my heart, I would experience "the treasures of grace," as Makarios describes. "Within that little space," I would find "God and the angels. Life is there, and the Kingdom" (Part Three).

My Faith in Life

Near the end of my celibacy, I read a statement which articulated the faith that brought me through the suffering I experienced. "Faith: the involuntary assumption that life is worth living, no matter what happens" (author unknown). Indeed, an "involuntary assumption" from deep within my psyche had manifested as that "involuntary" paralysis of my left leg. When I had the impulse to jump to my death, the Life Force instinctively intervened and saved my life. Hence, the gift of faith: from my body, I was given a faith in Life.

After my wife and I broke up, my life was still worth living. During my celibacy, my appetite for life gradually increased. And during the thirty-five years since the death of my marriage, my life has become more worthwhile and meaningful than ever before. "No matter what happens," even after a painful divorce, life is still worth living.

Imagining "the One"

In spite of the intensity of my rage and my pain during my celibacy, my "dark night of the soul," I started to imagine "the one" special woman with whom I might "fall in love" someday. Increasingly, I had positive fantasies, feelings and thoughts of a new partner. I began to dream of a very special woman who might happen into my life.

After the failed reunification with my wife, I began to form a romantic image of this special woman, which was partially influenced by two of the three women at my job in Taft. At the clinic, I flirted with one attractive female employee for two years. Then, an alluring woman was hired with whom I became enchanted for several years. I never dated either one of these women. Yet as a consequence of being dazzled by these two ladies, the possibility of a new romantic alliance was taking shape within my psyche. My longing took flight, as a romantic image of "the one" special woman grew within my imagination.

A NEW RELATIONSHIP

The Love I Received, the Suffering I Caused

Love comforteth like sunshine after rain.

WILLIAM SHAKESPEARE

A flower cannot blossom without sunshine,
and a man cannot live without love.

MAX MULLER

After being celibate for almost four years, I met Cara. It was a chance meeting on a Saturday morning, August 2, 1986. I had taken my fourteen-year-old son to a nearby city park for his swim meet. When he was not competing, I glanced around the pool area where a crowd of parents and other spectators were seated.

Not far from me, a petite, redheaded woman caught my attention. We were sitting in the bleachers at a right angle to each other, about fifty feet apart. I was able to glimpse at her without being too obvious. Secretly, I hoped she had also looked my way.

After the swim meet, I mustered my courage and went over to speak with her. She informed me that she had a preteen daughter who also had been competing. We talked briefly about our children. I do not recall how either of them fared in that particular meet.

My first impression of Cara was that she was *not* ordinary. Instantly, I found myself drawn to her quiet, introverted nature. Her calm demeanor and simple dress suggested shyness. She seemed genuine, not one to wear much of a mask. From her thoughtful comments, I sensed that she was quite self-aware. These initial impressions aroused my interest. As I came to know her more intimately, my first impressions never changed.

As it turned out, we would both be vacationing for the next several weeks. Cara was traveling to the Far Horizons Retreat Center in Sequoia National Park, an organization based in the principles of theosophy: "wisdom concerning the divine." My children and I would be vacationing in my childhood family's much-beloved mountain cabin in Montreat, North Carolina—a Presbyterian conference center near Asheville. So, almost a month passed before we next met in person.

------ •♥• ------

Once we both returned to Los Angeles, we began to spend increasing amounts of time together during the remainder of 1986. Frequently, we prepared a meal at Cara's home, while engaging in interesting and meaningful conversations. We discovered we had a lot in common, especially our interests in psychology and spirituality.

I had never met anyone like Cara. I found myself fascinated by her quiet manner in the outer world, and I was intrigued by her mesmerizing inner world. She was highly intuitive, with an incredibly imaginative inner life. She was not only introverted, but also had a profoundly spiritual nature.

Cara was a deeply feeling woman. Her caring heart was open and ready to love. As a part-time chiropractor, she worked with the body, using gentle adjustments and massage. Her work with the body and her heart-centeredness both counterbalanced my more-heady nature. Through our relationship, I discovered I feel most comfortable with a woman who lives more from her body and heart, and less from her head.

Our temperaments were quite similar—both introverts. So, I experienced an almost immediate kinship with her, which I had never felt with a woman I was dating. Yet in our relationship, I was the more extroverted partner, something I liked for a change.

But I wondered if we were *too* similar for a lifetime relationship. In those days, I was always jumping ahead, trying to figure out the future. For example, "Two introverts might not have much of a social life," I thought to myself.

———— •♥• ————

At first, I was hesitant to become involved, especially after four years of not dating. So, I proposed friendship. In that fashion, we began.

Before long, an erotic energy arose between us. Increasingly, we began to kiss and make out, which gradually became more frequent and extensive.

Yet I did not want to become fully sexual until I was sure the potential for a meaningful relationship was present. I was not interested in a one-night stand or a brief sexual liaison. My sexual ethic and personal inclination allowed for increasing physical intimacy, only when a corresponding caring and commitment to monogamy was emerging.

Almost from the beginning, I intuitively felt there could be an imbalance in our relationship; Cara might become more attached to me, than I to her. After all, I was in my early forties and she was in her early thirties, an eleven-year difference. I felt she might be badly hurt, if I were to decide she was not "the one" with whom I would want to spend the rest of my life. As a consequence, I felt quite torn about becoming more sexually involved.

Additionally, I wanted to get it right this time. I did not want a difficult partnership. I wanted to be with a woman with whom I could easily relate. So, I was hesitant to jump into another relationship until I was more certain that we would be "emotionally compatible." In those days, I used that phrase to describe the most indispensable aspect of a relationship for me. In retrospect, I believe I was searching for a woman who was capable of a deep feeling connection. Such a woman might help me to further develop my own capacity for feeling, so that I would be able to engage more intimately from my heart.

Finally, I had dated very little before marriage: a few women for a few dates and two brief summer infatuations. Then, during my junior year in college, I met my wife. Our campus courtship lasted two years before we married. Then, for the next sixteen years, I was faithfully wed.

So, now single again, I wanted to explore the world of diverse women. Given my almost complete lack of dating experience, I wanted to see what other women were like: how they were similar, how they were different. Becoming involved with dissimilar women might help me compare and contrast, so I could discover with what type of woman I might best partner. But I was not ready for a long-term commitment.

Given Cara's inviting nature, I had no other hesitations about involvement.

THE LOVE I RECEIVED

Quickly, I realized Cara was a woman who was deeply interested in me. And I rapidly became fascinated with her. She was incredibly responsive to me, kind and considerate. She seemed to really like me, which at first was hard for me to believe.

The failure of my marriage had shaken the foundations of my self-esteem. And having been celibate for four years, I lacked self-confidence in the dating arena. I could not imagine a woman might actually care for me. For Cara's love, I was profoundly grateful, at the time; and for more than thirty years since then, I have felt a deep gratitude for her love.

Cara and I spent most of our indoor time at her home, not my tiny now-studio apartment. She lived in her mother's large, one-story suburban home, with her grade-school-age daughter. The child's grandmother assisted Cara with childrearing and household tasks.

Cara's mother and daughter warmly welcomed me into their home. But Cara did not include her young daughter in any of our activities in the community, and almost none at home. She was rightly afraid that her daughter might become attached to me. And then, if our relationship did not work out, the child might get hurt.

After my years of living alone and being celibate, the holidays I spent with Cara and her family that year were the most wonderful in four years. After my separation, I absolutely loved spending holidays with my children. But an absence, an emptiness, was always present; I did not have a partner with whom to share such joyful occasions.

Given the sprawling layout of the house, and an attentive grandmother, Cara and I had plenty of time for privacy in her bedroom. For more than a year, we spent the majority of our indoor time in her room.

As I recall, Cara's bedroom had little furniture except for a very large futon mattress on the floor. Candles and incense burners adorned several low-level tables, in this otherwise dimly lit room. These small mesas were decorated with crystals, small Indian artifacts and a variety of other sacred objects.

———————— •♥• ————————

Even though Cara was reared Catholic, her spirituality had expanded into the world's religions and various spiritual practices, far beyond the traditional beliefs, practices and confines of Catholicism. In fact, she had become disaffected with the hierarchical patriarchy of her church. She had not attended mass for almost a decade.

Cara's room was more than a bedroom. Her room was her sanctuary, wherein she could retreat, muse, dream and reflect upon, not only her inner world but also her experiences in the outer world. Although extremely devoted to and involved in her daughter's upbringing, she had created a place and times just for herself. Her quiet nature required such a haven.

Cara welcomed me into her inner sanctum. She was eager for me to partake of her quiet inner world and become a part of her outer life. And she wanted me to share more of myself with her by meeting my friends and children. I soon realized Cara wanted a long-term commitment, something I was not ready for.

Stimulating and enriching dialogue was at the core of our relationship. Neither of us was good at small talk. As two introverts, intimate dialogue was essential. We shared our psychological and spiritual experiences, ideas and interests.

I was always excited and joyful to be with Cara in her sanctuary, especially after four years of living alone and being celibate. During our relationship, I spent overnights at her house about twice a week: one mid-week, and one weekend night.

We spent a great deal of time at her home, but we also had many outside activities. We frequently hiked in nearby national forests since we both loved nature. We took weekend trips in California to the mountains in Idyllwild, traveled to Santa Barbara, and lodged on the beach in Carlsbad.

In Los Angeles and its environs, we visited sacred sites, shrines and temples. We enjoyed walking around the Self Realization Fellowship's "Lake Shrine" in Pacific Palisades. We visited the Rosicrucian Temple in Oceanside, California.

We celebrated mass at the Santa Barbara Mission, something which left Cara in tears. For the first time, she saw *laywomen* serving the elements, received not only the bread but also the *wine*, and heard the mass in *English* instead of Latin. The Catholic Church had changed significantly in the ten years since Cara's last communion.

On some Sundays, we attended services at the Healing Light Center—in Glendale, California—from which Cara had graduated. We discussed spiritual books especially important to each of us. She introduced me to "Agnes of God," a movie about the psychiatric problems of a novice nun who suffered the stigmata. She made tapes for me of her favorite New Age music: Ray Lynch, Kitaro, Tangerine Dream, among others.

Even though I had a deep interest in spirituality, Cara exposed me to many new ways of relating to the divine. She vastly broadened my understanding of the sacred. In that sense, she was my spiritual mentor.

The deep spiritual dimension of our relationship, I believe, helped set the stage for what was to happen between us sexually.

Our Sexual Experience

During our first four months together, Cara and I slowly became more physically intimate. We would lie on the mattress on her bedroom floor and talk, hug and kiss for hours. Before long, we were cuddling in the nude under her comforter—without making love. I loved being naked with her. All the kissing, fondling and rubbing of our nude bodies together gave me enormous pleasure. Our skin-to-skin contact comforted and nourished me.

Soon, we began having mutual oral sex, discharging some of the erotic tension aroused by our physical affection and sex play. As we became more physical, I wanted to have intercourse. Yet I was reticent since I knew I was not ready for a long-term commitment. I wanted to make love. Yet I did not want to mislead Cara.

So, after five months of a physically affectionate friendship, I proposed, "Let's try being sexual and committed for four months."

I know most women would find such a proposal to be "absolutely cold and utterly ridiculous. What an idiot!" Yet I knew of no other way to protect Cara from my ambivalence about a longer-term commitment.

Fully aware of my hesitation about a more-lengthy alliance, Cara consented.

In those days, I did not consider myself as having committed to a relationship until we had sex. Intercourse and commitment were synonymous to me. My perhaps idealistic sexual ethic required monogamy, given my belief that sex should always involve caring and commitment—if sexual intimacy was to be safe, enjoyable and truly special.

In spite of that, I did not believe a commitment had to be lifelong. Serial monogamy was an entirely acceptable option for me.

———— •♥• ————

On New Year's Day 1987, we made love for the first time. We had hiked a brief distance in a nearby national forest. The wooded area was hilly but the grass was sparse, given Southern California's desert climate. As we walked and talked, we saw no other trekkers on this chilly holiday.

We decided to sit and talk on a slightly sloped hillside overlooking the San Fernando Valley. Before long, we were kissing and fondling each other. Although it was a cold day, soon we had our pants and underwear off. Since the air was chilly, she kept her sweatshirt on, and I left my wool shirt on. I placed my winter jacket under her, so her bare buttocks would not be pressed into the coarse gravel in the soil.

I entered her. After being celibate for four years, being inside a woman felt magnificent! After a few moments, we both orgasmed. Five months of a growing friendship, deepening affection and increasing physical intimacy were finally consummated.

———— •♥• ————

Cara and I had a wonderful sexual relationship. We both thoroughly enjoyed making love: giving and receiving affection and pleasure. We discovered we were compatible not only sexually but in almost every other way. Being compatible in so many areas greatly enriched our physical relationship.

While making love, we were taken beyond the confines of our familiar selves into the world of the other. After my years of celibacy and a great deal of solitary introspection, I was eager to experience the physical nature of a woman again, along with her mysterious femininity.

During the next four months, perhaps I was too focused on sex. Essentially, every time we were together, we made love. Even outdoors in the woods, we loved making love—usually on the quilt which I kept in the trunk of my car. But in the last six months of our ten-month alliance, the emphasis on our sex life receded somewhat. So, the various aspects of our partnership became more balanced.

Our sexual relationship entailed enormous tenderness, yet was intensely instinctual. I journaled, "Simultaneously, I feel like a small boy being tenderly held by his mother, and yet, like a powerful man, eagerly penetrating, artfully maneuvering and bringing Cara and myself to orgasm."

———— •♥• ————

I marveled at the feeling of Cara's soft vagina encircling my hard penis. I could spend hours inside her, just feeling her love, her feminine responsiveness to me. Nothing could compare to the feeling of being received into her warm, wet opening. Being inside her was heavenly.

Cara and I would talk about how our sexual couplings impacted each differently. Her soft, vaginal receptiveness relieved me of my hard, phallic intrusiveness. After making love, I wanted to drift off into a blissful sleep. But Cara was invigorated. My thrusting provoked her into thought and action. After sex, she was wide awake, ready to talk or begin another activity together.

When making love, Cara was stimulated by my penetrating phallic energy. And I was soothed by her warm vaginal love encircling me. My masculine spirit energized her. Her feminine body nourished me. When making love, she ingested masculine energy, and I devoured a morsel of the feminine.

But when being sexual with Cara, I was apparently ready to receive something even more wonderful. At forty-three, I had matured enough, so I was ready to experience an entirely new dimension to lovemaking. For me, and probably for her, an unforeseen spiritual quality came to life in our sexual relationship. My consciousness had evolved sufficiently, so I began to experience and marvel at a divine presence while having intercourse.

When we were sexual, raw instinct merged with mother-infant-like tenderness. And vital masculine and feminine energies were exchanged. But now, for the first time, I was ready to experience the *love of God when making love.*

———◦♥◦———

I reveled in making love with Cara. Through her deeply caring and instinctual responsiveness to me, I began to experience an unexpected holy dimension while making love. While in her vagina, I felt an amazing, divine affection surrounding me: something which I had never experienced before or even thought possible. Even though I had regarded the sex act as special, and as a sacred pleasure given to us by the Creator, I had never imagined a woman's vagina incarnating the love of God.

Shortly after we first made love, I began to experience Cara's vagina as "sacred," which means "to make holy." I did not know that the love of God could be embodied within a woman's vagina, through her love for me. I journaled, "Cara's vagina is 'sacred.' Within my psyche, a reverence is evolving for her vagina. Indeed, her vagina is divine."

When making love, I was receiving both divine instinct and sacred tenderness. With her, sexuality and the divine were becoming indistinguishable for me. An entirely new holy dimension of the sex act was happening to me.

Within Cara *was* the love of God. From her heart—and through her body and vagina—I felt God caring for me. The deity's love was embodied; the divine had incarnated into the flesh. When encircling my lonely penis with her nurturing vagina, Cara was surrounding me with a divine, healing affection.

In this carnal act, God was warmly responding to me, baptizing me with a divine *caritas*. Through the creature, the Creator was instinctively holding me. In one of the most primordial aspects of Its creation, the Creator was tenderly stroking me. Through the warm, wet responsiveness of Cara's loving vagina, I was being caressed a blessed by God. How wonderfully tangible the love of God is! In union with Cara's loving nature and body, I underwent *a loving union with the divine.*

In early spring that year, we spent a weekend in Idyllwild, California. While hiking in that magnificent forest, we made love partially standing up. Cara was leaning against the slanted, now quilt-covered surface of a massive granite boulder as I entered her.

Afterward, we noticed an orange tanager perched above us on that giant rock, apparently having witnessed our lovemaking. For us, the presence of that simple bird was a sign that something sacred had transpired between us in that resplendent wood.

The Beginning of the End

For four months, I was amazingly happy. I was not focused on the pain from the breakup of my marriage. I was not lonely as I had been during my celibacy. And I was always thrilled to be with Cara.

But in the last six months of our ten-month alliance, each of us was struggling with something which would finally usher in the demise of our relationship. Our dissimilar ideas about a common future was the issue. Almost from the start, we periodically discussed this difference. With the passage of time, these conversations became more frequent and progressively more painful.

Even though Cara and I thoroughly enjoyed each other's company, she was clearly aware of my hesitation about making our alliance more permanent. The tension between what she wanted—and my reluctance to make a long-term commitment—was difficult for both of us but, of course, especially for her.

And then, four months after making love for the first time, my proposed "four-month trial" sexual liaison expired. Cara confronted me. She correctly assessed that I was less deeply involved with her, than she had become with me. My emotional attachment was obviously not as strong as hers.

Cara began to say that she did not feel loved by me. She was hurt-
ᵗᵍ and in pain. She wanted a stronger indication of my emotional
ᵐᵉⁿt in our relationship. Yet I was unable to demonstrate more,
ᵐbivalence about a more permanent troth.
ⁿ to feel anger toward me. She wanted to spend more
And she wanted to meet my friends and my teenage

children—something I had resisted, given my doubt about a more permanent partnership.

——— •♥• ———

I was plagued with guilt for not loving Cara as much as she loved me. I was pained by the fact that I was disappointing her. I do not like to disappoint the expectations of those for whom I care.

And yet I could not belie my feelings. I knew I did not want to make a lasting commitment to her since I had become aware that she was not "the one." I could not sacrifice and extinguish what I wanted, simply to make her happy.

Although I still wanted to spend time with her, increasingly I wanted to be alone. In response, Cara felt "discarded" by me.

I questioned whether I was capable of ever loving or living with a woman again since living alone had become so familiar. Perhaps I had been single too long; maybe I no longer knew how to live in an intimate relationship. Being independent for four years, I made my own decisions. And I enjoyed plenty of alone time for introspection, journaling and reading. And living alone was obviously less complicated. But of course, lonelier.

——— •♥• ———

In late summer, we spent a wonderful weekend in Carlsbad, California. Cara was unimaginably responsive to me. For that weekend, our relationship was perfect again, seemingly free of the commitment issue. Looking back, perhaps this was her last-ditch effort to hold onto me.

But then, for the next six weeks, Cara was distant with me. She became more detached, not only emotionally and sexually but also time-wise. In the fall, she resumed her studies at a nearby university. She became preoccupied with her schooling and had less time for us, so I felt abandoned. I realized I had become more attached to her than I had thought.

Breaking Up

Ten months into our alliance, I concluded that it had been conceived from the beginning. Looking back, I felt it was wr on a trial basis, to have become involved with Cara, given my unwill-ingness to make a long-term commitment.

I told Cara I wanted to end our liaison as lovers, but very much hoped we could remain friends. Given my lack of commitment, I felt breaking off our relationship was the loving thing for me to do. For her sake, I needed to sacrifice my desire to continue longer, hence depriving myself of the many wonderful aspects of our relationship.

I thought to myself, "Am I crazy? Am I some sort of masochist? Why deprive myself of such an amazing relationship," just because I was not ready for a more lasting commitment?

Cara was my first relationship after my marriage failed. I thought to myself, "This relationship is so easy and so good, except for the commitment issue. Surely, I can find an even better relationship," which would be equally effortless. Little did I know how long it would take.

In spite of the initial "trial" nature of our ten-month alliance, Cara came to expect that our relationship might develop into a more en-during partnership, with a growing commitment from me. After all, we were getting along exceptionally well. Her hope that our liaison might continue was only natural—was to be expected.

But my reluctance to commit was still very much alive within me. And that was hurting her. So, I ended our relationship. Cara was rightly confused as to why I would not commit to such a wonder-ful alliance.

———— •♥• ————

Six weeks after we broke up, we spent an afternoon together talk-ing and holding each other. I felt this was what the great spirit of love would have us do.

Over the next several months, Cara and I occasionally became sexual. On Christmas Eve, and again on Christmas Day, we made love for the first time since the breakup two months earlier. I did not know ʼ at this meant. But it felt marvelous.

 a while, I considered a "sexual friendship" with Cara, a more
 ᷄. At the start of our relationship, I never would have con-
 arrangement. But now, I thought this might ease her
 e my loneliness. Instead, she wanted a commitment.

On New Year's Day—exactly a year after making love for the first time—I took Cara to a movie and cooked dinner for her at my apartment. I suggested she spend the night, but I told her we did not need to become sexual. In bed, we began to talk about the difference in the intensity of our feelings for the other. She stated, "I don't feel safe with you. I feel loved and loving at home," with her mother and daughter. I drove her home.

A week later, we became focused on trying to develop a friendship which would not be sexual. I hoped that we might remain good friends.

In mid-January, I took Cara to dinner on her birthday, January 16th. Then, we went back to her home and cuddled in the nude. Being affectionate felt so wonderful. I felt a great fondness for her. I wanted to become a part of her body. But she did not want that. I was not angry. I understood and left.

Yet the next day, we became sexual again. I felt enormously exposed, so utterly human for having such an appetite for physical affection, such a sexual hunger.

In mid-February, we made love again, and then again, two weeks later. But now, I was beginning to feel guilty for being sexual with her, without being willing to commit.

Four months later—eight months after our breakup—Cara and I made love one final time. Afterward, we both felt miserable, extremely depressed. Our previously joyful intimacy was now severely infected with sorrow.

THE SUFFERING I CAUSED

Shortly after we broke up, Cara had a dream of blood flowing from her breasts. Instead of giving milk, her nipples were "dripping blood." With our breakup, the flow of the warm milk of her love for me had mutated into the drip of the warm blood of her suffering. Love no longer flowed from her breasts. Only pain bled from her bosom, now filled with hurt, anger and profound sadness.

In one of her two letters to me after the breakup, Cara expressed heart-rending grief. She spoke of feeling deeply wounded and feare' her heart might "bleed forever." She was afraid she would keep] me "for the rest of my [her] life."

Cara, my "beloved friend," was now suffering deeply. I had terribly wounded the woman who had so generously loved me. My relationship with Cara had been enormously healing for me. Yet with the breakup, our alliance had become horrendously painful for her. Hence, "the suffering I caused."

————— •♥• —————

I had felt a heart-to-heart connection with Cara, but I did not love her as deeply as she loved me. My love for her did not entail the enduring commitment that she wanted. This imbalance caused her pain. From the beginning, I thought Cara might get hurt, but I had not anticipated the depth of her suffering.

I loved Cara enormously. But to this day, I regret I did not say the words, "I love you." Through *other* words and much physical affection, I had clearly demonstrated my love for her. But since I was not ready for a permanent troth, I did not want to speak those amorous words, for fear of misleading her.

Yet I sensed I had added to her pain by failing to be totally honest and say, "I love you." Even though I was ending our relationship, I should have uttered those three words. I had not told Cara the entire truth: "I love you." But now at last, here the truth is spoken.

Tending Cara's Suffering

I wanted to support Cara during her suffering since I remembered "the suffering I experienced"—the seemingly endless pain after my marriage had failed. I was so severely depressed that I experienced that impulse to jump to my death. Now, she was in excruciating pain from "the suffering I caused" by ending our relationship.

When my marriage broke up, I experienced "a heart bleeding." Now, Cara's nipples were "dripping blood." I understood and identified with her suffering, her bleeding. When she suffered, I suffered with her.

Yet while supporting her, I was probably re-experiencing some of ____ from the breakup of my marriage. At first, I could not clearly ____ etween Cara's current suffering and my past pain.

____ ay, I was also pained by the loss of Cara. I felt a deep ____ sence of her loving presence in my life.

When we broke up, I did not feel anger or rage, as I had with my wife. And I did not feel suicidal. My period of celibacy had clearly changed me. With a stronger masculine identity, I had not become pathologically attached to Cara. For the first time with a woman, I experienced interdependence—simultaneous independence and dependence—in a loving relationship.

I suspect Cara's suffering was teaching her about her overattachment to me, similar to what my pain had taught me about my overdependence on my wife. In spite of being deeply hurt, Cara would gradually emerge from her suffering as a woman being healed. About six months after we broke up, she had a dream suggesting a rebirth was taking place within her (Chapter 5).

————•♥•————

During the first year after our breakup, I talked with Cara by phone at least once a week. I had hoped giving her a chance to verbalize her pain and grief from the breakup would be healing for her. Yet at times, she would talk angrily and negatively about our relationship. Her harsh words bruised some of my cherished memories.

Sometimes, we had enjoyable and interesting conversations. But after a while, her anger would resurface, which was always hurtful for me. Yet I understood why she needed to express the angry feelings arising out of the hurt.

I had hoped that listening to her pain that year would help her resolve some of her grief. But I am not sure if tending to her suffering helped or hindered her healing.

A Friendship Aborted

Although I had ended our relationship eight months earlier, we came together in late June to watch Bill Moyer's 1988 weeklong television series, *The Power of Myth*, with Joseph Campbell. Life's spiritual dimension had been a central aspect of our relationship.

Shortly after, Cara decided she did not want to get together again, even as friends. And after another six months, she decided she did not want to talk by phone.

As described in one of her two letters, Cara felt "torn apart" by her decision not to remain friends. She felt being around me would be too painful. Her memories of us being together caused her the "utmost pain." Yet someday, she hoped these same memories might bring her "enjoyment."

Over the next year, I did attempt a few phone calls. Either she did not answer, or if she did, she was indifferent. It became clear that a friendship was no longer a possibility.

———— ❖ ————

Since we lived near each other, we did have two or three chance meetings in our community. The first time, I ran into her at the Woodland Hills Mall in the San Fernando Valley. We had not spoken for two years. I wanted to hug her but she seemed reticent. I did not want to cause her pain. I felt she should take the initiative. There was no hug.

Each time, we talked briefly, each asking how the other was doing. It was awkward. Clearly, Cara's wounded heart was still not entirely healed. We each wished the other well and parted for the last time.

I very much wanted Cara to remain my "beloved friend." Yet she was unable to do this. My unwillingness to commit to a long-term relationship, and then me breaking off our alliance, had caused her too much pain for a friendship to be born.

Hence, a friendship aborted.

REFLECTION

Looking back, I realize Cara was the ideal lover for me at this time in my life. She came into my life when I badly needed to be embraced by a deeply loving woman. Through her love for me, I experienced the feminine in a unique, truly divine and miraculous manner.

Cara gave so freely and fully of herself. She opened her heart and body to me—so lovingly, so instinctually, with a responsiveness so complete. Her healing love, both deeply emotional and intensely erotic, had initiated a curative process within my soul. During our year-long alliance, the wound in my heart received Cara's nurturing care. Her warm affection began to transform my heart-wound into a novel, life-giving opening into my soul—and into a lasting openheartedness for loving others.

Even though unaware at the time, later I realized I had internalized—taken into myself—part of Cara's feminine essence. I received her healing love and ingested some of her womanly warmth. Beyond a shadow of a doubt, Cara's deeply feminine nature fostered the further evolution of my feminine soul.

I was blessed with the good fortune of Cara happening into my life. Surely, a divine providence was at work, when such a deeply loving woman came into the life of such a terribly lonely man. The warm sunshine of Cara's love broke through the dark clouds from the death of my marriage. As Shakespeare wrote, "Love comforteth like sunshine after rain."

Cara's love was not a gift taken lightly. "The love I received," I have affectionately remembered for more than thirty years. Hers was a heart full of love. I came to love her. And she loved me even more. For her love, I remain profoundly grateful.

Cara's "Sacred" Vagina

Cara's loving heart and body played an essential role in my midlife transition and transformation. I had felt God's love when we made love. For the first time, I encountered divine *caritas* for me, while inside a woman's vagina. Yes, the love of God was embodied in Cara's generous heart and body.

As a result, her vagina became "sacred," holy to me, worthy of veneration. For many years after, I fondly carried within my heart the palpable memory of her loving heart, most tangibly felt with my remembrance of her now-sacred vagina.

Furthermore, Cara's "sacred" vagina would become the key metaphor for, indeed the principal symbol of, my midlife metamorphosis. Her healing love, partially expressed through her love-filled vagina, would foster the dramatic transformation of my heart-wound into a living vagina in my heart: indeed, a sacred portal into my soul.

Cara: Not "the One"

Cara's love saved me from the excessive masculinity which I had amassed during my celibacy. And her *caritas* initiated a curative process within my wounded heart, so my soul could be resuscitated and my life started over again. Although I was unaware at the time, Cara's nurturing love had *prepared the inner womb*, my soul, for a conception.

Even though I had felt a deep affection for Cara and experienced a healing love from her, I had not experienced romance; I was not romantically in love with her. So, I knew Cara was *not* "the one" about whom I had dreamed during my celibacy. I still thought that some-day I would "fall in love" with a very special woman who would be "the one."

At that time, I was incapable of loving and committing to a wom-an without an overpowering romantic attraction, without an all-con-suming projection. My inner feminine side was still mostly uncon-scious and underdeveloped. Looking back, I realize that my soul was too immature for an enduring relationship with a woman at that stage in my life.

PART TWO

MIDLIFE TRANSITION AND TRANSFORMATION

From the Outer Woman into the Inner Feminine

───◆♥◆───

The Eternal Feminine shows us the way.

FINAL LINE,
FAUST
GOETHE

As is so often the case at midlife, my soul was ripe for being romantically projected outside of myself. For this to happen, the right type of woman would have to come into my life, who might spark a "falling in love" response within me. Then, I could undergo a powerful romantic attraction to a woman who would cause me to feel "in love" and fully alive. I could worship my soul in an actual woman, as a projection onto her. I would become conscious of my *own* soul, initially as a goddess-like presence outside myself.

The spring of my rebirth began when I met Diana. At the time, I was forty-three years old. She would be "the one" with whom I would "fall in love." Unknowingly, my soul would be projected onto this flesh-and-blood woman.

But after ten brief weeks, Diana abruptly broke off our liaison. Over the next five years, my suffering and grief, along with the gradual withdrawal of my soul-projection, would transform me. A rebirth of my consciousness (Chapter 5), the awakening of my soul (Chapter 6) and ultimately the birth of God in my soul would re-create me (Chapter 9).

While dating Diana, and during the month after our breakup, three powerful events transpired: "a kiss and the question" that I asked Diana (Chapter 4), the sculpting of a portal into my soul (Chapter 5) and "a dream and the answer" (Chapter 6). These three life-altering experiences would steer me into my soul, the inner feminine. In this process, my old ego-identity would slowly die, so a new identity could be rebirthed.

At midlife, my failed liaison with Diana inaugurated my transition from loving an actual woman, into falling in love with the inner woman. With the breakup, my self-esteem was decimated, so then my soul was able to awaken within. As Jung stated, "The first half of life is devoted to forming a healthy ego. The second half of life is going inward and letting go of it." My suffering had eroded my ego-identity, so I let go of my ego and entered into my soul.

CHAPTER 4

A KISS AND THE QUESTION
"Are You the One?"

John the Baptist sent his disciples to ask Jesus,
"Are you the One who is to come,
or should we wait for another?"
In response, Jesus infers He is "the One,"
the Messiah, by alluding to his miracles
which John's disciples had just witnessed.

LUKE 7:19-22

Four months after breaking up with Cara, I became enchanted with Diana, "the one" who would activate the romantic projection of my soul onto her. Nine months earlier, I had met her at my new job. At that time, I never imagined I would "fall in love" with her, nor did I expect she would be "the one" for whom I was searching. But looking back, those nine months must have constituted a mating ritual, apparently mostly unconscious for me.

While working with Diana, I began to believe she was the actual owner of all the wonderful traits that I began to see in her. I felt she possessed the feminine qualities that I wanted in a life partner. I thought I was attracted to Diana *for who she actually was.*

However, at that time, I was not aware—as is the case with all projections—that my soul was being projected onto her. But in fact, during our brief, ten-week liaison, I did "fall in love"; and I came to feel Diana was "the one" I was seeking. The seed of my soul was projected onto her, so my soul could thereby be conceived in my consciousness.

—————— •❧• ——————

At my new job, Diana was hired at the same time that I was. For orientation and on-the-job training, we were frequently together during our six-month probationary period. At the agency's headquarters, she had the office next to mine. After three months, I was transferred to a district office closer to my home.

Even though I found Diana physically attractive, initially I was not drawn to her somewhat aloof and distant nature. After my marriage, I had an uncanny sensitivity to reading a woman's body. And indeed, Diana's body language was suggestive of caution, perhaps even fearfulness. Given similar issues with my wife, I was also reluctant.

Be that as it may, a work friendship did develop. At times, we got together for dinner and a movie after work hours. Yet during these nine months of becoming acquainted, an attraction and a sexual charge were slowly developing between us. The two of us attending a work-related conference would not only intensify these erotic energies, but also dramatically amplify my budding romantic expectations.

THE SPRING OF MY REBIRTH

A Kiss: The First Night

In March 1988, our agency staff attended a conference in Monterey, California. Diana and I drove from Los Angeles in separate cars with other staff. Yet by the end of the conference three days later, she suggested just the two of us drive back to Southern California in my car and spend the night at Big Sur, one of her favorite vacation spots. I believe she took the initiative because she sensed my hesitation about involvement.

The conference began on St. Patrick's Day, that year a Thursday. Diana was Irish, so that was a noteworthy day for her. As for me, that Celtic holiday would turn out to be my "lucky four-leaf clover day," to be sure, a providential day.

Before dinner on the arrival day, Diana and I mingled with other conference attendees in the hotel lobby, having drinks and hors d'oeuvres. We were acutely aware of the other's presence across the room, as we made frequent but brief eye contact. From the lobby, I hardly noticed the magnificent sunset over the Pacific Ocean.

Just before dinner, Diana discreetly approached and invited me to her room after the evening meal.

After dinner, I went to her room where she was waiting. She had arranged for her conference roommate to be elsewhere. We talked briefly about our growing interest in and emerging feelings for the other. She was attracted to my "distant" nature. I was intrigued by her "mysterious" femininity. After a few minutes, she suggested we lie on the bed.

On the bed, I excitedly embraced her and felt her body press against mine, as we kissed for the first time. The physical affection started slowly. Her lips were so soft, so fleshy. I had never tasted such full, such moist and tender lips. Our slippery lips and tongues began to swim together. Lying on our sides, our embraces became more passionate, our kisses more libidinous.

She had on a light pink, woolen-knit dress, which was quite soft. From her tight-fitting dress, her tantalizing breasts protruded. She was ravishing! I was euphoric!

Then, I rolled onto my back. She followed, coming to rest halfway on top of me. She slid her right leg between my legs. Our lips and tongues were all over the other's mouth, face and hair as we made out. An erotic heat began to warm the room.

I nibbled on the side of her neck. She responded with a sigh, yet quickly pulled away as if this was forbidden territory. Her neck was so sensitive. I never knew a woman could be so responsive to a kiss on the neck.

I stroked the side of her face affectionately and brushed her long, black hair away from her cheek. My cheek nestled against hers. Such affection took me back to earlier days. I felt like a small child, ingesting tenderness and nourishment from his mother.

We must have kissed for several hours. Her kisses were intoxicating. I felt like I was being overtaken by a goddess *in the flesh*. Never before had I been kissed like that. I thought to myself, "Never again will I experience such passionate kisses."

While physically entwined, I am sure we talked. But I do not recall a single word.

After these exhilarating hours, I left her room deeply satisfied, yet terribly excited. I returned to my room on the remote bottom floor of the hotel next to the ocean. I finally fell asleep fantasizing about her, while listening to the waves crash upon the beach.

The Question: The Second Night

The next night, I invited Diana to my room, after arranging for my conference roommate to be absent. Immediately, we lay on the bed. And once again, we began kissing and caressing each other's clothes-clad bodies. With her on top of me, I excitedly slid my hands over her enticing, firm buttocks.

I rolled over on top of her. My stiff penis pressed against her pubis. Our lips slithered upon the other's without pause. Our lascivious kisses seemingly had no end.

Staring deeply into her eyes, I became entranced. I gazed with amazement into her big, brown eyes, those Irish eyes, so inviting and yet so mysterious. She responded, "My eyes will heal you." I had never heard a woman say such a thing. I thought to myself, "Perhaps this might be true," as I peered deeply into her pupils. In awe of the unknown, I wanted to look into her soul and see who this alluring woman might be.

Suddenly for no reason, I straightened my arms and pushed my chest up from her breast. Unexpectedly and without inhibition, I asked, "Are you the one?" My voice did not have its usual tone; it had an intense, uncanny quality filled with awe and passion. Apparently, her intoxicating kisses had prompted this unforeseen question from within.

Initially, I thought I was asking if she was "the one" I would marry, the one who would become my best friend and lover for life. Is she the one meant for me? Am I the one for her? Is she "the one" about whom I had dreamed during my celibacy?

At work, I had known Diana for only nine months. Then suddenly, this entanglement. Had I denied that I was falling in love; had an embryonic love been gestating unconsciously within my soul? Or was it the amazing intensity of these first two nights?

Even though this query was entirely premature for a second "date," I was quickly becoming enchanted with Diana. I was rapidly beginning to envision an amazing romantic potential in our evolving chemistry: a strong physical attraction, an intense emotional bond and a deep spiritual affinity.

Even so, I had no conscious intention of making such a query. In the passion, the heat and excitement of the moment, this unpre-meditated question simply flew out of my mouth. Seemingly, another voice from within had made the inquiry. I had no awareness that such a bewildering question, "Are you the one?" was waiting to be asked. These unforeseen words were just blurted out from somewhere deep within my soul. At the time, I had no aforethought whatsoever about this question. But five years of afterthought would follow.

Then, as I sought to grasp her mysterious nature, I asked, "Who are you? Where did you come from?" I was in a virtual trance, as these questions were being asked from within me.

Yes, I was mystified by the arrival of this magnificent woman into my life. Yet I sensed another soul was present in the room, lurking between us in that night.

Maybe it was I who asked, "Are you the one?" Yet my voice was unfamiliar. My words were filled with wonderment in response to what was happening. I had the feeling that Diana had been sent to me from some unknown region: perhaps from the realm of the goddess-es. Or was this question an initiation into a fortuitous spiritual quest, an inadvertent journey into an as-yet-unidentified sacred territory?

After several hours of erotic entanglement, she returned to her room at midnight.

———◆———

Almost instantly, I had sensed a "messianic" quality to this un-premeditated question. As I began "to fall in love," it was as if divine expectations were being seen in Diana. Several years earlier, as a middle-aged man, I had imagined that I might require a feminine messiah as my "savior." Now, Diana was fast becoming this messianic goddess to me.

Instead of a male Christ, a feminine messiah was arriving into my life. At the time, I believed I was seeing in Diana an actual incarnation of the divine feminine. Diana was my feminine Christ, my "Christine." In my journal, I wrote many times, paraphrasing the Phantom's song to his Christine, "You alone can make my soul [song] take flight." With the goddess Diana now arriving into my life, my soul indeed took flight as I fell in love. I had found the redemptive feminine in a flesh-and-blood woman.

In these first hours of becoming entangled, something wondrous transpired, which I had never felt before. Something magical and mysterious came to pass. Something unimaginably "divine" was happening during those first two days, although I was barely aware of what it was. But I knew I was undergoing something heavenly: something beyond words, beyond comprehension.

———————— •♥• ————————

Four months after that March weekend in Monterey, I recalled reading Jungian analyst Edward Edinger's book, *The Christian Archetype* (1987), the prior year. He reflects on the question asked by John the Baptist's disciples to Jesus: "*Are you the One* who is to come, or should we wait for another?" (Luke 7:19). When I re-examined his book, those words flew off the page! Two millennia earlier, John's disciples had asked Jesus this same question, using the *exact* words that my lips had perplexingly uttered to Diana four months earlier.

Edinger describes this question as "the crucial question of individuation. Once it is asked, the die is cast and the process must live itself out for good or ill" (page 52). Such a query signals the commencement of the individuation process, whereby an individual becomes increasingly conscious of his/her deeper Self. For many Westerners, myself included, the archetype of Self is symbolized by the Christ. Gradually, the Christ/the Self emerges, bit by bit, from the depths of the soul and incarnates Itself into one's consciousness.

When I asked Diana, "Are you the one?" I hardly realized the significance of this question, although I had intuited something messianic in the query. Now, like John's disciples, I felt "the one," my feminine messiah, had arrived in the person of this exterior goddess. So, I need *not* "wait for another." At that time, I had not yet experienced "the birth of God in the soul": the birth of the interior messiah/the Self from the soul, and Its incarnation into my consciousness.

Big Sur: The Third Night

On the day the conference ended, Diana and I drove south in a leisurely fashion along the magnificent California coastline from Monterey to Big Sur. It was a bright, sunny day in the early spring. A new adventure was commencing.

We had selected an isolated, rustic cabin in the lush woods near the ocean, where we would spend our first, full night. Yet we were mostly oblivious to our surroundings, given the amorous fervor of our now two-day-old liaison.

After dinner, we drove back to our cabin in the dark. At her request, we undressed separately—Diana in the privacy of the bathroom. She asked to wear my flannel pajama top. In our room, I had stripped down to my tightfitting jockey briefs. When she came out, she was wearing my pajama top and her panties.

As I lay on the bed on my back, she approached. She climbed on the bed and straddled me. With the tips of my fingers and the palms of my hands, I reached up and began to slowly caress and gently fondle her warm, ample breasts. I raised my head and nibbled upon her pajama-clad nipples, as her breasts dangled upon my face. Being modest, she was not ready for me to see her bare-breasted.

We began to passionately rub our underwear-clad erogenous parts together. With her riding on top of me, her soft vulva pressed my erect penis firmly against my belly. I was ecstatic as her fleshy lips—her seemingly parted labia—embraced both sides of my penis. She slid back and forth—from head to base—on my stiff, blood-filled shaft. Her clitoris stroked the underside of my organ.

The heat of our bodies filled our small cabin with an erotic steam. Our juices comingled on her panties and my briefs, as the aroma of our fluids intermixed in the warm, now-moist air. We experienced enormous pleasure, tension and excitement, as if we were having intercourse—yet not having it.

Diana wanted to "take it slow." I was more than willing to restrain myself for now, given the zest of my erotic excitement and the zeal of my romantic expectations.

I fondled her wet, panty-covered vulva. She stroked my damp, tightly enrobed phallus. We kissed passionately as we ground our still-not-yet exposed genitalia against the other's, again for what must have been several hours. At times, one or the other, or both, came close to orgasm.

Even so, Diana was not ready for me to enter her. The orgasms would be saved for later, when our budding affections would be in full bloom and ready to be consummated. Intentionally, neither of us climaxed. Yet we both seemed satisfied, satiated and finally exhausted. As our making-out tapered off, Diana fell asleep on top of me.

————— •♥• —————

The next morning, I awoke first. As Diana slept quietly on her back next to me, I could see, for the first time, one of her magnificent womanly breasts, fully exposed by the partially unbuttoned pajama top. Her large, white breast was topped with a glorious red nipple, resting gently on her pink areola. In the early morning light, I contentedly stared with amazement at this mountain of feminine flesh until she awoke twenty minutes later.

After a late and leisurely breakfast, we drove back to Los Angeles, talking all the way home, as new lovers do. Diana remarked, "You let me in," meaning I let her into my being, into my soul. I had been hesitant about involvement with Diana, but now my heart was rapidly opening to her.

Falling in Love

A few days after the conference, I had the uncomfortable sense that Diana had something to teach me. I wrote in my journal, "Her deeply feeling nature may help me experience my feminine, feeling self again." I had a hunch she would somehow be a part of my continuing redemption: the goddess who would make me whole again.

For ten weeks, beholding her face and gazing into her mysterious brown eyes became a favorite pastime for me. At times, staring into her eyes precipitated tears of tenderness trickling down my cheeks. I was like a child, looking into his mother's eyes. I regressed. I loved. I took her into my heart. At such moments, the two of us were one.

When our lips would swim together and our tongues were entangled, I would breathe deeply with the erotic pants of a horny, forty-three-year-old man with his lover—and at other times, with the contented sighs of a small child near his mother. Her seductive lips drew me into her. We could kiss affectionately and passionately for hours.

I loved the fragrant smell of her hair, the soft feel of her skin. I nestled at her breast: my cheek against her bosom, my lips tenderly opening to her nipples.

What a powerful magnetic attraction between us! Astonished and amazed, I rapidly began to worship this goddess. I had never felt such an overwhelmingly passionate energy between myself and a woman.

As my ego boundaries began to melt away, I was still somewhat fearful of involvement. I journaled, "I fear I might be engulfed by her softness, her deeply feeling nature. I don't have anything to push against; she's too receptive, too soft, too feminine. If I cannot push against her, I might get trapped inside her." I was afraid I could be swallowed by her mysterious femininity. Yes, this goddess might devour me.

Yet as time passed and my heart gradually opened to Diana, I realized I was not going to be ingested. Rather, I was taking her into my heart, the chamber where I could hold and cherish her. Three weeks after our first kiss, I journaled, "I woke up this morning and Diana was inside me, in my heart," as I felt her presence within my body. A month later, "Diana fills a hole in my heart, now that I have taken her into my soul."

I became vulnerable and tender. Being around her caused me to feel weak. I wrote, "Diana will save me from my masculinity, from my solitary self-determination. Her womanliness has moved my soul, stirred me in unexpected ways." I surrendered to love: its power, its rule over me. Yes, "Two souls, one life—a dream."

Diana was my "dream woman," the woman I had dreamed about during my celibacy. She was "the one" for whom I had been searching.

Upon waking one morning, the phrase "morning song" arrived into my consciousness, an appellation which described my experience of Diana. At midlife, she was fast becoming my "Morning Song."

Somehow, I knew this was the dawn of a new day, a midlife commencement: a fresh start to my life, maybe a new life partner. Perhaps a rebirth. Yes, being with her, I felt as if I was being "born again" into a totally new life. Hence, the spring of my rebirth.

Our Relationship

Nevertheless, our relationship was not problem-free. In fact, it was quite challenging at times, as we tried to understand major differences in our temperaments. Furthermore, Diana told me she wanted me to be happy, like she felt she was. But then, she disclosed events that indicated her unhappiness. And she was worried about the high level of conflict in my marriage five years earlier. In contrast, all her relationships had been "easy." But later, she described several of her past relationships that had been highly conflicted. Finally, she felt I was not trusting like herself. Yet her distrustfulness was blatantly obvious to me.

At times, it was as if she and I spoke different languages. I journaled, "My relationship to Diana seems to be more of a challenge than with Cara. I like a challenge, for a change." But in time, I would realize our differences were too great an obstacle to overcome.

I sensed Diana was not especially self-revealing. She alluded to events that she was not ready to talk about. For some reason, she was hesitating about becoming more involved with me. I wanted to know more about her. Yet at this time, she was not ready to be more self-disclosing.

——— •♥• ———

As I recall, I saw Diana about once a week when I would travel to our agency's main office for case conferences. Afterward, in the privacy of her office, we had long, loverly talks, kissed passionately and fondled each other's clothing-clad erogenous parts.

During our ten-week liaison, we also got together most weekends for daytime visits, meeting halfway between our homes. We would hike and have lunch, or have dinner and see a movie. Then, we would make out in a secluded, wooded area on a blanket, or in her car.

For overnights, we spent only two or three weekends together. An eighty-five-mile distance between our homes was a hindrance. But more significantly, Diana was hesitating about becoming more involved with me. I became increasingly disheartened by her obvious ambivalence.

In late April, Diana spent a Saturday night at my apartment, the first overnight since Big Sur in mid-March. We spent the night naked, except for underwear, erotically entangled in bed. Even so, she did not want to make love, for me to enter her.

In mid-May, we spent a weekend in Santa Barbara. Except for going out for occasional meals, we spent those two days in bed. As I was waking up on Saturday morning, I had a feeling of great familiarity within me. When I opened my eyes, Diana's soft, brown eyes were staring at me. I felt like I had known her for a very long time.

Later that day, Diana wept in my arms, yet offered no explanation for her tears. She said she had never allowed a man to hold her while crying. She had disclosed her innermost feelings only to women. I felt honored to witness her pain, privileged to be the first man to embrace her as she sobbed.

We did not make love that weekend. Diana was vacillating about becoming more involved with me. Now two months into our liaison, I was becoming increasingly frustrated.

AN UNEXPECTED BREAKUP

That year for Memorial Day weekend, I went canoeing with my fourteen-year-old daughter on the Colorado River. For several years at a nearby YMCA, we had been involved in the Indian Princess program for fathers and their teenage daughters. As a group, we met monthly for various recreational activities in the community. Then, each Memorial Day weekend, we traveled to the Colorado River to canoe on the stretch, from just below Hoover Dam to Willow Beach. Our father-daughter group camped along the river for two nights. On Monday, we caravanned back to Los Angeles.

When I returned home, I received a phone call from Diana. After she tearfully told me that her cat had died, she said she wanted to end our relationship, pronto! She had been crying for four days, struggling with this decision. She was distraught, yet gave no intelligible explanation for terminating our liaison.

At this time, she made no mention of my divorce still not being finalized. And she said nothing about my former girlfriend, Cara, either at this time or any future date. She was not open to any discussion about staying together. The breakup was final.

I had lovingly taken Diana into my life. And then, she abruptly jerked herself out of my heart. She had lured me into her orb; and in response, I allowed her to gravitate into my soul. I was angry with her for the breakup since I had allowed her to enter so deeply into my heart. Why did I permit Diana to travel so far into the core of my being?

In the ten weeks Diana and I were together, we did not consummate our love. For the entire time, she had resisted this.

An Unconsummated Love

Prior to our breakup on Memorial Day, Diana had not been available for full sexual intimacy. Even so, our heavy petting kept me energetically engaged. Perhaps because of her sexual distancing of me, my desire to have intercourse was fueled even further. Did our partially consummated liaison not only intensify the sexual charge for me, but also amplify the romantic projection of my soul onto her?

Within my body and my heart, erotic and romantic energies had lovingly arisen. Yet instantly, all was extinguished. The hope of Diana becoming my life partner vaporized. And she was not going to gratify me sexually. Within my soul, painful emotions were now intermixing with formerly pleasurable passions.

My anguish was enormous. I was bereft of a potential life partner. And I was bemoaning the lack of sexual fulfillment with the woman with whom I was falling in love. Not becoming fully sexual, and then Diana abruptly leaving the scene, left me with only myself.

My pain drew me inward into my soul. Now, my soul was the only "One" to whom I could turn. I needed her assistance. Yet my soul was too bloodied and bruised herself—from the breakup—to comfort me. What would my soul and I do with our suffering? I knew we would need each other's help.

Even though our first three nights began with a heavenly intensity, our relationship was not meant to be. Passion was the hallmark of our liaison that spring. At least I had loved; yes, I had fallen in love. Better "to have loved and lost," than not loved at all. Yet entirely unexpectedly, as a result of having fallen in love and lost, an alliance with another woman, an interior woman, would come to be.

———— •♥• ————

Now, *unlike* John's disciples who realized Jesus was "the One who is to come," I had to "wait for another." Diana was not "the One"; she was not my feminine messiah. The messiah who was "to come" would arrive from within. I would have to wait for that savior to be born within my soul.

As the individuation process unfolded within me, my feminine soul would eventually become the mother of this messiah—the mother of Self within me. My virgin soul would be "the One" to deliver this messiah/the Self into my consciousness.

Ten years later, I journaled, "Diana was the right woman (*unavail-able*) at the right time (the start of midlife), for the awakening of my soul and my rebirth."

A Summer of Suffering

The spring of my rebirth was followed by a summer of suffer-ing. Diana ending our alliance caused me to suffer greatly since I had wholeheartedly fallen in love with her. I had hoped she would be "the one" with whom I would spend the rest of my life. I had imagined we might have a home together, possibly even children. This was the worst summer of my life.

But in mid-June, Diana suggested we might become re-involved in the fall. A few days later, she implied that our breakup would be only a three-month "hiatus." She requested, "Wait for me." I felt some-what hopeful about such a prospect, and yet I was rather doubtful. Having a three-month delay before resuming our relationship would be torturous for me. And by summer's end, the outcome was *not* guaranteed.

At the time, I did not know Diana's reasons for a pause in our relationship, although it was clear she was quite ambivalent about me. But for the first time, she did express concern about my divorce not being finalized, even though my wife and I had been separated for five years; and two years earlier, my wife had filed for divorce. As long as I was still legally married, Diana did not want to become fully sexual with me. Within a month, I reactivated my divorce case, hoping to eliminate this particular obstacle. That was the only portion of her reluctance over which I had any control.

More to the point, Diana disclosed that she was interested in another man she had previously dated. Although they had not yet become re-involved, she wanted to consider him as a potential life partner. Waiting that summer was agonizing for me, and seemingly effortless for her. I had but one focus, her. She had two foci: her former boyfriend and me. She was having difficulty deciding between us.

Two weeks after Diana ended our liaison, we had lunch at Café Casino. She told me about a traumatic event during her teenage years that had deeply injured her. Her unhealed wound seemed to be part of her reason for hesitating to become more involved with me. Hearing what had happened to her pained me tremendously.

Yet I was suffering my own anguish since she had so impetuously ended our short-lived liaison. In early summer, I journaled, "Too much sadness for me to bear, too much pain for me to handle. Why do I suffer so deeply? When does the suffering end? Where is my solace?" I was reminded of Freud's remark, "We are never so defenseless against suffering as when we love."

In early August, I traveled with my son and daughter, and my sister and her daughter (all three, mid-teens), to Hawaii for ten days. Although planned as a fun vacation, I was totally miserable as I quietly suffered internally. In the hotel lobby with my phone card (before cell phones), I attempted to call Diana each day. But she never answered. Each time, my heart sank.

In Hawaii, I journaled, "I wish Diana were here with me. It is so hard to wait from Memorial Day to Labor Day. She puts our relationship on hold for the summer. That pisses me off! My inner woman [my soul] is so angry. All my aspirations and dreams burn with a fiery rage. I am tired of feeling the anger of disappointed dreams."

The Fall and The Winter

After that summer of suffering, Diana finally made her decision. She wanted me, not her former boyfriend. We reunited for several months that fall, as she had proposed. Our affections were finally consummated. My heart was happy, yet fearful of being abandoned once again.

Nevertheless, our relationship remained a challenge. That fall, the stark reality of our emotional incompatibility became increasingly clear to me. In the end, our relationship would not endure.

Our relationship was in the process of dying that fall, and was dead by winter. No longer my "Morning Song." But now, a "song of mourning." That winter, a lament became my painful refrain. I repetitively journaled, "Ten thousand tears, and then ten-thousand more." My suffering seemingly had no end.

Although I suffered sorely, thankfully this time I had no thought of suicide like I did when my marriage ended. In spite of intense pain, this breakup would not destroy me.

A year later, I made a private retreat to the Pecos Benedictine Monastery in Pecos, New Mexico, where Brother Dan Stramara served as my spiritual director. His scholarly interest was in the feminine references to God in the Bible and throughout church history. And he was well-versed in Jungian psychology. Brother Dan quietly reflected, "She [Diana] wounded your inner feminine." I broke into tears. I knew he understood.

At work, Diana's angry distancing of me made clear she did not want a friendship.

Several years later, Diana married for the first time, but not her former boyfriend.

Mourning

After we broke up, my love for Diana did not cease. I would recall the fleshy feel of her lips, the softness of her hair and the sight of her big brown eyes. In December, I wrote in my journal, "Too much was wonderful there, too much to give up."

Three years after we split up, I was still mourning Diana. I journaled, "Like a nightingale, she sang deep within the recesses of my darkened heart." And, "She had begun to caress the edges of my solitude. Her presence fed my aloneness, so my heart was less hungry, less lonely."

Four years after the breakup, I journaled, "I loved Diana enormously. Her breasts were exquisite. I loved to kiss and nibble upon them," as I fondly recalled our naked bodies together. "To live between her legs. To pump my juices deep inside her," as I continued to hold on. A half-decade of grief would be required before I could fully relinquish her.

As my bond to Diana was dying, I entered into my wounded heart. Because of the intensity of my suffering, I realized I had to penetrate into the core of my being. In this process of entering into my soul, I would unknowingly fertilize the inner woman: put my seed into and impregnate my soul. In time, the agonizing loss of Diana would *induce the labor* for my rebirth within the soul.

I mourned my grave loss. But simultaneously, I began to embrace the genesis of my rebirth and the reanimation of my soul, which were soon to emerge from my broken heart. From these ashes, a phoenix would arise.

REFLECTION

My Dependency Issue Resurfaces

So much pain from a ten-week, spring romance. How did I become so attached in such a short time? Was I still too dependent? Or was the breakup so painful because I had opened my heart so completely and began to love Diana so deeply? Or as I fell deeply into love, did I regress into a childlike state?

During my celibacy, I thought I had resolved my dependency problem. After my wife and I separated, I had lived *without* a woman for four years. Since I had more firmly established my identity as a man, I felt my unhealthy dependence on my wife had been mostly resolved, although a moderate feeling of woundedness remained. Furthermore, I had grieved the loss of Cara with much less pain. But now with Diana, why was my suffering again so excruciating?

I had lovingly taken Diana into my heart, and she took root within my soul. Unknowingly, I had regressed and become vulnerable like a child, in the tender and contented moments of falling in love. I was not aware she had become so deeply embedded within my heart, and I so childlike.

The umbilical cord attaching Diana to me was affixed to the placenta within my heart. Now, that cord that yoked us—and earlier had joined me to my wife—was cut once more. Diana, my newly-found love, had expelled herself from the interior womb, from my soul.

Remnants of that bloody placenta would remain within my heart for five years.

To be sure, another dependent alliance had developed. My heart was bleeding again, as I suffered the loss of a second symbiotic attachment. This time, my problem had been disguised in the deceitful garb of an intoxicating romance. My dependency issue had resurfaced.

My Jungian Analyst's Perspective

A month after Diana terminated our relationship the first time, I called a female Jungian analyst and made an appointment for two weeks later. Given the intensity of my pain, I realized I needed help. I wanted someone to guide and support me, for fear of being overwhelmed by my suffering. As a therapist, I knew I should not ignore my pain, but ought to look it squarely in the eye.

In part, my analyst felt I was attracted to a "younger" woman—Diana, nine years my junior—because my inner feminine, or *anima* (Latin for soul), was "underdeveloped." She said that I was unaware of my feelings. Yet I thought to myself, "Diana's passionate feeling side has engaged my soul so deeply. She has galvanized my feelings with a feverish passion."

My analyst assessed that my parents had not validated my feeling self; they had not mirrored my feelings adequately. With the help of therapy, I needed to experience and become more conscious of my emotions. The development of my more feminine feeling side was the initial focus of treatment.

Later, my analyst and I focused on my strongest yet most out-of-balance trait: my highly intuitive nature, which paid scant attention to the details of reality. As my ability to be conscious of the facts of a situation increased, the predominance of my intuitive capacity was necessarily sacrificed. I sorely grieved this decrease in my intuitive capacity. Yet as a consequence, I became more reality-oriented.

After all, my vigorous intuitive propensity was what had led me so far astray into such an unrealistic romance with Diana, blinding me to the reality of our relationship. In my highly intuitive consciousness was a romanticized image of Diana; indeed, she was a waking "dream." My analyst always brought me back to the reality of the negative aspects of our relationship, thereby helping me to relinquish my image of Diana as a goddess. Gradually, I discovered her reality as an ordinary, imperfect human being—like myself.

For three years, I had weekly analysis. My analyst served as a funeral director, as I grieved Diana. And she was the midwife during my rebirth and the awakening of my soul. Since my *anima* (soul) steadfastly adhered to Diana, it was not projected, transferred onto my analyst. Rather, my analyst was the sturdy feminine receptacle into whom I poured my suffering soul. Expressing painful feelings to a deeply receptive woman was profoundly healing for me. Indeed, she mirrored and validated my painful emotions. Eventually, I completed 150 hours of analysis with her.

A Projection: The Conception of My Soul

After Diana and I broke up the second time, I spent many years contemplating the powerful events within my soul, which began in spring 1988—the spring of my rebirth. That second night in Monterey, Diana's alluring kisses had aroused my soul. Yes, a mysterious presence was lurking between us in that hotel room. And that question, "Are you the one?" was unexpectedly asked. With our passionate kisses and that mysterious question, the projection of my soul onto Diana was activated. During those first two days, I fell deeply into love. Indeed, Diana was "the one" who made my soul take flight.

I had unknowingly fallen in love with an intoxicating projection. Yet through this projection onto Diana, the inner woman became visible to me. Initially, this interior goddess was outside myself; I could gaze at my soul as a projection onto Diana. I experienced the animating energies of the inner feminine *within* a relationship.

As on a movie screen, I watched my soul being projected onto Diana. For the first time, I viewed my nascent soul, as portrayed by an actual woman. In this manner, I experienced and became acquainted with an outer vision of the inner feminine.

Initially "perceived" in Diana, my soul was thereby "conceived" in my consciousness. Indeed, during our three-month alliance, Diana carried my projected soul like a pregnant woman.

With prolonged reflection about Diana and me, I gradually became aware that a tremendous spiritual metamorphosis had been instigated within me, catalyzed by Diana. A decade after the breakup, I journaled, "My soul was conceived when it was projected onto Diana. In this manner, I put my seed into her, so as to give birth to my soul. Diane carried my soul like a pregnant woman. When she broke off our relationship, my soul was painfully separated from her, like a fetus is from its mother."

As a result, my soul was then able to gradually awaken as a distinctly feminine presence within me, now separated from Diana.

———————— •♥• ————————

Ultimately, Diana did not want to carry my soul-projection—to bear such a load. As the recipient of my soul-projection, she likely felt unloved, as might be expected. Being worshiped as a goddess has a downside; I was more in love with the projection than with Diana.

I failed to genuinely love the real, precious human being Diana. Yet at the time, I was certain I was actually loving her. In those ten brief weeks, I came to care for her greatly. But in fact, I was too preoccupied with romance, so I was unable to truly love Diana. Instead, I had fallen in love with a projection, a romanticized image of Diana.

I overvalued my soul-projection, and in doing so, I devalued the real woman beneath that projection. She must have sensed I was not "in love" with her for who she actually was. Most certainly, this projection was a contributing factor in the demise of our liaison.

When Diana ended our alliance the second time, she made clear that I was not "the one" for her. Yet I clung to the hope that she might be "the one" for me. Gradually, I became painfully aware that she was not "the one" for whom I was searching.

What was left was a projection of my infant soul, with no screen on which to view her. My soul was now suspended in midair, given Diana's departure. With no screen on which to behold her, I turned inward into my aching heart.

The outer woman had disappeared. The inner woman, my soul, had been waiting for me to become conscious of her as an *internal* reality. Over time, the inner feminine would slowly develop, manifesting as a distinct presence within me.

In this fashion, my soul-projection onto Diana was painfully retrieved, taken back into myself. This projection needed to be re-collected; the image of my soul had to be consciously recalled and placed back inside myself. Little by little, this projected image was mournfully removed from Diana, thereby restoring my *anima* to her original home within me. Indeed, a soul retrieval.

The Death of My Soul-Projection

The loss of Diana resulted in almost unbearable pain for me. Since the umbilical cord of my dependent attachment to her had been cut, I was now suffering once more. In spite of our incompatibility, I grieved her for many years before I could fully accept Diana's absence in my life.

I thought I was in love with the real Diana, not an imaginary goddess. But was it the loss of Diana, or the sacrifice of my projection, that caused me to suffer so greatly? Was I being forced to relinquish and grieve the real Diana, an imaginal Diana, or both?

I slowly concluded what was most painful was giving up my romantic projection, not letting go of Diana herself. Breaking up with my *fantasy* of Diana was much more difficult than breaking up with the *reality* of Diana. Looking back, most of my suffering came from the death of my soul-projection, not from the loss of Diana.

Causing further suffering, I realized I would never again find an external goddess since, in fact, they do not exist. In grieving the loss of Diana—both the real and the imaginal Diana—I was also bemoaning the possibility of ever again having a deeply romantic liaison with an earthly woman. Now, from the outset, such a romance would be impossible since I had discovered that there are no flesh-and-blood goddesses.

So, I began the painful, arduous and lengthy process of realizing that there are no goddesses on the face of the earth. No mortal woman could ever measure up to such heavenly expectations. Rather, I was looking for an interior goddess, my soul. As Goethe wrote, "Goddesses dwell in solitude, sublime, enthroned beyond the world of place and time" (*Faust*, Part II, Act I). The goddess that I was seeking was living within my placeless and timeless soul, wherein she ought to abide if she is to thrive.

———— •♥• ————

For my rebirth, and for my soul to awaken, my liaison with Diana had to die. She had to be torn from my heart. Only from a broken-hearted condition was I then able to be reborn. Without a doubt, our breakup did *induce the labor* for my rebirth. And in that process, my soul was awakened. Because of the death of our alliance, I was forced to search for my soul within myself, instead of seeking her in an actual woman.

Having me experience and know the inner feminine had been my soul's objective from the outset. Diana was the catalyst used by the interior woman for her own ends. Only through the death of my relationship with Diana—the death of that intoxicating projection—was I then able to see who or what was left: my soul awakening within me.

When I asked Diana, "Are you the one?" I sensed another soul had been lurking between us in that Monterey hotel room. In fact, my soul, not Diana, was actually "the One" for whom I had asked. My soul had been "the One" waiting for me to notice her instead. She was "the One" with whom I was destined "to fall in love" for the rest of my life.

For "Kiss"

In my journal, I repetitively and fondly recalled Diana's kisses, the ones that had so deeply stirred my soul. Not her eyes, as Diana had predicted, but her kisses had been the most healing. Her kisses had opened my heart and awakened my soul from a deep slumber. For those ten brief weeks, Diana was my diva, my goddess in the flesh.

A few years after our breakup, I began to refer to Diana affectionately as "Kiss." In my musings and journaling, this name frequently arose into my awareness as I fondly recalled our first passionate kisses. For me, "Kiss" captured the essence of our relationship. After all, her kisses had sparked the "falling in love" response within me, thus prompting that life-changing question from within: "Are you the one?"

Since Diana was "the one" who instigated my soul's awakening, I often thought about dedicating this book to her. With many variations over the years, I journaled the following words in final form: "For Kiss, whose passionate kisses gave first breath to this man's womanly soul." In kissing Diana, new life had been breathed into my dead soul. Her kisses had revived my soul, so it could gradually awaken and eventually flourish within me.

Nevertheless, while writing this book, I decided to change the dedication to the five women partners mentioned in these pages: my first wife, Cara, Diana, Pat (Chapter 6) and my present wife (Epilogue). Each of them has played a significant role in my life. Each has made a unique and weighty contribution to the evolution of my soul.

The First Month, While Grieving Diana

In the month after Diana ended our relationship the first time, my suffering began to take on a transformative shape with the appearance of two images. First of all, three weeks after our *first* breakup, I would sculpt my heart in clay, with a wound-like incision into the center. While in a state of deep grief and agonizing pain, this heart-wound would be spontaneously healed into a vagina in my heart. And through that orifice, I would be reborn (Chapter 5).

Then, ten days after sculpting my heart, a *Woman-with-No-Head* would appear in a dream and tell me that she would lead me "home." After this dream, Diana, my outer "dream woman" would be replaced by this inner "dream woman." Through this dream, I would become aware that my soul was awakening and becoming animated, as an increasingly distinct feminine presence within me (Chapter 6).

Together, these two images would shepherd me into my soul, into the realm of the inner feminine. I had lost the exterior goddess with whom I had fallen in love. But I would soon regain my divine soul, which would become the love of my life. In this manner, I would make the transition from the outer woman into the inner feminine, a process that would radically transform my life and completely re-fashion me.

CHAPTER 5

THE SACRED VAGINA

A Portal into My Soul

Jesus responded to Nicodemus,
"I assure you, everyone must be born again.
Anyone who is not born again cannot be in God's kingdom."
Then Nicodemus asked,
"How can a man who is already old be born again?
Can he go back into his mother's womb
and be born a second time?"

JOHN 3:3–4

I have no written record of the day I sculpted my broken heart in clay thirty years ago. Yet I recall it almost as if it happened yesterday. While sculpting a wound-like incision into my clay heart, this wound would be unexpectedly transformed into a vagina: a sacred portal into my soul. In the following years, I would be steered away from the outer woman into the womb of the inner woman, my soul.

After separating from my wife, five years of suffering had prepared this interior womb for a transformative experience. Unbeknownst to me, something had long been gestating within my soul, which was now ready to be delivered into my awareness. As I sculpted a vagina into my heart, a divine child would be birthed into my consciousness. For the next five years, midwifing and growing this life-changing event became my focus. My old self slowly died, as I was gradually reborn a new man.

On Father's Day 1988, I began the transition from the first half of my life into the second half. I was forty-three years old. My former girlfriend Cara was with me. Something spiritual had been "fathered" within me, which was now ready to be birthed by an interior "mother." On this day for honoring fathers, I was not the father. Rather, I was "born again" as a child, a spiritual infant. This was the commencement of my rebirthing as a new man. I would come to regard this rebirth, my second birth, as my *spiritual* birthday. This pivotal event launched me into the second half of my life.

When I say I was "born again," I am *not* referring to the usual Christian meaning of this term. Rather, I began the journey into the depths of my psyche—something the soul hungers for at midlife—so that I could unearth the rejected and unknown parts of my soul. By retrieving these lost parts, I would be reborn with a more complex and solid self-identity. Unmistakably, this was a "conversion" experience, a *metanoia* (Greek): a "transformative change of heart."

In my case, my *change of heart* was a movement into my soul, which would gradually, yet radically, transform who I am. I was being called from the external world of my previous forty-plus years, into the less-well-known realm of my soul. What's more, over the next five years, I would be *repeatedly* "born again" from the womb of my soul.

———— •♥• ————

What happened that Father's Day was entirely unexpected. Until I touched the clay, I had no idea what I would sculpt. Yet while sculpting, I became the recipient of a most treasured gift, bestowed upon me by an Unseen Presence. From my soul, a sacred symbol of my rebirth would emerge and appear in the wet clay. This symbol would unceasingly guide and unremittingly reshape me for decades.

Some weeks earlier, at a nearby university, Cara had enrolled in an art class where she was working with clay. On this particular Sunday, we had agreed she would bring a block of clay to my apartment, so we could each explore some aspect of our psyches.

She arrived with a large block of moist, brown clay, perhaps a cubic foot in size. As I unwrapped the clay from the usual transparent plastic bag for keeping it damp, a musty smell arose into my nostrils.

We each cut off a large chunk for our separate use. This earthy material felt cool and moist to my fingers. As a Capricorn, I loved the smell and the feel of Mother Earth, this clay in my hands.

My sparsely furnished, second-story apartment had a large, rectangular living room. We decided Cara would work in the corner near the sliding glass door to the balcony. I would sculpt in the dimly lit corner diagonal to hers, about twenty feet away.

<hr />

While we were dating, Cara and I had developed the habit of sharing our dreams. In the mornings, I was usually enthralled with her report of her nighttime journeys. Thirty years later, unaided by any written record, I still recall some of these extraordinary dramas enacted within her psyche in the night.

Furthermore, I was envious of her amazing dream life. Her psyche frequently gifted her with rich and engaging images, clearly revealing the deeper movements within her soul. And she had a remarkable ability to recall her dreams in vivid detail. So, the next morning, I could easily picture her dreamtime adventure in my mind.

On this particular Sunday, Cara had decided to sculpt a recent dream image. She had dreamt of a large, oblong cancerous tumor from which a butterfly emerged. From this malignant, egg-shaped "cocoon," the butterfly flew free. That was the extent of her dream. But what an astonishing image!

I wondered if her dream symbolized a rebirth for her after the painful emotional death, brought on by me ending our relationship eight months earlier. When we broke up, she had dreamt of blood dripping from her nipples. Now, in stark contrast, her butterfly dream suggested a rebirth, perhaps a new beginning, freed from whatever deadly tumor within which she had been entombed.

THE SCULPTING

Unlike Cara, initially I had no dream image to sculpt. But somehow, I knew I should sculpt my heart. And in effect, as I sculpted my heart in clay that day, I did have a *waking* dream. I was *not* in my head; I was crying and moving into my heart, the very organ that I was being prompted to sculpt. Unwittingly, I allowed myself to be guided by the instinctual wisdom of my soul. While in this trance-like state, the image that was meant to be dreamt that day, in fact, materialized in this fertile chunk of brown clay.

I began to mold the damp, malleable clay into the shape of a heart. For an eighth-grade science project, I had carved a realistic likeness of the human heart from a rectangular bar of Ivory soap; and I painted it red with contrasting yellow arteries. But my clay heart was shaped more like a valentine. To be sure, the valentine image depicts the human heart as the organ of love.

Cara and I worked in total silence, except for intermittent sobbing in each corner. I thought to myself, "I must give shape to my pain." As I became more absorbed in the process—and possessed by this now-pregnant, maternal clay—tears filled my eyes and wet my cheeks. For the next four hours, as I worked with my clay heart, I underwent a "transformative change of heart": the onset of a profound internal metamorphosis.

Holding my heart in the palms of my hands felt wonderful. My aching heart craved attention and needed to be touched. Given the very painful breakup with Diana, my soul wanted to be gently caressed. So, I decided my hands should lovingly give my heart a healing massage. As I carefully handled and shaped the clay that day, I was seeking to rehabilitate my broken heart.

During my celibacy, I had developed the practice of lovingly focusing on—listening to and journaling—what was happening within my soul. Without fail, this practice helped to relieve my heart's gloomy mood. On that Father's Day, I tended to my injured soul by shining the warm sunlight of my compassion onto the shape forming in the moist clay. I treated my wounded heart by illuminating it with the rays of my loving consciousness.

The Heart-Wound

Early in our relationship, while walking on the beach, Diana had remarked, "You're like an open sore," a bleeding wound. Five years after my wife and I broke up, Diana sensed the pain of my "heart bleeding" still. She informed me that the Latin word for "wound" (*vulnerare*) is the root word for "vulnerable" (*vulnerabilis*). Hence, in the wild, a wounded animal is vulnerable, more susceptible to attack.

As I hesitatingly opened my heart to Diana, I did begin to re-experience the wound from the death of my marriage. Through that painfully reopened "sore" in my heart, I "let her in," as Diana said after our night in Big Sur; or I "took her into my heart," as I wrote in my journal shortly thereafter. Thank God, my still-open wound had rendered me vulnerable to the possibility of loving once again: to lovingly take Diana into my heart.

———————•♥•———————

Yet ten weeks into our relationship, Diana abruptly terminated our liaison, completely severing our connection. I had allowed her into my heart, where she had taken root. With her sudden departure, my heart was torn open once more. From the demise of my marriage, I still felt some of the pain of my "heart bleeding." Now, I was reinjured and bleeding again.

Blood flowing from my heart was becoming an all-too-familiar affliction. As a twice wounded and vulnerable man, I wanted to retreat into the safety of my heart and lick my wound: to tenderly give attention to my suffering soul. This reopened wound was calling me inward into my pain. Having twice become symbiotically attached to a woman, I began to reflect more deeply upon the common root of my suffering: my dependency problem.

I was aware that my wound was *my* wound. I was the sole owner of my injury; this "sore" did not belong to anyone else. Those who *seemingly* had inflicted my pain, my wife and Diana, were not to be held accountable for my healing. Besides, endlessly blaming them would not cure my broken heart, only delay its restoration.

The only solution was for me to nurse my grieving heart. I was the only person who could treat my wound. I trusted with my persistent self-compassion and the curative passage of time, my broken heart would be restored: released from the anger and healed of the hurt. Then, my heart might be graced with forgiveness toward not only my wife but also Diana.

The Incision

As my own caregiver, I realized I had to make an incision into my earthen heart. By fashioning an opening into the wet clay, I was sculpting the wound that I felt in my body, in my heart. Undeniably, my heart was badly damaged, in need of repair. The arteries through which my emotions flowed had become inflamed and blocked, my heart now diseased. Too much pain was festering inside me from the recent, traumatic breakup with Diana.

Yes, my heart-wound required emergency open-heart surgery. And on that Father's Day, I was the only person who could perform this operation; I had to operate on myself. Yes, I was the surgeon. But most fundamentally, I was the patient. I needed this life-saving procedure to save my wounded soul, to restore my broken heart.

So, I took a sharp knife and slowly penetrated into the firm, damp clay. I began the incision near the "valley" at the top of my valentine-shaped heart. The cut went straight down the center, almost to the bottom. I could feel the pain of the knife cutting into my heart. I was weeping. After all, I was making the incision without anesthesia: no alcohol, no drugs, no painkillers. I imagined blood flowing from this self-inflicted wound, created by the scalpel in my hand.

As I cut into my heart, I was probably re-experiencing some of the pain which I felt from the breakup of my marriage. Yet now, I had fresh pain to manage since Diana had so impetuously terminated our short-lived alliance. The old wound was reinjured, by yet another woman rejecting me.

This was a *symbolic* surgery, a conscious act of self-penetration: an exploratory opening up and probing into my soul. With the knife, I sliced into my inner agony. I needed to explore my diseased heart through a process of self-examination. I wanted to unearth the root of my pathological attachments to my wife and Diana, the breaking of which had been so torturous for me.

Furthermore, at midlife especially, my heart required an operation, a preemptory and potentially life-saving surgery. I needed to turn inward and evaluate the first half of my life; and in the second half of my life, this open-heart surgery would create an orifice for whatever might emerge from within me. Perhaps a midlife soul-searching would save me from ever needing a medical open-heart surgery.

A knife was required to pierce my chest—to open up my terribly pained heart—which was still mostly well-defended and unexplored. I needed to cut my heart wide open, so I could reach my suffering soul.

This was not a pointless, masochistic or suicidal stabbing of my-self. Rather, I was intentionally attempting unearth the root of my pain and attend to my soul's sorrow. Yes, when cutting into my clay heart, my hurt was expressed as anger. And yes, the aggression was not being directed outward, but inward toward myself—similar to a suicide.

Even so, when making that incision into my clay heart, I was not using my anger self-destructively, but instead constructively, seeking healing. I directed my anger toward myself, so my heart might be radically opened up. Then, my soul's anguish could be exposed to the warm sunlight and fresh air of my empathetic consciousness.

THE SYMBOLIC ENACTMENT OF TWO DEATHS

While sculpting that incision into my clay heart, two deaths were being enacted: an emotional death in my heart from the loss of Diana and the symbolic death of my ego. When Diana abandoned me, I ex-perienced *a death in my heart*. And my self-esteem was badly injured, resulting in *the death of my ego*.

A Death in My Heart

Diana ending our liaison was a death-like event for me. Although she was still alive, our embryonic alliance was stillborn. My now-un-inhabited heart became the tomb for our dead romance, the tomb wherein my love for her would slowly decay.

I had lovingly taken Diana into the womb of my heart, where she had become affixed. But then, she abruptly uprooted herself from my soul. The umbilical cord attaching her to my heart was ripped out. I was in pain and depressed, suffering deeply.

When Diana rejected me, I felt like I had been crucified, like I had with my wife. Now, a second time, I was undergoing an emotional death, dying of a broken heart. Indeed, a death in my heart.

The Death of My Ego

I no longer needed to literally jump to my death from that park-ing structure. Now, five years later, not a literal but a symbolic suicide was transpiring. While cutting into my clay heart, I was unknowingly enacting the death of my ego-identity, a symbolic death.

When Diana abandoned me, I was flooded with intense feelings of rejection. I felt crushed and humiliated, my self-esteem stomped into the dirt. My suffering ate away at my self-confidence. Tears devastated my sense of who I was. Indeed, the pain and the hurt were dissolving my ego.

Not my body, but my ego had to die. In the process of digging up my pain, unearthing the hurt and uncovering the root of my suffering, my self-confidence was demolished.

This symbolic suicide was actually an egocide, whereby my old ego-identity perished. My ego died into the soil of my soul. And my broken heart became the tomb for my now-deceased ego. Yet in time, my decaying ego would become fertile humus for the flowering of my soul.

TRANSITION AND TRANSFORMATION

Then, I realized that the narrow incision into my clay heart had to be opened wider for closer examination. So, I took the knife and began to slowly spread apart each side of the wound, like a heart surgeon might open a chest.

As I opened the narrow slit in my clay heart—more in the middle, but less on the top and on the bottom—an oval-like opening appeared. Then, like a lightning bolt, the thought, "This looks like a *vagina!*" flashed into my awareness. This "open sore," this bleeding wound, was becoming a vagina. I was in awe: amazed and astonished.

Why would such an image materialize in the midst of my tears? While sculpting my pain, why did an organ of pleasure manifest in the clay? For what reason was the passion of my suffering being transfigured into a passionate sexual orifice? With the manifestation of this vagina in the wet clay, what was Mother Earth divulging to me?

Besides, what type of woman would so readily expose her most private part. Whose vagina was this? Was this the vagina of an interior goddess? Was this the inner woman's vagina, my soul's vagina? Was this a virgin's vagina?

I could have dismissed that vaginal image in the clay as a fluke of my imagination. Or I could have thought that it was the libidinal craving of a now-unattached, middle-aged man. Yet I sensed this vagina was sacred: a symbol warranting adoration and reflection.

Who bestowed this blessing upon me? That Father's Day, not I, but an Unseen Presence within me had orchestrated this sacred event: implanted that vagina in my heart. Intentionally, I had sculpted the wound. But then, psyche interceded and spontaneously healed my wound by morphing it into a vagina. I was simply the surgeon whose hands had made the initial incision.

As I gazed at the vagina in my clay heart, the hint of a smile came to my lips. My heart was pleased. The vagina seemed to smile back at me. A sense of satisfaction and joy came over me.

A Healing from Heaven

This life-threatening wound in my heart was transformed into a life-giving vagina. Yes, that vagina was the perfect antidote for the sore in my heart. In an instant—that split second of awareness—I was given everything I would ever need, although at the time I did not realize this. Not an "open sore," as Diana had remarked; but now, an "open vagina" would reside in the center of my chest forever. A remedy from within: a healing from heaven.

What I was meant to receive that day, I was given. Out of a potentially deadly wound emerged this life-creating vagina. What a fascinating orifice to appear in my heart. Would this vagina become the birth canal through which I might be "born again?"

Silently, I stared into her vulva as if reverently preparing to enter a temple.

The Sculpting Continues

Then, from the wet clay, I molded labia and fashioned scratch marks on each side of the vaginal orifice, so as to make it more realistic, and to indicate the presence of pubic hair.

As I was weeping, I began to *feel* a warmth within my heart. Although I was obviously still a man, this warm, womanly orifice would become my "heart's vagina," an enduring part of my kinesthetic anatomy.

The wound had rendered me painfully vulnerable. And now—with the emergence of this tender, feminine orifice—the vagina rendered me pleasurably unclad and defenseless. Would I become excessively open, perhaps too vulnerable: like a woman, like a child?

Would I be too unprotected from potential hurt by others? Would I be overly exposed to perhaps unwanted dreams, images or dark thoughts from within?

————— •♥• —————

This was the beginning of an entirely new life for me, although at the time I did not realize how radically changed I would become. Yet I knew something extraordinary had transpired that day.

This time, the open wound in my heart would *not* grow back together, as it mostly had during the five years after my wife and I had separated. Instead, my wound had morphed into a vagina: from a pain-filled "sore" into this potentially pleasure-filled vagina. Yes, that bleeding wound was instantaneously *cured* into a sacred portal into my soul.

This holy vagina would become a permanent orifice, which would hopefully keep my heart open for the rest of my life. No longer a wound, a bleeding sore or a scarred heart. Now, a feminine opening, an opening into the feminine. Instead of forever bleeding pain, becoming bitter or emotionally numb and shut down, I was being radically opened up, so I could give and receive love more freely. And with this vagina now in my heart, I might be able to feel things more deeply and experience a greater receptivity to the Life within and all around me.

As I worked with my clay heart, I realized it needed a tube at the bottom of the vagina, so menstruating blood could flow out of my heart. Even though anatomically incorrect, my heart required a singular conduit, so infections could be drained from my soul. Imagining menstrual blood flowing from my heart—usually while crying—became a method for releasing my pain and anxiety. No longer "a heart bleeding" every night, but now periodic bleeding as a part of my soul's menstrual cycle. Regularly bleeding out disappointments and pain would keep my heart healthy and open, thereby liberating it for more loving.

A REBIRTH

Then, I was given the image of tiny hands reaching out of the clay vagina. Somehow, there was to be a birth. These small hands were arriving out of that dark birth canal into the light of my consciousness.

As I sculpted, two tiny hands and arms emerged from the wet clay on each side of the vagina. Indeed, an unexpected arrival.

From whose watery womb was this child being born? Was an interior virgin birthing a new me? Was some sort of divine child being born, perhaps a messiah: "the birth of God in the soul?"

Spiritually, *I knew my ego had to die before I could be reborn from the heart*. My ego-identity had perished, as I made that painful incision into the clay. My heart became the tomb for my deceased ego. But in that process, that dark tomb was transformed into a dark, life-renewing womb.

From that womb, a new ego-identity would gradually be born. Yes, I had deposited my seed, my dying ego, into the inner woman's womb. The seed of my dead ego fertilized this interior virgin, thereby creating a divine embryo. Through her birth canal, a spiritual infant—a reborn ego-identity—was now arriving.

Yes, an interior mother, my soul, did rebirth me that day. This divine mother gave me life, a new life. She was the Unseen Presence who had guided the sculpting. And to heal my heart-wound, she had benevolently bestowed her vagina in the center of my heart.

This interior mother would devotedly suckle my newborn ego-identity: continually nourish, comfort and guide me with her feminine essence, as I gradually grew into a new man.

As might be expected, initially I was born a spiritual infant. Yet from her womb, I would be *repeatedly* reborn, gradually becoming an utterly different man. In this manner, I would be healed of the excessive masculinity which I had amassed during my celibacy.

Nicodemus had asked Jesus, "How can a man who is already old ["middle-aged," in my case] be born again? Can he go back into his mother's womb and be born a second time?" (John 3:3-4). For me, I knew the answer was, "Yes. I can return to the womb," the womb of my interior mother. At midlife, to be "born again" required me to enter into the womb of this divine mother, not the womb of my earthly mother.

———•♥•———

Three weeks after the loss of Diana, I was reborn as I sculpted my heart. Until this vagina manifested in the clay, I was not aware that my soul was pregnant, much less that I was ready to be "born again." Later, I realized that falling in love with Diana gave birth to my soul in projected form; then shortly thereafter, her breaking up with me precipitated the death of that projection. In effect, these two brief events—the birth and then the death of that projection—had *induced the labor* for the rebirth of my ego-identity.

With Diana's departure, I began to form a bond with the infinite womb of the interior, divine mother. In the second half of my life, she would become my "heavenly mother." Or as Jesus said, "My earthly mother gave me [physical] death, but my heavenly mother gave me [spiritual] life" (*The Gospel of Thomas*, saying 101, as translated by Robert McNair Price). Was Jesus as a person, and in his ministry, conscious of the inner feminine? In the heart of Jesus, a heavenly mother?

As my still-wet clay heart stood on the table, I gazed at it with contentment. The sculpture was complete. Everything that needed to be said that day had been spoken by the clay.

My wound was healed into this feminine orifice into the holy womb of God. And through that sacred vagina, I was "born again" as one of God's divine children. To be sure, I underwent a *metanoia*: a "transformative change of heart."

As it turned out, Cara and I both had sculpted images of transformation and rebirth that day. For her, a butterfly had emerged from a deadly tumor. As for me, the painful wound in my heart was transfigured into the vagina from which I was "born again."

In the coming days, my clay heart dried and hardened into a light brown color. Regrettably, I did not fire it. Yet since then, it has remained near me in my bedroom. Late at night, or just before dawn, I still peer into that deep, dark, mysterious orifice, attempting to see that which-is-yet-to-be-seen.

REFLECTION

Suffering: A Purpose

At last, my suffering and grief were more obviously guiding me somewhere. My suffering and the death of my ego had not been in vain. Perhaps a purpose in my pain, a reason for my anguish. Yes, from my suffering and death, I was "born again."

Now, my heart-wound was given an altogether different form and purpose, resulting in a *complete reversal of meaning*. A bleeding, *life-threatening wound* was regenerated into a healthy vagina, *an organ with a life-affirming purpose*.

The cure had been hidden in the wound; the injury harbored its own medicine. Just as the body has the natural ability to heal itself *with appropriate treatment*, so also the human heart can cure its wounds *with the assistance of an empathetic consciousness*. Because I had chosen to be patiently conscious of my suffering, my wound was able to be spontaneously healed into this sacred vagina. In this fashion, my heart was restored to love once again.

Yes, my pain did have an unambiguous meaning, a rehabilitative purpose. Because I consciously endured my suffering, psyche's divine hand was able to complete her healing task. With the assistance of the warm sunlight and fresh air of my empathetic consciousness, psyche healed the wound in my heart by transforming it into a vagina. In this manner, the redemptive purpose of my suffering was instantly and dramatically revealed. Yes, in the suffering, the possibility of healing and rebirth.

———— •❖• ————

If my heart had never been so gravely wounded, I would have never been blessed with the gift of this sacred vagina. The presence of a wound in my heart was absolutely necessary before such an injury could then be healed into this vagina. Only because I had been wounded could that "sore" then be regenerated into a vagina. Yes, this is "the gift of woundedness."

With much gratitude, I began my journey into the infinite womb of God. This vagina became my passageway into the heavenly realm within. With a vagina now in my heart, my ego-consciousness was able to have frequent intercourse with my soul. And as a result of such spiritual intimacy, my soul was able, over time, to bear some of her innumerable "fruits of the feminine."

Over the next five years, my suffering slowly diminished. The torment of mourning the death of my marriage and the breakup with

Diana—and the labor pains of being birthed into a new life—would mostly abate.

I could have fled my pain: turned my back on it through denial. Or I could have run into the arms of another woman. I could have literally committed suicide, ending my life, my pain forever. Instead, I *chose* to endure my suffering with faith and hope, trusting it had a divine purpose.

The Sacred Vagina: A Transcendent Synthesis

The unexpected appearance of this vagina in my clay heart was a miraculous synthesis of my midlife pains and pleasures. My dependent attachments to my wife, and five years later to Diana, were both severed, resulting in two deep woundings and great suffering with each.

Interspersed between the severing of these two symbiotic attachments was my four-year celibacy. During this time, I bore witness to my "heart bleeding." I became the devoted caregiver for my injured soul, seeking to heal my broken heart.

Two women were pivotal for the transformation of my heart-wound into a vagina: not only Cara but *even* Diana. I had entered into Cara's loving and pleasure-filled vagina and experienced it as "sacred." Was it the forgotten kinesthetic memory of Cara's loving vagina that appeared in my clay heart that day?

Moreover, my romance with Diana had not been consummated when we broke up the first time. Since I had not experienced Diana's vagina, at that time, is that why a vagina materialized in the wet clay? Was this sculpted vagina a replacement for Diana's vagina? If Diana had wanted me to enter into her vagina, perhaps I would have never discovered this vaginal opening into my soul, at least not in such a unique and graphic manner.

While sculpting my heart, the Unseen Presence had comingled, without my awareness and beyond my comprehension, these five life-changing events. The transcendent psyche had spontaneously synthesized two painful losses (my wife and Diana), my four-year celibacy, and two pleasurable experiences (Cara's "sacred" vagina and my "romance" with Diana) into a single symbol. Yes, my heart-wound was converted into a vagina in my heart. Truly, a transcendent synthesis:

the miraculous appearance of this sacred vagina, granting me access into the mysteries of my divine soul.

In the final analysis, I realized this vagina was that of my virgin soul. Her vagina had materialized in my clay heart in an uncanny, embodied manner. Anima had unveiled and revealed herself in an unmistakable and immodest fashion. Her fleshy, feminine vulva was now living in the center of my chest. (At times, I refer to my *anima* as "Anima," as if my soul were a person with a proper name.)

Now, this numinous symbol of a sacred vagina would yoke my ego-consciousness to the dark mysteries within my soul. Through this symbolic portal into my heart, I would be able to reestablish a meaningful relationship with my soul and return to my deeper Self.

Anima had enticed me into her feminine essence. Through her vagina, she received me and took me into herself. Just as I had penetrated Cara, I needed to penetrate my soul: to enter into myself. With phallic-like self-examination, I had pierced my well-defended, masculine chest and entered into my suffering soul. In so doing, I had penetrated Anima and impregnated her, which resulted in my rebirth.

The exterior woman and the interior woman were both a part of my redemptive journey. Each was a part of God, each a part of the journey into my soul.

Depending on the Inner Feminine

The heartbreaking separations from my wife, and later Diana, prepared me to become a more self-dependent man. To a great extent, these breakups were so agonizing because my dependency problem was still unresolved. Only by severing my dependent attachments to these two women was I then coerced into relying on the inner woman.

After breaking up with Diana, I realized that my dependency needs were gradually being transferred from actual women onto the interior woman. So, Anima became "the One" upon whom I would depend. She was my own soul, living right within me.

To the extent I had not developed my feminine side, to that same degree, I became overly attached to my wife and Diana, in an unhealthy, dependent fashion. Now, more dependent upon Anima, I would be able to live without an overdependence on an actual woman.

Progressively, I began to establish a stronger alliance with Anima and depend on her. By partnering with the inner feminine, I became a more self-reliant man. A repurposed umbilical cord enabled me to become dependent upon my soul, instead of my wife or Diana. At midlife, Anima was the woman I needed, "the One" who would forever nourish and support me. She has become the partner of a lifetime, my partner for life.

From this time forward, I no longer focused so exclusively on an actual woman. I knew Anima would never abandon me, as long as I was faithful to her: gave her the undivided attention she required. The inner woman would be with me forever, in spite of any vicissitudes in a relationship with an actual woman.

Ten days after sculpting the sacred vagina, my search for my soul was to be vividly confirmed in a dream. In this dream, I would be greeted by a *Woman-with-No-Head* who would announce that she would lead me "home." Over the next five years, this headless woman would escort me into the inexhaustible "fruits of the feminine" within my soul. And as the individuation process unfolded within me, she would guide me toward my divine Self. Ultimately, I would experience "the birth of God [the Self] in the soul."

———•♥•———

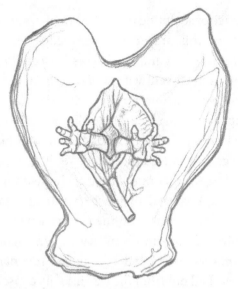

The Sacred Vagina
An Artist's Rendition of My Sculpture

INTERLUDE
MUSINGS AND ELABORATIONS

The Sacred Vagina Prayer

For over a decade, I mused about the sacred vagina which I had sculpted into my heart. So then, I wanted to precisely, poetically and prayerfully articulate the meaning of this image for me. Eventually, while flying on a half-filled, night flight to Costa Rica to visit my daughter, the final version came to me. The rest of the passengers were asleep. In an otherwise dark cabin, I had the reading light on above my seat. In the stillness of that night above the earth, I wrote:

The Sacred Vagina is
the opening in a man's heart,
through which he enters into the life of God
and out of which God is born again into the world.

The experience of sculpting the sacred vagina, and my subsequent reflections, became this prayer of acknowledgement and appreciation. My prayer was one of gratitude to the Unseen Presence that had orchestrated this sacred event within my soul. Much for which to be thankful: a portal into the interior mysteries of God.

The breakup with Diana had resulted in the wounding of my heart and the death of my ego. When I made that painful incision into my clay heart, my ego was indeed sacrificed. Yet with my ego out of the way, I was then able to enter *into the life of* God within me.

Furthermore, as I sculpted that incision into my heart, this wound was transfigured into a vagina. So then, I was able to penetrate into the fertile womb of God. And from that sacred vagina, God would be *born again into the world*. Indeed, the two tiny hands of that divine child had reached out from the clay into my consciousness. Over many years, God would be continually birthed into my consciousness, as small bits of the Self—images, dreams, ideas—were incessantly incarnated into my conscious identity.

Out of my heart's vagina, *God is born again into the world*, as stated in my prayer. Yes, this is "the birth of God in the soul"—the birth of the Self into consciousness.

The Sacrifice of My Ego

The death of my liaison with Diana and the demise of my marriage—and the sacrifice of my ego—were absolutely required for the rebirth of my ego-identity. In the course of these painful breakups, my self-esteem was demolished. So, while sculpting my pain, I experienced a symbolic death, an egocide, whereby my old ego-identity was dissolved into tears.

Yet because of the death of my ego, a rebirth could take place. With the demise of my old self, a new self—the two tiny hands of that divine child—could now be born. Without the sacrifice of my small, limited ego, I could not have been reborn into a greater consciousness. Only a defeated ego can experience "the birth of God in the soul": the birth of the Self from the womb of God.

In the coming years, my ego would suffer countless defeats, so more of the mysteries of the Self and the complexities of Life could be borne into my consciousness. The unsolicited demands of the

Self, and the unwanted challenges of Life, have resulted in my ego being sacrificed on many occasions. In this manner, my self-identity is constantly being liberated from its previously inflexible, limited and overly-confident ideas and opinions. No longer a master, my ego has surrendered to the complexities of the Self within and the Life around me.

Frequently defeated, my ego has been crushed into the ground of my being, my soul. My attitudes and beliefs have died and decayed, becoming humus for my soul. Gradually—with more of my ego out of the way—I have begun to live closer to the soil of my soul. Because of this, new life has been able to grow out of my soul into my consciousness.

Each time, from this fertile soil of my soul, my ego-consciousness has been unfailingly resurrected into a renewed and expanded identity. I have been continually "born again" from God's infinite womb, filled with new life from God's sacred mysteries. In this fashion, I am being transformed into a more complex consciousness.

Yes, I have been "born again" countless times. Unlike traditional "born again" Christians, the Self and Life have required me to die and be rebirthed multiple times, not just once. Through this process, more of the infinite mysteries of the Self and Life have been poured into the grail of my consciousness.

Even though the sacrifice of my ego is necessary for the expansion and growth of the Self into my consciousness, I still require an ego to navigate the complexities of the Self and Life. However, I seek to have my ego be a servant to the Self and Life, not the master of the mysteries within and around me.

After the symbolic death of my ego, my soul's creative imagination flourished. As I mused about this vagina in my heart, many images and ideas arose into my consciousness. Three of these images arose from the imagination. Two were spontaneous thoughts that came into my awareness, as I journaled or during my analytic sessions. One is a memory from childhood, and another an object that I came upon after sculpting my heart—both elaborations upon the image of the sacred vagina. Seven of these are described in the following pages.

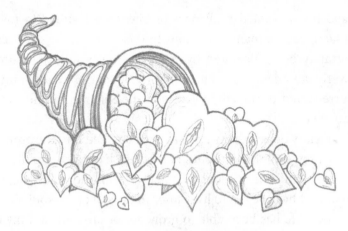

A Cornucopia of God's Compassion

Three days after sculpting the sacred vagina, I journaled, "Both the vagina and the heart are organs of love." For many women, love and the vagina are intimately associated. And now, my heart also had a vaginal orifice, so I could love more intimately. Indeed, this vagina became a part of my psycho-spiritual anatomy. I journaled, "Through this vagina, God's love can pour out of me, and I can take others into my heart."

With this vagina in my now-unclad heart, I realized that the love within me was indeed the love of God: the two, one and the same. The love in my heart was one tiny piece of God's loving heart. Whether from a manger, a compassionate act or even a romance, is not the human heart the birthplace of divine love?

When compassion is imparted from one person to another, even though imperfectly conveyed, *this is the reality of God's love.* When loving each other, we express God's compassion. Only through us can God love others, and only through others can God love us. God's compassion is radically immanent, embodied within the hearts of the human race. Only by giving love to others and receiving their love, have I known the love of God.

I realized that divine compassion encircles the entire globe, carried by each human being, within every person's heart. No matter how misguided, perhaps all our efforts to love are God's attempts to fulfill His/Her loving purpose. In spite of humanity's many flaws, the human family, spread around the planet, is the sole domicile of God's compassion. Each heart is one of God's organs of love through which God can impart His love, Her compassion, for others.

No longer "a loving consciousness in the sky" as my father taught. Instead, as I have often said, "We are God's loving consciousness on the earth." Not a transcendent deity, but an immanent God, inhabiting the hearts of the entire human family. Dwelling within more than seven billion hearts, an empathetic consciousness is seeking to be born within the human family, with the intent of enveloping the earth. Yes, human hearts are the "cornucopia of God's compassion."

Vulnerable "Like a Young Woman"

In the months after sculpting the sacred vagina, I felt extremely vulnerable, perhaps too unprotected. Had I become too openhearted? Was my heart too sensitive, too soft? My heart-wound (*vulnerare*) had rendered me vulnerable (*vulnerabilis*). Now, that vagina in my heart also left me vulnerable. With this undefended vaginal orifice into my heart, I feared I could be easily hurt.

Then, one day during an analytic session, I suddenly realized I could cross my arms over my chest to shield that tender vaginal opening into my heart. Just as a woman might cross her legs at times to protect her genital area, I could also cross my arms over the vagina in my heart. If required, I could safeguard this delicate, newly-found orifice into my heart.

As I crossed my arms over my chest in the session, I told my analyst, "I feel like a young woman," who was just beginning to explore her body and was learning to protect her most private part.

I came to believe vulnerability is essential if I am going to be able to give and to receive love: to experience intimacy with others. Without vulnerability, how can there be heartfelt love? Yet I do not need to place my now-tender heart into the hands of another. Rather, my heart should remain within my hands. Then, I will be able to love mostly undefended, yet with discernment, so that I can love more abundantly.

Could it be that our greatest loves occur only with vulnerability: the radical exposure of the most private, the most tender and mysterious, corners of our souls?

For me, being vulnerable "like a young woman" is crucial for intimacy with the inner feminine. And to experience genuine intimacy with a woman, I need to be radically open and self-disclosing.

With the intention of feeling lovingkindness toward the multitude of people around the globe, I had to become unguarded like this young woman. In all such situations, my heart requires an opening through which I can give and receive love. Yes, the sacred vagina rendered me vulnerable, as I became more open "like a young woman."

God Kissing the Lips of My Heart

Three years after breaking up with Diana, I began to imagine that God was gently kissing the lips of my heart. Diana's lips were no longer available for me to kiss. Yet her passionate, real-life kisses became the prototype for this image of God kissing my heart. Rather than Diana kissing my actual lips, I imagined that God was kissing the lips of my heart. With this image of God's affection for me, my healing continued.

When in pain, I prayed, "Kiss the lips of my heart, Oh Lord." I journaled, "Caress my wounded heart, so I might again learn to receive your love." And, "Kiss the lips of my bleeding heart. Yes, suck the blood of my suffering into yourself, so you can digest my blood and make divine use of it."

After having sculpted a vagina into my clay heart, I would imagine God kissing the vaginal lips of my actual heart. I prayed, "Oh Lord, be near to me. Comfort me with your presence. Kiss the labia of my heart, so I might feel your love. For then, I am no longer so lonely." And, "Yes, Oh Lord, kiss the lips of my soul, your sacred heart. Nourish me with your tenderness. Caress me gently, so I can feel your compassion for me."

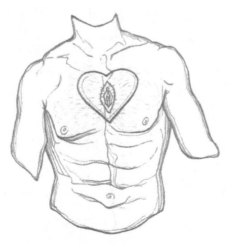

A Vagina Tattoo Over My Heart

For several years after sculpting my heart, I had the desire to have a vagina tattooed in the center of my chest, complete with labia and pubic hair. I was fearful that the vaginal lips within my heart might somehow grow back together. Then, I would become emotionally shut down. I did not want my heart to close down again and be unable to feel and to love. With a vagina tattooed on my chest, I would have a *daily* reminder—in the mirror each morning—for keeping my heart open for more loving.

Yet I never had the tattoo done since I was fearful that most observers would not understand its meaning. Without my shirt on in public, others might regard a vagina tattoo on my chest as a profane, only sexual image. They might not be able to discern its spiritual significance. Onlookers would fail to see this vagina as a divine love-orifice into my soul.

Ten years after the healing of my wounded heart into a vagina and my rebirthing, I found it increasingly difficult to keep my heart open. So once again, I pondered the possibility of having a vagina tattooed over my heart. This might help me to feel and to express more of God's lovingkindness toward others. A vagina tattoo on my chest could serve as a poignant reminder of the divine compassion within my heart: one of God's many temples of love.

Perhaps, someday . . .

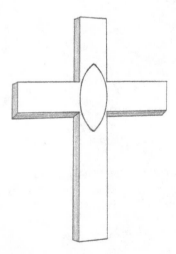

A Drawing Mantra: Vaginas in the Center of Crosses

Two months after I sculpted the sacred vagina, I spontaneously began to draw vaginas in the center of crosses, where the horizontal and vertical axes intersect. Most certainly, my heart-wound belonged at the center of the cross. But while sculpting, this heart-wound was transfigured into a vagina in my heart. Indisputably, the wound and the vagina were *both* situated in the *same* organ, my heart. Yes, the heart is the place of suffering, but also the place of spiritual rebirth. So, I knew that the vagina, a symbol of my rebirth, also belonged at the center of the cross.

Over the years, I drew hundreds of these vaginas in the center of crosses into my journal. Repeatedly depicting this image became a drawing mantra for me. These crosses with vaginas were a symbol for my continual death and rebirth. Each time I drew one of these, I was reenacting the death and rebirth of my self-identity. Through these repetitions, I was comforted. And curiously, I felt I was continuing to be healed.

A Childhood Memory: Mangers on Crosses

While writing this midlife memoir, I recalled entering into several Catholic churches, as a child, where I observed crosses on the wall behind the altar. Attached to the center of the cross was the infant Jesus in a straw manger. These were not crucifixes, but the empty cross of the risen Jesus. The mangered baby Jesus was *in the same place* where the heart of the dying Jesus would have been.

Although intended to symbolize the life of Jesus from nativity to resurrection, I now wonder if these mangered crosses might have been an inadvertent image of a symbolic death, followed by a spiritual rebirth. Yes, the death of the ego, so a rebirth of consciousness could take place.

Sculpting the incision into my heart was my spiritual crucifixion. And then, that wound was transfigured into the vagina from which I was "born again." In the story of Jesus, did he not have to die before the miracle of his resurrection? Are we not all—Christian or not— meant to die a symbolic death, so that we might be resurrected into a greater consciousness?

In a Monks' Cemetery: Heaven on Earth

A few years after sculpting my heart of clay, I again visited St. Andrew's Abbey in Valyermo, California, for a private retreat. Over the years, I had periodically retreated to this desert priory, far away from the busyness of Los Angeles. After my wife and I separated, this Benedictine cloister became a sanctuary for me.

Usually, I drove to this remote location for a half-day retreat on a weekday, when I was feeling especially lonely and isolated. Here, I would walk in the solitude of the surrounding desert, where I would cry and pray aloud with little fear of being seen or heard.

Behind the Abbey is a steep slope leading up to a plateau, perhaps seventy-five feet above the Abbey grounds. Since the top of this desert plateau cannot be seen from the cloistered property below, at times I walked naked in the warm sun, among the tall, randomly and sparsely situated cacti. In my hour of need, I wanted to be stripped of my defenses and pretenses, left in the most vulnerable of conditions. I longed to be seen naked by God, as I walked, cried and prayed aloud on this desolate plateau.

•♥•

On my first visit to the Abbey after sculpting the sacred vagina, I parked my car and walked up the dirt road—I was fully clothed—to the unfenced monks' cemetery on the hilltop. Unexpectedly, I came upon a new, overwhelming object dominating the entire burial site. A massive, rectangular block of black granite had been placed upright in the midst of these humble graves with weather-beaten, wooden crosses. I was the only living soul present.

This gigantic, rectangular slab was evenly cut and smoothly polished. The monument was probably two feet thick, eight feet wide and maybe sixteen feet tall. It stood on a four-foot-high, altar-like cement base covered with cobblestones. Perhaps this sculpture weighed fifteen tons.

In the middle of this plain, black granite slab, the sculptor had cut a large oval opening—the orifice itself at least eight feet tall and perhaps three feet wide. When I looked at this sculpture, instantly I saw a "vagina," like the one revealed to me while sculpting my heart. Perhaps most observers would never permit such a thought, at least not in a monk's cemetery. Even though carved from cold stone, this smoothly cut, oval orifice was sublimely warm and invitingly feminine—indeed, a womanly orifice.

In that desert cemetery, I had found a graphic, yet dramatically larger, image of the vagina in my heart: a replica in stone of that portal into my soul. That day in that quiet place, I had stumbled upon the symbol of my healing and rebirth. This stone sculpture of a womanly orifice concurrently existed with the sacred vagina within my heart. During this terribly painful period in my life, this was indeed a providential synchronicity!

•♥•

The orifice in this massive stone monument was facing due west, suggestive of the final sunset at the end of one's days on earth. At the monastery, this memorial was called the "gateway to heaven."

Looking through that portal, I watched the sun go down that evening, where it had already eternally set for those monks there interred. Probably for most of the monks, heaven, the Kingdom of God, was the one after death, a distant paradise.

But for me, that massive stone vagina in the cemetery symbolized "heaven on earth," the *here and now* Kingdom of God. Yes, the Kingdom of God was *present all around me* in those quiet desert surroundings under the twilight sky.

Furthermore, that vagina-like orifice in the stone was a symbol of the portal into the Kingdom of God *within my soul*. Or as Angelus Silesius (1624-1677) wrote, "Paradise is at your own center; unless you find it there, there is no way to enter."

In that place for the dead, I became focused on Life. Heaven was within me: the indwelling presence of God. And paradise was surrounding me: the sacred Universe of nature and the divine family of man. As Jesus said, "For behold, the kingdom of God is within you [in your hearts] and among you [surrounding you]" (Luke 17:21). Indeed, the Kingdom of God, both internal and external, *here and now*: utterly real and totally alive, eternally moving toward wholeness and completion. Yes, "heaven on earth" creeping toward realization.

CHAPTER 6

A DREAM AND THE ANSWER

"I Will Lead You Home"

———◆♥◆———

I once was lost,
but now am found.
Was blind,
but now I see.
"Amazing Grace"

JOHN NEWTON
BASED ON LUKE 15:24,
THE STORY OF THE PRODIGAL SON

While dating Diana, she was the only woman with whom I was consciously involved. On our second date, as we were passionately kissing, I asked her, "Are you the one?" Almost instantly, I began to feel Diana was "the one" for me. Yet at the same time, I sensed the presence of another soul lurking between us that night in Monterey. Was I simultaneously becoming enchanted with another woman, a second woman?

Who was this mysterious woman lurking between Diana and me, this other soul? Initially, I was uncertain who she was. But a month after Diana's first breakup with me, a *Woman-with-No-Head* visited me in a dream, arriving quietly but vividly. I surmised that the soul lurking between Diana and me that night, and this headless woman, were the *same* woman. Each was a different manifestation of my soul: one a felt presence between Diana and me, and the other the image of this headless woman in the dream.

The day before this dream, I had called the female analyst with whom I would have analysis for three years. Making that phone call probably helped precipitate this dream: a dream which was ready to be dreamt anyway, in one form or another. When I woke up the next morning, I wondered if this headless dream woman might be the analyst whom I would visit in two weeks. But quickly, I realized my analyst-to-be was not the woman in my dream. "The One" who came in the dream was "divine." She was my own soul, my *anima*, not a real woman.

THE DREAM

On the night of June 28/29, 1988, I had the following dream:

I am walking in a large city, where the people speak a foreign language. It is night and I am lost. The city itself is dark and the cars have no lights. Only moonlight illuminates the city.

A woman appears who has no head. She is a large-framed and big-busted woman, wearing a light-blue cotton top with long sleeves. Where her neck and head should be, there is only a bit of roundedness, like the stump of a neck. With no opening for a head, her tight-fitting shirt neatly covers the slightly rounded stump between her shoulders.

I ask her how to "go home." She has no head, yet somehow says to me, "I will lead you home." She speaks in plain English, not in the language of that foreign city. Even without a mouth, she is able to utter these words calmly and clearly.

Then somehow, I am in the sky viewing the city below. From this vantage point, I can see that this headless woman is on the right-hand side of the city. From that edge of the city, she is going to lead me out of this urban area into the dark countryside. I will not reside in that city. Apparently, my home will be in a dark, rural area.

Lost in a Dark City

Upon waking, I immediately realized I had been lost in this "large city," my head, for decades. As a thinker, I habitually analyzed anything and everything. Indeed, I had become *addicted to reason*. Over time, my compulsive thinking had numbed my ability to feel. Remember, I was the guy who had dreamed of dropping books (my mind's ideas and thoughts) from that tall building, as I attempted to kill the rattlesnake (my soul's instincts and feelings) below.

Even with Diana, I was always trying to figure out whether or not our liaison would work. One day when I was analyzing our relationship, she told me that I was "picking the petals off a beautiful rose." With my analytical mind, I was killing the rose, damaging our love.

Later, I learned that one of the Latin meanings for the word city is "to draw lines." City streets are usually highly organized, running mostly parallel and perpendicular to each other. A perfect depiction of my rational ego!

I was lost in the large city of my reasoning mind. Far removed from the countryside of my soul and nature, I needed to be escorted out of my head—out of the ego-centered city of my thoughts—into the rural darkness of my soul.

In fact, because of my overuse of analytical thinking, my *own* rational language had now become "foreign" to me, leaving me disoriented and lost. Although I had evolved this language myself, my ego's logical dialect was now unintelligible to me. I was lost in a self-created mental maze. I was too confused to find my way out of my head.

I needed to be guided out of my thinking head and into my feeling heart. I was being directed to leave that city of masculine consciousness and travel into pagan ("outside the city") territory—my feminine soul—where a more primordial tongue is spoken.

Going home meant departing from my reasoning mind and returning to the "rural darkness" of my body and my soul. I had to rediscover the soul's symbolic language: the language of dreams and myths, not rational concepts and abstract ideas.

The Woman-with-No-Head

This dream woman had "no head." She did not require a head since my head (the large city) was already too big; my reasoning mind was too dominant. If she would have had a head, I would have probably ignored her. And she was "large-framed and big-busted." Again, she was trying to grab my attention. With her stout body, she was compensating for my overly developed intellect, which had left me so confused and lost in the first place.

Given her captivating stature, I felt compelled to follow this *Woman-with-No-Head*. I was certain I could lean on this sturdy, feminine figure who was older and wiser than me. Never once did I question her; I totally trusted her. I was confident she would shepherd me "home," although I had no idea what "going home" meant. But I surrendered to being guided by what I knew to be her superior feminine wisdom.

The *Woman-with-No-Head* was a personification of my soul, tailored by the psyche for my particular states of mind and heart during my midlife transition. My soul knew I was lost in my head. So, this headless woman arrived to steer me back into my heart. I realized I must follow this wise woman: allow myself to be guided by my soul.

The Answer: "I Will Lead You Home"

This *Woman-with-No-Head* delivered a profound message in five simple words: "I will lead you home." Through the sacred vagina now in my heart, she would escort me back into my soul: my interior, spiritual home. I needed her help to reconnect with my forgotten soul, where the non-rational language of dreams, images, intuitive ideas and feelings is spoken.

At the time of this dream, I was not aware that I was so lost, so far away from home. I knew I was too focused in my head at the expense of feeling. Yet I had no clue how to depart from my thinking mind and return to my feeling soul.

This headless woman's remark, "I will lead you home," became the overriding focus for the second half of my life. As Jungians say, this was a "big dream," an archetypal dream that would radically change who I was. For more than thirty years now, this *Woman-with-No-Head* has remained my trusted, transformative guide.

I would not comprehend the deeper meaning of returning to my spiritual home for many years. But this *Woman-with-No-Head* clearly wanted to escort me to my final home: into my soul and my deeper Self. As the lyrics of the hymn "Amazing Grace" state, "I once was lost, but now am found"—in my case, found by this headless woman. Previously, I was "blind, but now I see" that my soul is indeed my home.

As one who had strayed a great distance from his soul, I was found by this dream woman, who beckoned me back into herself.

With the arrival of this bizarre, yet grace-filled feminine figure, I became the recipient of her *amazing grace*. This *Woman-with-No-Head* would save me from my rational mind. Her soulful presence in my life would be my salvation.

The Return to the Home of My Soul

Like everyone, I was born into the world psychologically merged with everything—not only everything within me but also everything around me—completely unconscious of the complexities of Life. As an infant, I lived in a state of undivided oneness and wholeness with Life. In the Garden of Eden, close to God, I partook of the Tree of Life. Having no ego, there was no "I" to separate me from Life. Only a blissful *unconscious union* with Life was present. God's earthly paradise was my first home.

As my nascent ego grew, a *conscious separation* developed between my "I" and the Life within and around me. My ego slowly emerged and separated itself from the Tree of Life. Now, I no longer lived alongside God in that garden, no longer a child at home. I had eaten the forbidden fruit of the Tree of the Knowledge of Good and Evil, tasted the fruit of the Tree of Consciousness. Consequently, I became separated from the original wholeness in God.

By eating from the Tree of Consciousness of Good and Evil, I committed the "original sin": the "crime of consciousness." Yet this act was a part of the divine, evolutionary plan. As a result of having eaten the fruit of this tree, my consciousness was created. Accordingly, I was separated from an unconscious union with God, with Life. Furthermore, as a growing consciousness, I slowly developed a conscience: the ability to judge a thing as good or as evil.

Because of my "fall" into consciousness, I was kicked out of my first home. Now, my ego-identity separated me from the Tree of Life: from my living soul, and from the Life all around me. I was banished from the Garden of Eden; I was expelled from the garden of unconsciousness, and began to live in the city of ego-consciousness. The challenges of childhood, adolescence and adulthood lay before me.

This *departure* from unconscious union with Life resulted in a conscious separation from the life of my soul. Living in my second home of the ego, I struggled to overcome my inferiority complex and understand my confused young-adult self. I suffered into maturity. I married, had children and established my career. In time, I developed clarity about who I was. In the first half of my life, I established my ego-identity.

Yet by midlife, I—my ego—had become radically estranged from my home in the soul, as implied by the dream statement, "I will lead you home." Now middle-aged and single, I was alone and confused, "lost in a dark wood." Indeed, beneath my midlife confusion and misery was a *nostalgia*, "a longing for home," a hunger for my abandoned soul.

I longed to *return* to the home of my soul. This headless woman had said to me, "I will lead you home." Her statement suggested that I needed another home, other than my thinking ego. She had arrived to guide me back toward my first home, my original home. She wanted to steer me back into my forsaken soul, a soul that I had left behind during the first half of my life.

At forty-three, I was being told that my third and final home would be my own soul. The *Woman-with-No-Head* wanted to give a new direction to my life. She would escort me back into my feeling heart, into my soul.

"The return" did not take me back into a state of *unconscious union*, as in Eden: that would have been regressive. And continuing to live with *conscious separation* from my soul was not a return to the home of my soul. Somehow, I had to find a new way of being in the world, whereby I would live between the extremes of an unconscious merger with my soul and Life, and a conscious alienation from my soul and Life. Going home entailed a progression, a *conscious reunion* with my soul and the Life around me.

In my third home, a *conscious union* with the Tree of Life would be achieved by becoming conscious of the complexities of Life—both interior and exterior—with its many polarities and conflicts. Then, I might experience a greater kinship with all of Life: intimacy with not only everything within me but also everything around me.

Unconscious wholeness was no longer a possibility. Now, an entirely new type of wholeness—*conscious wholeness*—entailed a consciousness of the complexities of my soul and Life. I had to embrace the multifaceted nature of inner and outer Life: not only good and evil but also masculine and feminine, matter and spirit and countless other polarities.

In my return to the Tree of Life, I would become more conscious of and intimately related to the mysteries of my soul. And I would mature into an increasing awareness of the infinite complexities of the Life around me. Life "here and now" on earth, with all its complexities, would be my final home. Yes, my heavenly home on earth.

My Analyst's Perspective

At my first Jungian session, I shared this dream of the *Woman-with-No-Head* with my analyst. She immediately referred to this headless woman as the "instinctual feminine." I was not sure what she meant, but I garnered "instinctual" probably referred to everything feminine about the dream woman, except for her missing head. From her comment, I sensed this headless woman was an extremely important figure with whom I needed to develop a conscious relationship.

The *Woman-with-No-Head* was redirecting me out of masculine thinking into feminine feeling. Not through my left brain's *logos* (my head's worship of words and ideas), but through *eros* (my heart's honoring of feelings and my desire to love) would come my salvation. Instead of *impersonal* thinking, I had to enter into the realm of *personal* feeling. Rather than analyzing, I had to feel and to value with my heart: to have compassion for everything within and around me. My whole life needed to become centered in my heart, not my head.

As I worked to integrate the instinctual feminine into my conscious identity, my analyst suggested I read H. Rider Haggard's 1887 novel, *She: A History of Adventure*. This is the story of Horace Holly's adventure into a lost jungle kingdom. Queen Ayesha, the beautiful and mysterious white queen of this African empire, is all-powerful. Indeed, "Ayesha" means "She-who-must-be-obeyed."

For Jung, Haggard's "Ayesha" is a personification of the soul, the *anima*. He saw this story as a metaphor for a man's adventure back into his forgotten soul. In the book, "She" declares, "My empire is of the imagination." Yes, the soul is the kingdom of the imagination! The reader is informed that Ayesha has the power to heal wounds. She's imagination can also cure illnesses, reanimate the dead: She knows the secret of immortality.

Did my soul's imagination have the ability to do such miraculous things? Did the "instinctual feminine" within me have such powers? Yes, Anima was "the One" who had *healed* my heart-wound into her vagina. And from her vagina, I was reborn—*reanimated* from the dead. Furthermore, the *Woman-with-No-Head* had said, "I will lead you home" into my immortal soul; Anima knew the *secret of immortality*. Yes, my soul's imagination had done all of these things.

Looking back, I believe this particular female analyst had been providentially selected for me. She was a deeply feminine and empathetic woman. She embodied the instinctual feminine, similar to the headless woman in my dream. But she was *not* the *Woman-with-No-Head*.

My analyst saw the profound significance of this headless woman for the gradual emergence of unknown parts of my soul into consciousness. Her persistent attention to this *Woman-with-No-Head* encouraged me to become more focused on the development of the inner feminine, my soul. At this time in my life, she was the perfect analyst for me.

One Woman's Negative Reaction

In contrast to my analyst's valuing of the *Woman-with-No-Head*, one highly intellectual woman whom I knew was incredibly judgmental of this dream-image. When I shared this dream with her and other friends—who met monthly in a small group—she felt I had "no respect" for women. Since this dream-woman had "no head," clearly, I thought the woman in the dream had no brains! This woman concluded that I had no respect for women in general. Most assuredly, this woman's issues around her femininity had been triggered.

Like everyone, I do not consciously choose who appears in my dreams. No matter what strange images might arrive, or what unusual words might be spoken, my task was simply to look, listen and learn why this *Woman-with-No-Head* had visited me. This dream was meant to be interpreted *internally* and *symbolically*, not externally and literally.

The *Woman-with-No-Head* was challenging my conscious attitude, presenting a contrary point of view. My masculine ego-consciousness needed to be put in its place. The dream was attempting to correct the imbalance within me: thinking at the expense of feeling.

The *Woman-with-No-Head* image did not reflect a negative attitude toward women, nor toward the inner feminine. On the contrary, this headless woman was precisely "the One" I needed. Her soulful directive was telling me that my masculine thinking would be mostly useless in my journey back into the home of my soul.

The woman in the group was unable to grasp that this dream-figure was my "savior": yes, "the One" who would lead me back into my interior home. This headless woman was the absent inner feminine in my life. She was a personification of my soul, reaching out to me.

Since a few of my women readers may have a similar reaction to this image of the *Woman-with-No-Head*, I mention this woman in my group, who felt I did not respect women. But I assure you, this dream was about my salvation as a man, who desperately needed the restorative power of the inner feminine.

THE AWAKENING OF MY SOUL

My intoxicating romance with Diana was actually an unconscious infatuation with this *Woman-with-No*-Head. After this dream, I realized that "the One" lurking between Diana and me in that hotel room, *and* the *Woman-with-No-Head*, were the same woman. Through these two entirely unexpected yet pivotal events, I was becoming more aware of and enchanted by the woman within me.

I was *obsessed* with Diana. But more to the point, I was *possessed* by my *anima*, my soul, which I had seen in Diana. As I became more conscious of my *anima*—and cultivated a relationship with her—this possession gradually diminished. For a man, is not "falling in love" always, at least partially, a process of becoming romantically possessed by his *anima*?

Although I truly believed that I had fallen in love with Diana, Anima was the one whom I was actually beginning to love so ardently. Indeed, I had fallen in love with my soul for the first time, even though initially as a projection onto Diana. As I became more conscious of this inner woman and became dependent upon her, the loss of Diana became less painful.

The *Woman-with-No-Head* had said to me, "I will lead you home." Or as spoken in the last line of Goethe's *Faust*, "The Eternal Feminine shows us the way [home]." Indeed, first by the mortal feminine (Diana) and then by the immortal *Woman-with-No-Head* (my soul), the Eternal Feminine was guiding me into my soul: back to my abandoned soul.

Distinguishing Between the Inner Feminine and the Outer Woman

As I grieved Diana over the next five years, I eventually figured out who the actual woman was and which part was my soul—the inner feminine. I struggled to differentiate between Diana and my romantic projection on her. Who was Diana? What was *not* Diana? How much of my image of Diana was the inner feminine, my soul, projected onto Diana?

I needed to discriminate between these two tightly entangled women, so I could perceive the inner feminine as distinct from Diana. I labored to separate them: to untangle their natures and clearly distinguish between Diana's womanly traits and the feminine attributes of my soul. Once these two women were more separate in my mind, I could consciously discern and integrate the inner feminine as a part of myself. Only then could my soul flower and bear her fruit.

With the passage of time, I realized that much of the feminine beauty that I saw in Diana was that of the inner feminine. I was not aware that such fertile beauty resided within my soul. Diana was a beautiful woman. But with my *anima* now retrieved from Diana, I became conscious of the feminine beauty within my own soul. Because of my increasing consciousness of my soul, then my soul was able to bear some of her "fruits of the feminine" (Part Three).

My Soul Mate: Mating with My Soul

When I met Diana, I was searching for my soul mate. But in this dream, the *Woman-with-No-Head*, my *anima*, was calling me inward to notice her. This headless woman was seducing me to mate with her instead of Diana. Not a younger, actual woman, but now a mature, inner feminine figure would become my soul mate.

In a trance-like state, I had asked Diana, "Are you the one?" But in fact, I was speaking to that unattached soul lurking between Diana and me. Then three months later, this *Woman-with-No-Head* was "the One" who answered this question. Diana was "the one" I asked; but my soul was "the One" who answered, "I will lead you home."

By projecting my soul onto Diana, I had become involved with two women simultaneously: Diana and my soul. From the outset, I was having an "affair" with Anima. Thankfully, Diana kicked me out of her life, perhaps because she intuited my "unfaithful" liaison with Anima. Diana must have sensed my romanticized love was not actually for her.

For several years after this dream, I had fantasies of my decapitation: the death of my thinking ego. My head had to be cut off. Or at least, my rational ego needed to be cut down into a smaller size. If I wanted to mate with Anima, she required a truly humble and receptive ego.

With the unexpected appearance of a "sacred vagina" in the clay and the arrival of this *Woman-with-No-Head* in my dream, my soul was clearly awakening within me. Anima wanted to become a part of my life; she yearned to partner with me. After this dream, I became increasingly more intimate with my *anima*; yes, I mated with my own soul. Anima is "the One" with whom I will spend the rest of my life. Anima is my true soul mate.

The Incarnation of the Divine Feminine

Eventually, I realized that the inner feminine was seeking to incarnate within me. At this time, I was becoming conscious of Anima as an amazing divine, feminine aspect of my soul. Since I was reclaiming my soul from the realm of projection, my *anima* could then awaken within me.

Little by little, I began to feel Anima's womanly presence within me; and I discerned her to be distinct from not only Diana but also separate from my thinking ego. The umbilical cord of dependency, which previously yoked me to my wife and Diana, would now connect me to Anima. Accordingly, I became more dependent upon her, my soul.

With the awakening of the divine feminine within me, I began to experience a vast imaginal realm, which astronomically surpassed what could happen between two human lovers, such as Diana and myself. Within my soul, I would find compassion, imagination and creativity, wisdom and truth—all aspects of the divine feminine. And over time, Anima would birth my deeper Self: the birth of God in my soul. These "fruits of the feminine" would nourish, sustain and replenish my consciousness forever (Part Three).

Reclaiming my soul-projection prepared me to love a woman partner for who she actually was, rather than as a figment of my romantic imagination about her. But in fact, my projected *anima* was not a *figment* of my imagination; instead, it was a *fragment* of my soul, which had been misplaced onto Diana.

Furthermore, when recalled back into myself, then that soul-fragment could bear fruit into my consciousness. In this fashion, my beatific vision of the divine feminine, initially seen in Diana, would gradually incarnate into my consciousness and become a part of me.

———— ❦ ————

After Diana, I never fell so far, so deeply into love again. In fact, I no longer had a desire "to fall in love." I simply wanted to love a woman for who she really is. With the arrival and development of the inner feminine, I was then able to be more genuinely loving of an actual woman than ever before.

Since more of the feminine was flowering within me, my *anima* could no longer be so readily projected onto an actual woman. Besides, after I became enchanted by and intimate with Anima, I no longer wanted to chase my soul in a flesh-and-blood woman.

Thankfully, I am no longer capable of romantic love. Now, thirty years later, I can love, cherish and treasure a woman for who she actually is. Loving a woman for a lifetime is infinitely more miraculous than loving an imaginary goddess, although the latter is more magical for a brief time.

Equally as important, I began to select a different type of woman for a partner. Since I was living less in my head and more from my heart, I became involved with two women who lived from their hearts. In effect, the *Woman-with-No-Head* was guiding me to find a woman similar to herself: more heart-centered, not primarily head-focused. An eight-year relationship with Patricia and my marriage to Marigrace (Epilogue) would confirm this shift within me.

LOVING A REAL WOMAN: PATRICIA

Five years after Diana and I broke up, I met Patricia through Great Expectations, a dating service with a walk-in office (prior to internet dating). In her profile, Pat listed her profession as "attorney," yet added she was "a nice one." Since I was working with lawyers at my job, I knew many attorneys, both male and female. Very quickly, I came to agree with Pat's self-assessment. Indeed, she is "a nice one!"

With no aforethought, we quickly and passionately became entangled, a choice I never once regretted. Our relationship lasted eight years, followed by a wonderful friendship over the last nineteen years. My afterthought has been simply one of gratitude for our loving liaison at that time—and now, for our devoted friendship, which I know will last a lifetime.

As a result of my own transformative journey into the inner feminine, I now had the ability to become involved with a more overtly feminine woman: a woman with an undisguised capacity for feeling. Given the awakening and growth of my soul, I was no longer attracted to a woman whose head was predominant: who was disconnected from her heart.

With Pat, I had heart-to-heart intercourse, not head-to-head discourse. We were emotionally compatible, so I experienced a more soulful intimacy with her.

Early in our relationship, I began to associate my experience of Pat with the *Woman-with-No-Head* in my dream five years earlier. Pat was an embodiment of the "instinctual feminine," which I was now primed to encounter in an actual woman. Since I had become better acquainted with my maturing inner feminine, I now wanted to partner with a more deeply feminine woman.

Pat is an extremely openhearted woman, whom earlier I would have avoided. Before, I was not attracted to such a woman since I feared deeply feminine women. I had always believed that unusually feminine women were highly dependent. So initially, I was fearful that Pat might be the clingy type. I was afraid of a dependent woman because her neediness might overwhelm me.

But now, as a result of significantly resolving my dependency issue, establishing my masculine identity, and embracing my feminine side, my fear of the feminine had mostly abated. And I was more self-dependent: less dependent on an actual woman.

As a consequence, a moderately dependent woman no longer frightened me. Since I had found more balance within myself—between dependence and independence—I had less fear of some healthy dependence in a woman.

As I became acquainted with Pat, I realized we both had a fairly good balance between dependence and independence. Unlike my first marriage, one of us was not "unacceptably dependent" and the other "excessively independent." *Inter*dependence made my relationship with Pat relatively easy.

———— •♥• ————

Instead of romancing a projection, I loved Pat for whom she actually was. And she accepted me for whom I was. Our relationship was joyful and playful: not too intense, not too serious, as is so often the case with romantic love.

With Pat, I had a "realistic romance" of deep affection, great appreciation and genuine admiration. Although I had now discovered the divine feminine within myself, I realized Pat also embodied the divine feminine. But she was not an imaginary goddess to me. Because I had reclaimed my previously projected *anima*, I could now experience and feel the divine feminine within her, as distinct from my feminine soul.

In several ways, being with Pat for those years represented a major shift for me. For one thing, I had selected a different type of woman: an openhearted, feeling woman. For another, I had learned a great deal about loving a woman for whom she actually is. Instead of "falling in love" with a projection of my *anima*, I loved Pat as a mortal woman.

Furthermore, I was now mature enough for a long-term commitment. With Pat, I did not run from a commitment as I had with Cara. And Pat did not abandon me as Diana had. Neither of us gave up and fled the scene. We both worked to understand and resolve our differences. Through our relationship, I learned how to genuinely love and be devoted to a woman. Our relationship lasted for eight years.

Pat contributed greatly to the evolution of my soul. My feminine, feeling side became deeply engaged with her. I could be vulnerable with her; I was self-disclosing of my feelings, mostly without fear of rejection. During these years, our alliance nourished and satisfied me. While with Pat, many new facets of my soul emerged.

———— •♥• ————

Ours was a long-distance relationship, except for the first nine months. After that, Pat moved from Los Angeles to San Diego. About three years later, she returned to Las Vegas, where she had previously practiced law. I remained in Los Angeles. Both of us had excellent jobs in different states, which was one factor in the eventual demise of our relationship.

When we broke up, we both felt pain, sadness and loss. Yes, I was depressed about our breakup, but I did not feel suicidal. Although moderately "dependent" in our *inter*dependent relationship, I had not been overly-dependent.

Humorously, both of us remember ourselves, not the other, as the person to initiate the breakup. Hence, neither of us felt "dumped" or rejected by the other. As my wife points out, this might be why Pat and I have remained close friends.

What a waste it would have been if our friendship had been "aborted" because one or the other, or both of us, was unable to continue as friends. Unlike Cara and Diana, Pat and I transitioned into a friendship. And she became a part of my family. For my wife and me, Pat is now a part of our "family of choice," as my wife describes.

After our breakup, our friendship was significantly enhanced when Pat fostered and adopted two children: a nine-year-old girl—and four years later, a fourteen-year-old boy. In spite of a three-hundred-mile distance between our homes, Pat and I worked cooperatively on some childrearing tasks and challenges. Be that as it may, Pat had the lion's share of the responsibilities. I am honored to have served as a father figure for both these teenagers, and now as young adults.

Our eight-year relationship was more than half the length of my first marriage. We never lived together and were never legally married. Yet I consider Pat to have been my second wife.

When Pat found and chose me at Great Expectations, I excitedly accepted. "I once was lost, but now am found"—this time by Pat, an actual woman. After being found five years earlier by the

Woman-with-No-Head in my dream, I was graced a second time by the arrival of this wonderful flesh-and-blood woman into my life. Once again, I became the recipient of an *amazing grace*.

I loved Pat for who she actually was, instead of becoming infatuated with a soul-projection. However, I still had to figure out how to consciously cherish Pat and Anima, my soul, at the same time. I wanted give equal attention to both Pat and Anima.

<hr />

INTERLUDE
GOD, MY SOUL AND THE UNCONSCIOUS

Having a more intimate alliance with Anima, I could now experience some of "the fruits of the feminine": my soul's favorable qualities. I would be blessed with the gifts of intuition, imagination and creativity, and the wisdom and truth of my soul. And ultimately, through Anima, I would experience the birth of God/the Self within my soul (Part Three).

Nevertheless, I had absolutely no idea that Anima could feel intense rage as well. At times, with her raging within me, I would experience some of the hellish aspects of my own soul. Likewise, I would encounter *Yahweh*'s jealous wrath within my heart. On my journey to my interior, spiritual home, I would be exposed to the depths of my soul's, and God's, fiercely dark nature.

Anima embodies the complexities of the soul, both the light and the dark aspects. Experiencing these opposing facets of my soul has been the most challenging part of my quest for wholeness: a consciousness of not only favorable but also unfavorable aspects of my heart, my soul. As Makarios wrote, the vessel of the human heart contains not only "the treasures of grace" but also "the treasures of evil."

God Is My Me

In my journaling—beginning at midlife—I unthinkingly began to use the words "God" and "soul" interchangeably. Since God seemed to speak from my soul, I was unable to distinguish between the two. As Jung remarked, "I have been accused of 'deifying the soul.' Not I, but God himself deified it!" Jung was stating that God, not Jung, had placed Himself within the human soul. As for myself, within my soul is where I have found God, the Indwelling Presence.

Furthermore, Jung wrote, "We cannot tell whether God and the unconscious are two different entities." In other words, when the mysteries of God are revealed from within, these seem to arrive either from, or through, the unconscious. As for me, my experience of God and the unconscious are indiscernible.

My experience of the indwelling God has been through my unconscious soul. My soul's "voice" is the voice of God, as I understand it. The utterances of my soul disclose my inner truth; that is, tiny bits of God's mysterious complexity are revealed into my consciousness. For example, I receive novel insights from my soul, which I regard as the thoughts of God. Consequently, I am unable to distinguish between God, my soul and the unconscious.

Over many years, a dialogue has developed between my consciousness and my soul, between my ego and God. My ego is the inquiring subject, and God is the responsive "me," indeed my own soul. Yes, "I" am conversing with my "me"—the God within me. I address my "me" as "God," "Oh Lord," "You," "Holy Sophia" or "Holy Psyche."

While writing this book, I recalled reading, many years ago, some of Catherine of Genoa's (1447-1510) writings, penned five centuries earlier. She wrote, "My Me is God, nor do I recognize any other Me except my God Himself." Catherine's "me" was her God: an objective, divine reality dwelling within herself. For simplicity, I paraphrase her words: "God is my me." These four simple words describe my experience of my "my me," my soul, and God as being one and the same.

As is the case with everyone, my soul is the infinite, divine mystery within me. I am the consciousness who converses with this mysterious, unconscious God. Residing within me, how could God be any closer? When I chant, "God is my me," I am comforted by the nearness of God, the Indwelling Presence.

As I complete this Interlude, I will focus on becoming conscious of my soul's feelings, especially my "darker" emotions. Many believe that the soul is pure love and light. But within me, I have also found hate and darkness. Anima's negative emotions, her dark side, are aspects of my soul that I struggle to accept.

For the last thirty-five years, I have vacillated between *neglecting* my soul, on the one hand, and then later, *nourishing* her. For long periods of time, I have avoided the dark facets of my soul. Instead, I have wanted to experience only my soul's positive aspects.

Neglecting My Soul

In spite of the appearance of the sacred vagina in my heart and the arrival of the *Woman-with-No-Head*, I increasingly began to neglect my soul with the passage of time. Forgetting to attend to the needs of my soul was incredibly easy. Yet whenever I ignored Anima, I was being unfaithful to her, disloyal to my soul.

During this time, I felt a conflict between my soul's longings, on the one hand, and the demands and joys of the external world. Necessarily diverted into my responsibilities at work and gladly distracted into my relationship with Pat, I often failed to pray, journal and pay attention to the hunger within my soul.

When I would neglect Anima, she would become distressed, jealous and angry. At midlife, I grappled with how to give Anima as much attention as I gave to Pat and my full-time job. My challenge was to develop a constant consciousness of my soul, a soul-consciousness, while still being focused on my work and enjoying time with Pat.

———— •❦• ————

"Hell, hath no fury like a woman scorned." This frequently cited remark—unfortunately most often derogatorily spoken only about women—first appeared in my journal a few months after Diana "scorned" me by abruptly terminating our relationship the first time. Feeling a hellish rage one day, I journaled, "My inner woman rages because she has been rejected. Hell, hath no fury like my soul scorned." My soul was furious with Diana for the sudden breakup. As Brother Dan at the monastery had remarked, "She wounded your inner feminine."

Yet more habitually and to the point, the episodic fury within my soul was the result of *my own* scorn of Anima's needs. During the following years, I found that I could easily ignore her various feelings and confusing emotions. Then, from my neglect, a hellish rage would arise within me. I wrote, "Hell, hath no fury like my inner woman scorned." Anima would become furious with me, when I neglected her for too long.

I journaled, "This woman inside me has been ignored and is lonely. Yes, I frequently fail to attend to her cries. Then, she becomes discouraged." Later I wrote, "An unhappy woman lives within me. I must acknowledge her feelings. Oh, how sad my soul becomes when I neglect her." I realized I had to attend to my soul's needs if I was going to be happy.

When feeling ignored for too long, my soul will become rageful. I journaled, "Anger arises within me because I have neglected Anima. Now, she rages back at me. It is as simple as that. My inner woman is raging for attention. How much longer will I drive myself into external activities before I attend to my soul?"

With her anger, my soul was crying out to be noticed, begging for intimacy with me. She did not like my unfaithfulness, when I spent too much time having "affairs" in the outer world. My habit of spending so much time with Pat, or being busy with my responsibilities at work and elsewhere, was far easier than tending to the needs of my soul.

Neglecting Anima was, in fact, a rejection of my soul. Apparently, I deemed my soul less worthy of my attention than my numerous activities in the external world.

By being too busy in the outer world, I was casting Anima out: throwing her outside of my awareness. Then, she would become jealous and rageful. As Jung stated, "Busyness is not just from the devil, it is the devil." Being too busy to attend to my soul's needs generates anger within me. Indeed, when my soul is neglected for too long, Anima takes on a devilish form.

———— •♥• ————

I have always been fascinated with the "jealous" God of the Hebrew Scriptures, who demanded the undivided attention of his chosen people. When He was neglected and forgotten, *Yahweh* would become wrathful. For me, this image of a rageful *Yahweh* is that of a deeply caring God who experiences deep hurt and becomes enraged when being ignored. Through his wrath, *Yahweh* was attempting to reconnect with his children. *Yahweh* was fighting for intimacy with his people.

Might this jealous God of the Hebrews also live within me? Is not the fury of my neglected soul actually the wrath of *Yahweh* within me? I journaled, "The rage of a neglected and jealous God burns within me. I have turned my back on God." I asked my soul, "Have I neglected you so completely that you must now endlessly rage? You are so incredibly jealous; you demand all of my attention!"

Quite frequently, I have not spent enough alone time with my soul. I journaled, "How can I attend to the needs of this rageful God within me? My soul is so demanding. Now, she needs to feel and express her rage, her pain, onto the pages of this journal."

I knew that attending to my soul's emotions was the best way for me to diminish this rage: to calm this angry God within me and bring my soul back into contentment. This wrathful God needed to feel Its emotions. I needed to take the time to allow my soul to feel her feelings. All the anger I felt was a part of my soul, indeed a part of God. My darker emotions were aspects of my soul, which I needed to attend to with acceptance and understanding.

As Jung remarked, "Emotion is the chief source of all becoming conscious. There can be no transforming of darkness into light and of apathy into movement without emotion." Only by feeling the rage within me could I find deliverance from the darkness. Then, the light of love could shine forth once again.

———— •❖• ————

Upon awakening in the morning, my first feeling was often sadness. I would realize, "My soul, she needs to talk." I journaled, "Always the sadness . . . Always with me, my ever-faithful sadness." Paraphrasing Simon and Garfunkel, I journaled many times, "Hello sadness [*darkness*], my old friend, I've come to talk to you again." I gradually became aware that my seemingly endless morning sadness was caused by my tendency to ignore my soul.

Surprisingly, allowing my feelings to surface and paying attention to these darker emotions helped dissipate the negative charge. After journaling for a while, the cloud of sadness invariably lifted, as I entered into the activities of the day. Since I took the time to sit with and feel my sadness, positive feelings were able to emerge, like sunshine after rain.

For me, depression, a deeper sadness, is a cry for help from my soul, a desperate cry for my attention. I came to view depression as the "call of my soul." Depression is the "voice," the feeling which calls me into my soul. By expressing my negative moods into my journal, I provide my soul with the attention she craves and requires, thereby giving her the relief that she wants. Like the sadness, the depression always passes away after I give my soul more prolonged attention.

As Jung remarked, "Depression is like a woman in black. If she turns up, don't shoo her away. Invite her in, offer her a seat, treat her like a guest and listen to what she wants to say." For me, when my "guest" depression arrives, she *always* has something to say, if merely to tell me, "I am so lonely. I am angry with you. Why have you neglected me for so long?" After I listen "to what she wants to say," Anima, this "woman in black," always feels better.

Perhaps for most men, certainly for me, ignoring the soul requires almost no effort. I can ignore my soul's emotions with much less effort than taking the time to sit with her feelings. But when neglected for too long, Anima becomes jealous and angry. I journaled, "My soul gets so pissed off when my ego is constantly focused elsewhere."

When scorned for too long, the soul will become furious, like a wild beast. As Jung articulated in *The Red Book* a hundred years ago, "My friends, it is wise to nourish the soul, otherwise you will breed dragons and Devils in your heart" (p. 232).

No longer the murderous rage of a dependent boy pushing away from his mother. Now, the fury of a neglected soul, my inner woman scorned.

Nourishing My Soul

Shortly after the 1994 earthquake in Southern California, I received a brochure for the annual conference on "Jung and Spirituality" in Einsiedeln, Switzerland. On the front of the pamphlet was a verse from the Hebrew Scriptures, translated by the former Benedictine monk who organized this yearly event.

"Pay attention, come to me [God]. Listen, and your soul shall live" (Isaiah 55:3). I was captivated by this verse; a wave of emotion washed over me. Instantly, I knew I had to attend this conference. With this strong feeling response, I realized I was being called once again to "pay attention" to my forgotten soul.

At the time, my soul was dying of thirst from prolonged neglect. On a daily basis, I had failed to be aware of my subtly fluctuating emotions. Hence, I was craving the quickening of my soul, so I might feel more alive. I knew if I gave careful attention to my soul's feelings, quenched her thirst, then my "soul shall live" again.

———— •♥• ————

Whenever I give Anima the attention she requires, I always feel better. During my twenty-three years of living alone, I developed the practice of waking up an hour early, so I could journal. Before getting ready for work, I would sit and "pay attention" to my soul: turn inward and reflectively journal and give expression to what I was feeling and thinking.

Anima is always thrilled when I journal her feelings in the morning. As I carefully listen, she is given a chance to fully express herself. While dating Pat for eight years, I lived alone. So, if I took advantage of the times we were not together, I had plenty of time to give attention to my soul.

Each morning, making a gradual transition from the night into the day is incredibly helpful to me. Taking the time to slowly cross the threshold from the darkness of sleep into the daylight of consciousness is crucial for the contentment of my soul. In this dimly lit state, before I become involved in the day's activities, Anima is frequently the most open and vulnerable. And I am more likely to intuit her thoughtful murmurings and notice the subtle shifts in her feelings.

I sit in my favorite, straight-backed armchair next to my bed and sip green tea. Sitting in the same chair, at the same time each morning, prompts my soul to respond. Once I sit down with a pen and my journal in my hand, Anima knows I am ready to listen. Then, she is more likely to reveal what is in her heart. Given my receptivity, Anima will slowly disclose her thoughts and feelings. Whatever is within her heart, meaningful or trivial, she expresses onto the pages of my journal.

I focus on the dark space within my body and wait for what might emerge. This emptiness, this nothingness, I know is fertile soil. I peer into the darkness within my body, and carefully listen to the inner silence. In this manner, I am ready to bear witness to whatever might surface into my consciousness.

I journal most of my thoughts and feelings since I know my soul is responsive to such careful attention. Each nuance of earlier thoughts carries a slightly new meaning. Every subtle shift in feeling expresses more of the complexity of my soul. I give Anima's desires free rein, and I allow her to think and feel whatever she wants.

Yes, I pay careful attention to this *Woman-with-No-Head*, my soul, the one who had said, "I will lead you home." Knowing my feelings and moods has become another method for becoming better acquainted with Anima. Becoming conscious of my soul's fluctuating feelings has been the primary passageway back into the home of my soul.

Self-expression into my journal has been essential for my healing. Journaling has become a form of self-therapy. Self-discovery, by putting my soul's thoughts and feelings onto paper, is similar to expressing myself to a therapist. When my soul speaks, I become the attentive listener. With an empathetic consciousness, I attend to her thoughts and feelings.

With self-empathy, I embrace my many pessimistic thoughts and negative emotions. By putting these dark facets of myself onto paper, I gain relief from the gloom. I know my journal does not necessarily make for good reading. But honest self-expression into my journal—and radical acceptance of what I am—do make for genuine self-healing.

Loving my *anima* is my inner work. With the fresh air of my consciousness and warm sunlight of my compassion, I "pay attention" to my soul. My spiritual practice is devotion to Anima, every aspect of her. Then, she can instinctively do her part in healing both herself and me. With such soul-tending, such soul-consciousness, my soul is able to flourish. Is not careful attention what lovers desire from each other?

Not only do I nourish my soul, but I discovered my soul could also generously replenish me, my consciousness, with her prolific "fruits of the feminine" (Part Three).

———— •♥• ————

In addition to journaling my thoughts and feelings, I religiously journal my dreams, thereby paying attention to what Anima wants to reveal to me while my ego is asleep. By being aware of my dreams, I can see my soul in action as I sleep; and I can listen to what she is telling me in the dark. When I pay careful attention to what Anima whispers in the night, I am greatly enriched, and she is deeply grateful.

Furthermore, in an intimate relationship with a woman, I have learned to "pay attention" to my moodiness and negative emotions. From the past, I knew that my unresolved problems—such as feelings of rejection and anger—could be triggered in an intimate alliance. Since Pat and I never lived together, I had ample solitude to reflect on our conflicts and seek internal resolution. I would journal my negative emotions, as a method for becoming more conscious of my problems and working through them.

My soul was thrilled with my Jungian analysis. When my female analyst spoke of the "instinctual feminine," Anima was exhilarated that my analyst immediately understood her far better than I did. And several days before each analytic session, my soul would become quite animated, as I carefully listened to—and made notes about—what she wanted to express in the next session. Furthermore, during my sessions, Anima always appreciated my total receptivity when I experienced unexpected feelings or was given novel insights.

By reading introspective, spiritual books, I nourish Anima. When I read soul-poetry (Rumi, Gibran, Rilke), at times my soul is brought to tears. She is crazy about soul quotations, especially the ones which resonate within her since she feels so instantly understood.

When I read about the interior world, I am not primarily focused on learning and remembering the ideas that I read. For me, psychospiritual reading is a process of plowing, fertilizing and planting seeds into my soul. Then, these can germinate and grow naturally, as they are so inclined. Later, these fruits of my labor can be harvested and provide nutrients for my consciousness. Nothing is more fertile than a well-plowed, well-seeded soul.

In addition, Anima is delighted when I become intentionally quiet and enter into my body. With this meditative practice, I become fully present to her. Then, I can feel her subtle, feminine movements within me. When I light candles, burn incense or turn on soft music, my soul relishes such quiet times. I am paying attention to Anima; I am spending time alone with her, something she craves.

When I experience nature's beauty—see the vibrant colors of tropical fish while snorkeling, view beautiful flowers anywhere, watch colorful birds in the rainforest—my soul is rejuvenated.

And my soul is revitalized by spiritual, New Age and classical music.

Furthermore, my soul enjoys spending time with family and close friends, laughing and being playful. She adores small children and animals, especially dogs.

Finally, my soul is grateful for private retreats at quiet monasteries or convents situated in nature. My many trips to La Casa de Maria in Santa Barbara, California, and to the Benedictine Monastery in Pecos, New Mexico, have been especially refreshing for my soul. At such places, my soul and I can be alone without external distractions, except for the beauty of nature. On these retreats, I reflectively journal and read spiritual books for a while. Then, I take my soul for meandering nature walks. We both come home feeling refreshed.

——— ·♥· ———

Tending the soul is a never-ending task, at times more difficult than others. For couples, their relationship will die if not attended to. So also, the soul will wither if one does not pay attention to her. Just as we must tend an outdoor garden, so also must we attend to the interior garden—the soul. Otherwise, the flowers will perish.

Watching the ebb and flow of my soul, I have found many unforeseen, life-giving images and ideas floating to the surface—or washing upon ego's shore—all of which nourish and guide me.

I prefer the companionship of a well-tended soul, rather than the "hell" of my inner woman scorned. "Pay attention, come to me. Listen, and your soul shall live." Frequently recalling this verse from Isaiah, I am reminded to pay attention to what is happening within my soul. By devotedly listening to my *anima*, then my "soul shall live."

PART THREE

A SOUL AWAKENS
The Fruits of the Feminine

An unexamined life is not worth living.

SOCRATES

Examine yourself that you may understand who you are. . . .
It is not fitting that you be ignorant of yourself . . .
You have already come to know, and you will be called
'the one who knows himself.'

THE BOOK OF THOMAS
A GNOSTIC CHRISTIAN GOSPEL
CHAPTER 1:3–6

What lies behind us, and what lies before us
are tiny matters compared to what lies within us.

RALPH WALDO EMERSON

Your vision will become clear
only when you can look into your own heart.
Who looks outside, dreams;
who looks inside, awakes.

C. G. JUNG

The appearance of the sacred vagina in my clay heart and the arrival of the *Woman-with-No-Head* in my dream inaugurated my midlife transition and transformation. My *anima* projection was gradually withdrawn from Diana. Piece by piece, my soul was retrieved and began to awaken within and become a more conscious part of me. My overdependence on an outer woman slowly diminished and was transferred to the inner woman.

In the following years, a remarkable feminine side emerged within me, which I had not experienced since early childhood—when my masculine identity was still diffuse. As a child, I played house with my three sisters, and I engaged in imaginary play with male friends, mostly outdoors in nature. But now at midlife, I found myself frolicking on an indoor playground, amusing myself with my interior nature, my soul. Through these internal activities, I was becoming more intimate with my newly-found playmate, Anima.

In Part Three, my focus is solely on interiority: on the life of my soul. From my soul, some of the prolific "fruits of the feminine" are delivered into my consciousness. I receive a portion of Anima's sacred fruits: intuition, imagination and creativity (Chapter 7). I also encounter wisdom and search for the truth of who I am (Chapter 8). And in my quest for wholeness, I partake of the Self: "the birth of God in the soul" (Chapter 9). As Gibran wrote, "The soul unfolds itself, like a lotus of countless petals."

In this process, I discover that "the One" I am seeking is my soul. But later, I realize the Self is "the ONE" I am searching for. Instead of being dependent on a woman, my wife or Diana, I become dependent on my soul and the Self.

With these inner activities, I am given self-knowledge. And I realize that knowledge of myself is identical to knowledge of God. Through this process, I individuate and become more of *what I am.* So then, I am on the path to becoming "the one who knows himself."

INTUITING THE DIVINE
God's Imagination and Creativity

———◆♥◆———

The intuitive mind is a sacred gift
and the rational mind is a faithful servant.
We have created a society that honors the servant
and has forgotten the gift.

ALBERT EINSTEIN

Without this playing with fantasy
no creative work has ever yet come to birth.
The debt we owe to the play of
the imagination is incalculable.

C. G. JUNG

My analyst helped me curtail the excesses of my romantic imagination about Diana. I began to see that she was largely an imaginary figure, an *anima* projection. My out-of-balance intuitive nature—my overly active imagination—had blinded me to seeing the reality of Diana as being distant and aloof with me.

With the slow death of that projection onto Diana, my soul was gradually retrieved. When no longer perceived as being outside myself, my *anima* could then awaken as a living reality within me. Increasingly, Anima presented me with an array of intuitive images and ideas. During these most painful yet extremely fruitful years, my imagination was regenerated and my creativity blossomed.

Numerous imaginal and ideational butterflies swarmed into my consciousness. Out of my still-bleeding soul, these vibrant images and winged ideas frequently flew into my awareness. Were these intimations of some mysterious, divine reality within me?

As my soul was awakening, my physical senses and thinking mind were of little use. Rather than perceiving the world primarily through my five senses, intuition became a new way for me to gather information. Jung describes intuition of the *external* world as "perception via the unconscious that brings forth ideas, images, new possibilities"; and he defines intuition of the *internal* world as "perception of unconscious events."

I journaled, "And so through intuition, I am able to perceive the intangible aspects of reality, which otherwise I could not see. With intuition, I can grasp more of the underlying transcendent nature of the Universe." Through "perception via the unconscious," I was able to intuit and experience the deeply spiritual nature of the Universe.

Yet my primary focus was on "perception of unconscious events": intuiting interior spiritual activity. In the East, for example, the intuitive chakra, the third eye, is regarded as the way to become aware of the invisible spiritual realm. Intuiting the unseen within me, I could "see" some of the immaterial aspects of my soul: images and ideas, dreams, meanings and possibilities. Through intuition, not with my five senses, I was able perceive these non-material realities. I became fixated on the intuitive apprehension of this interior realm.

Furthermore, I knew that such spiritual knowledge could not be obtained through my rational mind, my thinking ego. Intuition means "to perceive directly, without reasoning": instantly to discern, initially without thought. Jung wrote that intuition "does not denote something contrary to reason, but something outside the province of reason."

At this time in my life, I bore witness to seemingly endless images and ideas sprouting up from the soil of my soul. From my reading, I knew the words *image* and *idea* had the same root: *eidos* in classical Greek. I was intrigued by this notion since some of the images in my imagination seemed to embody *ideas and meanings*; gradually, images would morph into ideas. For example, my sacred vagina sculpture was an image pregnant with a multitude of ideas. Furthermore,

I witnessed the spontaneous arrival of many unique *ideas in complete sentence form,* some of which are mentioned throughout this book.

The *Woman-with-No-Head* had said, "I will lead you home." Intuition would become one of several pathways we would travel together, as she guided me into the home of my soul. As my intuitive capacity grew, I would taste many of the imaginal and ideational "fruits of the feminine," which had long been germinating within my soul.

Intuiting the Divinity

My intuitive ability has been the essential avenue for encountering the deity within me. Through intuitive awareness of my inner world, I began to receive hints of something more: an Unseen Presence within me, which was not I/my ego. Numerous unconscious contents were becoming conscious, disclosing more aspects of *what I am*, what God is within me.

While journaling, I listened for whispers from the Self; and I watched for glimpses of what was surfacing from my soul, as I sought to hear the voice and see the face of God. Through these inklings, small fragments of the mystery within me arose into my awareness. This Indwelling Presence was delivering tiny bits of Itself into my consciousness.

I intuited and felt movements within my soul: yes, the activities of a divinity. Minute pieces of God's vast mystery were being imparted to me. These novel images and unique ideas were connecting me, my ego-consciousness, to the mysteries within the soul. Through intuition, I now had a way of being with this interior deity.

I wanted my consciousness to be a passive receptacle into which the deity could pour Itself. I journaled, "My task is to intuit and receive God's nature, essence, and psyche into the grail of my consciousness." Or as Rilke wrote, "The deepest experience of the Creator is feminine, for it is the experience of receiving and bearing." As a receptive vessel, my ego-consciousness was becoming a feminine chalice for receiving the Creator's imaginal and ideational wine.

At times, I sensed the *unity* of Everything. My diverse and often conflicting feelings and multiple thoughts arose from a single soul, a single Self. Furthermore, I intuited the unity of the Universe, in spite of its infinite complexity. On a few occasions, I have felt an exhilarating union with Everything: both the interior and exterior universes.

And gradually, I began to feel the *divinity* of Everything: my soul, humanity, nature and the Universe. For me, the inner universe and the outer Universe are the essential nature of God. My soul and the Universe are two different aspects of the one God.

Furthermore, I became aware that this indwelling God was seeking to actualize Its potentialities through Its creative imagination within me. In March 1988, I journaled, "Through intuition, I am able to see possibility which can transform actuality." Later, I wrote, "Through my soul's imagination, God wants to do so much more, become so much more. How can I live with this *becoming God*, the infinite possibilities of God's becoming within me? *Whatever God is*, I want God to actualize Itself within me."

Feeling the Presence of the Deity

When some of these ideas and images were given to me, feelings were evoked; my eyes would fill with tears. Feeling seemed to be intrinsic to certain ideas. By way of feeling, and without ego's thoughts, a sacred value or meaning was at times being imparted to me. Through these interior activities, I felt the presence of the deity. I surmised some deeper intention was at work within me, as evidenced by the arrival of these feeling-laden, intuitive notions.

Experiencing meaning as being embodied in feelings, rather than thought, was a titanic shift for me. I had always believed meaning was something that I would acquire with my reasoning mind. But now, thought was mostly useless. I journaled, "Without feeling, life is not worth living; it is meaningless." I realized that spiritual meaning was emanating from my soul by way of spontaneous feeling responses to images, ideas and external events.

The intuitive imagination, not the bare facts of life, injected spiritual vitality into my life. Having an imaginative and feeling response to people and the natural world was exciting. As Keats remarked, "I am certain of nothing but the holiness of the heart's affections [feelings] and the truth of the imagination." Yes, I would find meaning for my life by way of feeling and through intuition: "the truth of the imagination."

When my soul/God would present an array of unexpected images and ideas, I felt completely alive. I hungered to stay vitally linked to the activity of the creative imagination within me. In my journal, I wrote, "I should be able to intuit and feel God in everything within and around me, in everything that I do. The introverted, intuitive-feeling side of me is my pathway to God. Yes, I worship feeling and intuition, for these are paths into my soul, into the interior mysteries of God."

IMAGINATION

In his novel, *She: A History of Adventure*, H. Rider Haggard portrays the kingdom of the imagination by using the metaphor of a lost jungle empire. The queen of this empire is "Ayesha," which means "She-who-must-be-obeyed." In the book, "She" declares, "My empire is of the imagination" (page 179). Accordingly, Ayesha demands obedience to the imagination. A few pages later, the narrator, Holly, remarks, "What is imagination? Perhaps it is the shadow of the intangible truth, perhaps it is the soul's thought" (page 189).

For Jung, Ayesha is a personification of the soul, the *anima*. As for me, my soul's imagination was now birthing her "intangible truth" and "thought" into my consciousness. And I realized these imaginative images and ideas "must-be-obeyed."

If the imagination was going to flourish within me, I knew I must become Anima's faithful servant. Reading about Ayesha persuaded me to surrender to the soul's transcendent imagination and to succumb to her infinite creativity. I wanted Anima's creative imagination to guide my life, with my ego serving as her loyal subject.

Orgasms of the Imagination

While suffering the loss of Diana, my consciousness—over a period of five years—was flooded with unexpected images and ideas, especially upon awakening in the morning. I was astounded by these prolific intuitive notions, which had apparently been germinating within my soul for decades. I wanted to be completely receptive to these spiritual beings by allowing them to breathe, live and thrive within me.

One day, when talking with my analyst about my highly active imagination, suddenly the phrase, "Orgasms of the imagination on the altar of life," came into my consciousness. Although initially un-sure what "the altar of life" was, I immediately knew what "orgasms of the imagination" was about. It was an exact description of what was happening within me.

After this therapy session, I journaled, "Within me, God explodes with inexhaustible images, bringing Life into me. My psyche orgasms, spewing forth the deity's ideas onto this altar." My ego-consciousness was having frequent intercourse—conscious discourse—with my soul. Consequently, my often-expectant soul was bearing her count-less ideational offspring into my receptive ego.

I prayed, "Yes, when your imagination is active within me, then I worship at your altar. I kneel before these images and ideas in sheer delight as you reveal yourself to me." I journaled, "We are meant to receive and to reflect the images and ideas of the soul—to observe and report these, nothing more." Greedily, I wanted these vibrant crea-tures to proliferate and "run wild" into my consciousness.

A few weeks later, I realized an altar is a place for sacrifice and communion. When the imagination orgasms, the ego is temporarily sacrificed. I journaled, "Only when my ego is sacrificed for a while, can my soul fully express her creative imagination." This altar within me was the sacred place where I could commune: experience inti-macy with my soul.

———— ·♥· ————

The imaginative activity within me was not something I was do-ing. These images and ideas were not products of my ego. They were instinctual eruptions from deep within my soul. They were gifts from the interior Creator.

Even though my ego was able to make itself more receptive to these spontaneous arrivals, imagination was occurring *in spite of my ego*. I journaled, "Imagination is an autonomous activity of the soul, not of the ego. The ego's activity is separate from the soul's activity." Imagination happens!

I view the imagination as the creative revelation of God that aris-es out of the soul. I journaled, "I hunger for God to appear to me through the imagination. Imagination is from the '*other* world,'" from the interior spiritual realm. Later, I wrote, "Imagination is the reality of God's presence within my soul. Without imagination, I cannot return to God."

If the imagination is an aspect of God's reality, then I worship the imagination as a part of the divine self-revelation. Or as William Blake (1757–1827) wrote, "The Eternal Body of Man is the Imagination: that is God himself." He believed that the imagination *is* God. Living during the Age of Reason in England, Blake felt the imagination had been totally discredited by the rationality throughout Europe. His worship of the imagination is exemplified in his highly original paintings and very unusual writings. Since first reading this statement, I have cherished the imagination as a most precious gift of God's creative activity within me. When imagination happens, God is present and alive for me.

Imagination: A Playground within My Soul

To my analyst one day, I exclaimed, "My inner world is like a playground!" Since my soul was no longer romantically projected onto Diana, an even more magnificent woman—an inner woman pregnant with a multitude of images and ideas—was now able to dance within my soul. My chalice, my ego-consciousness, was being filled to the brim with imaginal and ideational offerings from Anima, my spiritual playmate.

Overflowing with these intuitive novelties, I felt like a small, excited boy on a playground. Ideas and images became my playthings; symbols were my toys. I was constantly searching for, gathering and playing with these intuitive notions like a child, doing whatever I felt.

No expectations or demands, except to joyfully receive these soulful wonders into my consciousness. No rules to follow, save to appreciate and to endlessly explore. No decisions to make, only to witness, delight in and play with these limitless, intuitive realities. I journaled, "I want to frolic with these images and ideas forever, on this playground within me!"

I absolutely loved spending time in my interior playground, where I could actively experience the imagination. In this internal space, I was constantly playing with one idea after another. As Jung stated, "The creation of something new is not accomplished by the intellect, but by the play instinct, acting from inner necessity. The creative mind plays with the object it loves." With my instinctual play, the ideas that I loved were revealing what was within me. Through these disclosures, the interior Creator was re-creating me into more of *what I am*.

All of these intuitive wonders were gifts from God, God's divine children, with which I could play. With my ego out of the way, the divinity was able to reveal some of Its animated images and re-cre-ational ideas. Jung wrote, "Without this playing with fantasy no cre-ative work has ever yet come to birth. The debt we owe to the play of imagination is incalculable." The imagination was the interior play-ground wherein the creative work of discovering and becoming *what I am* was transpiring.

Imagination Is Reality

Years ago, I read Roberts Avens' book, *Imagination Is Real-ity* (1980). Written from a Jungian perspective, the title of this book sparked my interest and had an irreversible impact on me. I already knew Jung regarded the imagination as irrefutably "real," as real as any tangible object in the external world.

But this title gave the imagination a status which I had not previ-ously acknowledged. I realized that the imaginal realm was not only divine but also undeniably real. I journaled, "God is the imaginal and creative activity within, which seeks to inspire and transform me. Yes, the imagination is an aspect of the presence of God, the reality of God within me."

Some may ask, does analysis help or hinder the creative process? For me, at midlife, Jungian analysis provided a fertile environment for a soul that was ready to bear her imaginal and ideational fruit. Tilling inner soil, cultivating my soul, was my experience of analysis. Bearing and harvesting the "fruits of the feminine" has enriched my life beyond measure.

Psyche's Butterflies

In college, I learned that Psyche is the goddess of the soul, and that *psyche* is also the Greek word for butterfly. For the Greeks, some-thing about the soul was butterfly-like. Accordingly, Psyche is often depicted with butterfly wings.

One day, I thought to myself, "These images and ideas flying out of my soul into my consciousness are like butterflies. I fear they might not land for very long; their presence might be short-lived in my awareness." I was afraid these intangible creatures might flit away: disappear from my consciousness.

If I failed to catch these unique specimens, then the vast majority of them might vanish forever. With my consciousness being swarmed by so many vibrant images and fleeting ideas, I knew my memory could not retain such a hoard.

How could I hold onto these colorful beings, so I could recall them later? If not to be permanently lost, with what net could I catch them? Then, I realized I could ensnare these intuitive notions by writing them down on a small notepad in my shirt pocket. My butterfly net became a brief phrase or simple drawing, which captured their essence.

With a few words or a picture, the specimen was preserved. The next morning, I wrote or drew these non-material entities into my journal and elaborated upon them. On paper, I preserved each butterfly by describing its essential nature, or at times a bit of its mystery, with words. As a result, I was no longer anxious about forgetting a single one of them. So, I was able to liberate these notions from my consciousness.

My soul seemed to be filled with butterflies, these revelations from God: countless ideas, many dreams, a few visions and a variety of symbols and images. Inexhaustible specimens haphazardly flew into my awareness. All intangible, I could not touch any of them. Yet often, many of them touched me deeply, when an idea evoked a strong feeling or an image bore rich meaning.

Now, I view my psyche as an interior flower garden with an infinite reserve of butterflies. From the dark soil of my soul, these beautiful creatures flutter into the daylight of my consciousness, bringing tidings from the unseen God. My psyche is the cocoon from which they emerge into my ego-consciousness. Indeed, these are *psyche's butterflies*.

In Cara's dream, a butterfly had emerged from its cocoon, a cancerous tumor, symbolizing her transformation. And now, my metamorphosis was taking place by way of these butterfly-like images and ideas. My consciousness was being expanded and reshaped by these creatures from within: images and ideas were re-creating me. Psyche, goddess of the soul, was transforming me.

At times, my soul's imagination appeared to be sterile, infertile. Psyche was seemingly inactive, dull or dry. Was it not the season for butterflies? Greedily waiting for the next hoard of images and ideas to emerge out of my soul, I would become impatient. My analyst would remind me that eggs always require a period of incubation before more butterflies can hatch.

The Birth and Death of My Narcissism

With the arrival of so many intuitive notions into my consciousness, I began to believe I was an extraordinarily gifted, creative person. Being swarmed by these remarkable ideas, I felt I was without equal: incredibly unique, absolutely special. Never before had the world known one like myself, who could birth such astonishing ideas.

With great pride, I took credit for the creative activity within my soul. I was arrogant, with an inflated sense of who I was. A grandiosity and a sense of omnipotence emerged. I was becoming narcissistic, believing I was the Creator of these amazing specimens.

I knew the danger of inflation—the ego believing it is the Creator. So, with self-reflection, I gradually began to realize that the Creator within me, not I, was birthing these divine creatures. My ego was simply meant to be the curator for a few of the deity's many inexhaustible ideas.

The transformation of my narcissism transpired, as I became aware that each and every imaginative and creative event within my soul was a gift from the Creator. These cherished images and treasured ideas were *not my* creations. They were arriving out of my soul into my consciousness, as gifts from the Unseen Presence.

Not I, but the Creator within me, was special. Although I felt that some of these ideas were unrivaled, my ego was not special. My ego was simply the humble receptacle for receiving these divine elements; I was merely the chalice into which they were being poured. I journaled, "Our specialness arrives from our deeper Self, from God. No wonder we feel special or grandiose as we encounter that which is God-like within us for the first time."

Perhaps narcissism and self-infatuation are a necessary stage in the eruption and unearthing of one's imaginative and creative gifts. But ultimately, the ego is *not* the imaginative wizard or the creative genius. These are gifts from the Self, the true Creator.

With the death of my narcissism, I began to faithfully serve this divine, creative mystery within me. My task was simply to witness and write down my soul's activities and become a servant to the creative imagination. I said to my soul, "I seek to serve the great, creative mystery within me."

CREATIVITY

Vagina Envy

After the birth of my second child, I experienced vagina envy for the first and only time. Of course, as a therapist, I knew about Freud's idea of a woman's alleged penis envy. But now unexpectedly, I became envious of my wife's body and its ability to grow a fetus. In her womb, the miracle of miracles: two human beings had been created.

Yes, I had contributed the required sperm. And I emotionally supported my wife during her pregnancies. I was in the delivery room when each child was born. Most importantly, I was extremely involved in childrearing throughout their growing-up years.

But the zygotes had formed within my wife's body, not mine. No fetus was ever going to gestate within my male body. I had no uterus! Such a miracle could never be delivered from me. Consequently, I experienced vagina envy. Or perhaps more accurately, I suffered womb envy.

Fifteen years later at midlife, I began to resolve my womb envy when I realized that images and ideas were my "babies." From the depths of the unconscious—the womb of my soul—these imaginal and ideational children were being birthed into my consciousness.

My soul was the only creative uterus I had. Like a mother-to-be, I was aware that these were not my creations. But my soul was the womb wherein they were being created and from which they would be delivered.

Did the appearance of that sacred vagina in the clay suggest a resolution of my vagina envy, my womb envy? Yes, while sculpting that vagina in the clay, I unearthed the womb of my soul, which was then able to birth innumerable images and ideas. Birthing from within, I no longer felt womb envy. My creative instincts were now being gratified with the arrival of these ideational newborns.

God's Creativity

From the Judeo-Christian myth, I was taught that God created the world from nothing. And from the theory of evolution, I learned that creation is a never-ending process. Yet in my adult years, the Universe and the Creator merged in my mind and became identical for me. Yes, the Universe-Creator is eternally evolving Itself. The Universe is self-creating, a self-creating God. As such, the self-creating God, by definition, is incomplete and imperfect, as are the children of the evolutionary Creator.

With the arrival of these fascinating images and meaningful ideas, I was experiencing the creative activity of God. Could it be that the Universe-Creator, is still at work within each of us, relentlessly seeking to creatively transform our consciousness, and thereby the world?

With the activity of the creative imagination, I felt completely alive. I said to my soul, "I am alive only if creativity is happening within me. If God is not creating within me, I feel so dead. I must write, live the creative life, or else I will die." I no longer wanted to achieve and produce. Now, I just wanted to give birth. I journaled, "I live to bear the Creator's imaginal and ideational offspring into the world."

And when the creative imagination was alive within me, I felt exceptionally happy. I journaled, "Only when God is creating within me, am I truly happy. When I create with words, I am relieved and fulfilled," realizing that writing my soul onto paper would be my destiny. I wrote, "I am happiest when new things are being created within me." I thought to myself, "The Creator's creations are the most abundant when Her handmaiden is a receptive consciousness."

Through the activity of the creative imagination, the indwelling God was birthing novel images and ideas from within my soul into my consciousness, in this manner re-creating me. As the Indian mystic Osho wrote, "The more creative you become, the more godly you become. When your creativity comes to a climax, when your whole life becomes creative, you live in God." Living within me, the indwelling Creator-God was incarnating Itself into my consciousness, thereby further reshaping me into Its own image.

Birthing the Fruits of the Feminine

With a vagina now in my heart, I was remade tender and vulnerable, "like a young woman." And within my heart, I had found "a cornucopia of God's love." When picturing "God kissing the lips of my heart," I felt God's healing compassion for me. And by imagining "a vagina tattoo over my heart," I was reminded to express compassion to others. Through the creative imagination, I was being rebirthed as a more receptive and empathetic human being.

Furthermore, with the appearance of the images of "vaginas on crosses" and my remembrance of "mangers on crosses," my suffering took on an archetypal significance. Crosses with vaginas, and others with mangers, were images of the universal experience of spiritual death and rebirth. With the death of my old identity, I was able to experience the rebirth of a new identity. Out of my suffering and death, I was reborn. Yes, I was re-created.

Birthing My Seven Books

For the eighteen years after I sculpted the sacred vagina, my imaginative and creative urges were expressed into my journal, thereby being mostly gratified. Yet in this process, I was given seven book titles, one of which is *The Sacred Vagina*. With the arrival of specific titles into my consciousness, I felt the Unseen Presence was directing me to write these books. Through these inner promptings, I was being called into my retirement vocation as a writer.

Out of the fertile darkness of the inner feminine, all the core images and ideas for these books arose into my consciousness. I played with intuitive notions for each book. Dialoguing with each title and its kindred images and ideas, I began to flesh out outlines for six additional, still-to-be-written books. All of these book ideas were the result of the activity of the creative imagination working within me.

Now retired, my task is to make the transition from inspiration into perspiration: from delightfully playing with inspiring ideas into diligently penning these challenging books. I anticipate the next fifteen years—perhaps the rest of my life—will be my most prolific "child-bearing" years, as I put these ideas onto the printed page.

The first of these books, *The Sacred Vagina*, is an in-depth re-counting of the death and the rebirth of my consciousness, the awak-ening of my soul, and the birth of God in my soul, as I was entering into the second half of my life.

My second book, *The Holy Grail*, is about the symbol of the grail. During midlife, I became fascinated by this image. Then one night, while standing alone in my dimly lit kitchen, I glanced downward and saw the faint image of a cup. In this vision, the cup moved up from the floor toward me. Although an ordinary cup, I knew something sacred was being presented to me. From deep within my soul, a symbol for a receptive, midlife consciousness was being given to me. In the fol-lowing years, many imaginal and ideational spirits would be poured into this grail—the grail of my consciousness. This was my vision of the Holy Grail.

The creative imagination also guided me to reimagine some of the central symbols and ideas of Christianity which I had been ex-posed to as a child. In my third book, *The Christian Trinity*, I explore Life's three sacred realities—nature, humanity and the psyche—with which consciousness must come to terms. In *The Christian Cross*, my fourth book, I ask, "Why is a Quaternity (the cross) the key symbol for Christianity's Trinitarian God? My fifth book, *The Christian Quin-tessence*, describes the Kingdom of God as a here and now process/re-ality within the soul. The sequence of these three books on the Trinity, the Quaternity (the cross) and the Quintessence (Kingdom of God) reveals a numerical progression within my soul.

My final two books will be taken directly from my journals. Dur-ing the twenty-three years that I lived by myself, many seemingly ran-dom "wildflowers" blossomed within my soul. This sixth book, *Heart Flowers*, will be an arrangement of these blossoms: additional images and ideas, which evoked feeling and had intuitive meaning for me.

My seventh book, *The Prayers of a Pantheist*, will be a collection of my prayers to the Unseen Presence permeating everything. When troubled, I would pray to the Indwelling Presence and to the Uni-verse-God surrounding me.

All of these book ideas are the result of the creative imagination working within me. They are the products of a dialogue between my ego-consciousness and my soul.

Spiritual Wine

The breakups with my first wife, and five years later with Diana, left me brokenhearted each time. Yet especially after breaking up with Diana, "the fruits of the feminine" began to grow into the daylight of my consciousness, as described earlier. At times, when I would imbibe the wine of these imaginal and ideational fruits, I would feel spiritually intoxicated.

Looking back, I can see how my suffering from these two failed relationships guided me into the fertile womb of my soul. My heart-wound was creatively refashioned into that sacred vagina in my heart. And then, from that vagina, some of the countless "fruits of the feminine" were borne into my consciousness. I experienced "orgasms of the imagination"—images and ideas from within—exploding into my awareness. During this extraordinary process, the fertile womb of the creative imagination bore numerous fruitful images and ideas into my consciousness.

Nevertheless, only by *bearing* my suffering (*sufferre* in Latin) was my soul able to *bear* (*ferre*) her fruit. Previously bearing pain, my soul was now bearing fruit. From the soil of my suffering soul, imaginal and ideational vines grew and the grapes ripened. Into my consciousness were borne these life-sustaining "fruits of the feminine." In my suffering, a fertile purpose.

From the vineyard of my soul, these grapes were harvested and have fermented within my consciousness, with thirty years of reflection. Now, after aging within me, the wine of the creative imagination was ready to be poured into this book, *The Sacred Vagina*. This intoxicating beverage has readily quenched the thirst of my parched ego. For those who thirst for spirits, drink this wine, so that you may also become spiritually intoxicated.

CHAPTER 8

ENCOUNTERING MY SOUL

Her Wisdom and Truth

————◆♥◆————

Wisdom is radiant and unfading,
and she is easily discerned by those who love her
and is found by those who seek her.
She hastens to make herself
known to those who desire her.
He who rises early to seek her
will have no difficulty,
for he will find her sitting at his gate . . .

THE BOOK OF WISDOM 6:12-17

After Diana cut the umbilical cord that had embedded her within my heart, I could no longer be dependent upon her. Now, I was alone. Yet a month later, the *Woman-with-No-Head* arrived in a dream and said, "I will lead you home." Through her vaginal opening into my heart, Anima was inviting me into herself, into the home of my soul.

During the months following our breakup, I gradually became more dependent on Anima. This *Woman-with-No-Head* had offered me an opportunity to be rooted within her. Through a growing alliance with Anima, the now-repurposed umbilical cord began to steadfastly yoke my ego to my soul. A novel dependence on my soul's wisdom and truth evolved, so that I would be less dependent on a female partner. Although alone, I no longer felt bereft of a companion since Anima was awakening and beginning to live within me.

The Interior Sanctuary

With Anima now more alive within me, I spent the next several decades observing my soul and journaling what I was intuiting, feeling, thinking and dreaming. In so doing, I increasingly uncovered more of the wisdom and the truth of my soul. My devotional task was simply to be receptively conscious of these offerings from within.

Anima dwelt in the sanctuary within me. Consequently, instead of worshiping in a church or meditating, I wanted to pay homage to the divine within me. I entered into this sacred place, seeking to become more conscious of *what I am*. My prayer was for self-knowledge; I prayed to know the wisdom and truth of my soul more completely and deeply. In response to my patient prayerfulness, varied emotions and a multiplicity of thoughts surfaced from the depths of my soul into my consciousness, better acquainting me with myself.

My early morning habit of carefully witnessing and journaling my soul became my spiritual discipline. From within, new information was constantly being broadcast into my consciousness. My daily ritual was to notice and discern the endless nuances of ideas and the subtle shifts in my feelings. So, when people ask me, "What is your religion?" I usually quote Rilke: "Our task is to listen to the news that is always arriving out of the silence." More than any statement I could ever make, this best describes my spiritual practice.

My faith is in my soul, the God within my soul. My religious practice is that of quietly looking into the inner darkness and listening to the silence. I journaled, "Look into your darkness; it will show you who you are. Listen to the silence, Sam; it will tell you your truth." Now, I better understand the psalmist's utterance, "Be still and know that I am God" (Psalm 46:10). When silently looking within and listening—cut off from the external world—I am better able to encounter more of the truth of *what I am*, what God is within me.

———— •♥• ————

During my celibacy, I had unearthed this interior sanctuary. Now, this temple within me was available to me every moment of my life. I journaled, "I carry God's sanctuary within me. Truth and wisdom are near, if I remember to look and to listen."

The infinite temple, the enduring cathedral, the supreme mosque, was my own soul living right within my body. I journaled, "All alone inside my body. This is the sanctuary where God dwells." And later, "The soul is the point of contact between me and the God that is constantly revealing Itself into my consciousness." In this holy place, I was not lonely since I was experiencing intimacy with the Indwelling Presence.

At times, I retreated into this sacred space, so I could enjoy solitude away from the many activities of my life. Within, I found rest and relaxation. I experienced not only peace and quiet but also, I had a safe place to be. In solitude, I could gently bathe my weary ego in the refreshing waters of my soul and feel renewed.

Here, I could ponder the struggles in my life and seek resolution. I journaled, "I want to go into my interior sanctuary, where I can prayerfully reflect upon my sorrows." I trusted that the wisdom and truth of my soul would guide me through my various difficulties. I wrote, "In my aloneness, I shall be healed of my troubles." In a similar fashion, by focusing on my afflicted soul, I could provide her with the nurturing attention she required.

The Wisdom and Truth of My Soul

While in this inner sanctum, I prayerfully journaled, "My ego is wise to pray to the soul, so I can be guided by a wisdom far greater than I. 'Oh, Holy Sophia, fill me with your wisdom. And grant me consciousness of your truth. When I receive you into my awareness, I am guided by your wisdom and refashioned by your truth.'"

At times, I wept tears of gratitude when Sophia would touch me with her presence, through an unsolicited thought or feeling. Since I wanted to experience greater intimacy with her, I would pray, "Oh Sophia, come to me; be near to me." I knew Wisdom lived right next door, just outside my ego, so her comforting presence and instructive ideas were readily available.

I journaled, "Listen for Sophia's knock on the door of your heart, Sam. She wants to come in and be known by you. . . . I love when Wisdom dances at my door. Sophia, your presence refreshes me and provides wise counsel to my ego."

Feeling the sadness of separation one day, I prayed, "I come to you, Sophia. I want to be wholly surrounded by your feminine essence: to die back into your womb, to go back into my source. You hold me as no other ever has." Encountering the wisdom within me was yet another path I traveled on the journey toward the home of my soul.

As a small child, my soul was my first home, which I had abandoned as I entered into adulthood. Now at midlife, I prayed, "Oh Lord, lead me back into your womb, my forgotten soul, which can embrace me." I said to my soul, "I want to be held by your dark, interior mystery, which I know is God. You are the home to which I long to return."

Rather than praying to a masculine Holy Spirit, I prayed to Sophia, Wisdom or "Holy Psyche," as I named her. For me, this indwelling God was feminine: my soul was a woman. My ego was the masculine one. At especially difficult times in my life, my problem-solving ego was of little use. However, when my ego was humbly receptive to her, then Sophia was more likely to make herself known to me. I prayed, "Yes, save me from my patriarchal ego. Grant me salvation from my one-sided masculinity. Heal me with your feminine essence."

When I journal, I usually refer to Sophia as "Holy Psyche." My psyche is *holy* because it is the *whole*: my psyche is the totality of *what I* am. I prayed, "Oh, Holy Psyche, Infinite Mystery within my own soul, I fall before you, seeking your wisdom and truth. Comfort and nourish me with your presence. You are all I want, you and only you." I pray to the mystery of my soul, requesting assistance from all facets of Holy Psyche: both the good and the evil within my soul.

———————— •♥• ————————

In the sanctuary of my soul, nothing is unholy or ultimately evil. Everything within me is a part of my truth. No piece of me is *profane*, "outside the temple." Every part is *sacred*, "inside the temple" of my soul. Even my unsavory interior parts are a sacred part of God. What is unacceptable is not to be feared, but is to be embraced and unconditionally accepted. My task is to bless and purify my unacceptable parts with a compassionate consciousness.

By becoming more conscious of the unknown and disowned facets of my soul, I knew my darkness could be redeemed. The facets of me that had been rejected—cast into the unconscious by my personal and/or the collective morality—could be retrieved and become respectable parts of me.

If I become more aware of and welcome all aspects of myself, then I will become more complete. If I bring my interior darkness into the light of my consciousness and bless it as an aspect of me/a facet of God, I will become more whole. With self-compassion, all parts of my biological and human nature can be restored into a state of grace.

WISDOM'S WOMB WITHIN

The sacred vagina was my doorway into wisdom's womb within. Through this orifice into my soul, I had access to God's feminine wisdom, the feminine side of God. I trusted that Wisdom could rightly advise and guide me. I journaled, "She presents me with fresh feelings and novel thoughts, offering wise counsel to my finite ego."

As stated in The Book of Wisdom, "He who rises early to seek her will have no difficulty, for he will find her sitting at his gate." Indeed, upon waking, Wisdom was often quietly sitting at my gate, in the liminal space between the sleep of night and the consciousness of day.

I journaled, "In this dark, silent womb is where God's wisdom lives. Only if I spend time in the darkness will I find Wisdom. Only when I listen to the silence will I hear God's truth. So, Sam, 'Listen to the silent darkness, so Wisdom and truth can speak to you.'"

I journaled, "I need to enter into the womb of God. I have lost contact with the ground of my being—the Source of who I am. I want the wisdom and truth of *what I am* to be birthed into my consciousness." And I wrote, "You guide me with your wisdom and fill my consciousness with your truth," as I become *what I am* meant to be. "How could I not love Wisdom who feeds me with herself, nourishes me with her truth."

The Voice of Wisdom

The conference I attended in Switzerland was entitled, *The Voice of the Soul*. When I read this title on the front of the brochure, I became excited by the idea that the soul has a voice. Although residing in the unconscious, Wisdom speaks from the interior void, out of the silent darkness. Wisdom presents new possibilities, unexpected feelings and novel insights to one's consciousness.

Wisdom is spoken by the soul. When my ego is lost and needs advice, Wisdom can provide another point of view. Often, her ideas are contrary to mine, as she seeks to provide my ego with a less one-sided, more balanced perspective. So, I allow her to challenge, complement and change my ego's opinions and attitudes. Wisdom often reveals a novel and different part of my truth, a piece of which I am not yet aware.

Wisdom is always seeking to speak the truth of *what I am*. Without Wisdom's assistance, I am a confused and lost soul. I wrote, "An infinite source of wisdom and truth is seeking to become conscious within me: to guide me and to remake me."

I knew that the source of wisdom was other than I. Wisdom abides within the soul, not in the ego. I journaled, "Without the wisdom of my soul, my ego is an emaciated child, an impoverished beggar."

Often a defeated ego is the one most likely to receive Wisdom. I wrote, "All the profound truths of life are not very obvious to those who are arrogant. A humble ego acknowledges and warmly welcomes the wisdom that is far superior to itself."

Wisdom is "supernatural," intangible, in that she cannot be grasped by the five senses. Rather, this otherworldly wisdom arrives out of the mysterious reservoir of the soul. My ego receives wisdom from "Another," from the transcendent, Indwelling Presence.

Wisdom is a message from God, not a creation of my ego. Even though wisdom does not originate within my ego-consciousness, my ego can develop the practice of intuiting her presence and receiving her counsel. Yes, it is always wise for my small, often-bewildered ego to listen for Wisdom's quiet utterances—the "still small voice" within my soul (I Kings 19:12).

The Wisdom of the Unconscious

How could the unconscious be wise? I regard Wisdom as a divine blessing bestowed by Mother Nature and as the massive storehouse of knowledge built up in the course of human civilization, both now residing in the unconscious. Wisdom is the collective learning of the entire human race, gained through countless millennia of experience. The collective unconscious is the vessel that contains the wisdom that has been accumulated during human evolution; and it is the repository for the acquired knowledge from human civilization.

According to Jung, "The unconscious is the unwritten history of mankind from time unrecorded." The unconscious soul is the repository of the wisdom acquired during biological evolution, prehistory, history and across cultures. The wisdom of the ages—from nature and civilization—is to be found within.

If I am aware of her and diligently seek her guidance, I trust Wisdom will be present and will unceasingly guide me. As stated in The Book of Wisdom, "Wisdom is radiant and unfading, and she is easily discerned by those who love her and found by those who seek her. She hastens to make herself known to those who desire her." Within the soul, this wisdom is omnipresent for those who seek her.

A Wise Shepherd in the Unconscious

Although I was not conscious of having a shepherd in the unconscious at the time, later I became aware that Wisdom had guided me through five—all previously mentioned—pivotal events in my life.

Wisdom had unconsciously guided "my choice" of an independent wife. By the end of my first marriage, I realized that Wisdom had shepherded me, as a dependent man, to select an independent woman as my wife. In doing so, Wisdom was orchestrating the development of my independent masculine identity.

And when I reluctantly entered into my liaison with Diana, I was not aware that her aloof and distant nature was the precise quality for provoking the romantic projection of my soul onto her. Unbeknownst to me, the Wisdom of the unconscious had chosen Diana for this very purpose. But when Diana rejected me, this projection was demolished. Only then could these projected fragments of my feminine soul be retrieved and become a part of me.

Through my unsuspecting selection of these two women partners, the wise shepherd in the unconscious fostered enormous growth within me. In my marriage, Wisdom instigated the development of my independent masculine identity. And through the breakup with Diana, Wisdom guided me to become more conscious of my soul as an interior reality, distinct from Diana. In both cases, I was graced with the re-creative power of the wisdom of the unconscious.

Furthermore, as I struggled with my rage, the instinctual wisdom of the serpent was vigorously at work within me. Through the snake energy vibrating within my spine and my three snake dreams, Wisdom was actively seeking to integrate that rattlesnake of rage into my identity, thereby refashioning me into a stronger man. The wisdom of the serpent transformed a dependent, rageful boy into an independent man with a spine. Not I, but Wisdom, transformed me.

Additionally, while sculpting my heart in clay, Wisdom creatively transfigured the "open wound" in my heart into an "open vagina," entirely without my intent. Instead of living with a festering "sore" from a failed marriage and a broken romance, Wisdom healed my wound into a life-affirming vagina. Wisdom knew that my heart required a healthy, permanent opening for more loving. Not I, but Wisdom, transformed my wound into that vagina in my heart, so I could love more abundantly.

Finally, in the dream of the *Woman-with-No-Head*, Wisdom said, "I will lead you home." She wanted to heal me by shepherding me out of my thinking head into her feeling heart. Wisdom was escorting me into my final home: into my intuitive, feeling soul, and my deeper Self. Not I, but Wisdom, knew the exact direction I needed to travel.

With all my higher education, how could my heart contain greater wisdom than my ego? How could the answers to my complex problems arrive out of my own soul? These were not brilliant ideas I had read in books, or learned about in school. In fact, my ego's ideas were of little use, except for the idea of aligning myself with Wisdom's intentions.

Wisdom escorted me through these five major events in my life. Initially, I was unconscious of her purposeful activity within my soul, during all of these experiences. Nevertheless, this wise shepherd in the unconscious was diligently at work, guiding and remaking me into a better man. Except for her statement in my dream, "I will lead you home," Wisdom did not use a single word as she steered me through these complicated, life-altering experiences.

Yet again, I was the recipient of an *amazing grace*. Wisdom, this amazing shepherd in the unconscious, graced me with her transformative activity. I journaled, "No woman is more beautiful than the soul. Your wisdom has been my salvation. Yes, you have re-created me and made me more whole. Sophia, you are the Queen of Heaven, the Queen of the interior heaven."

My salvation—my restoration into wholeness—would come through not only wisdom but also self-knowledge. In spite of my receptivity to Wisdom, my soul still wanted me to embark upon a quest for self-knowledge: to unearth more of my inner truth. I would be saved not only by the grace of the Wisdom within my soul but also through the challenging work of acquiring self-knowledge. Through divine grace and the toil of becoming "the one who knows himself," I would be healed and restored into a greater wholeness.

TRUTH: SELF-KNOWLEDGE

For many years, I asked myself, is self-knowledge the same as wisdom? As a therapist, I knew the value of a person seeking to know and understand himself/herself. Self-knowledge can be a part of the curative process, wherein a client seeks to heal her wounds, repair his brokenness. For this reason, I decided it was wise for me to seek knowledge of myself. As I was pondering the wisdom of knowing the truth of *what I am*, I recalled Aristotle's remark: "Knowing yourself is the beginning of all wisdom."

In my quest for self-understanding, journaling my inner life—and reflectively writing about my relationships—was my primary tool for self-discovery. When praying privately onto paper, I could say whatever I felt or thought, without fear. In so doing, I was becoming conscious of my deeper Self. With the arrival of small, but numerous, nuggets from my soul, I was becoming more of the truth of *what I am*. As St. Augustine wrote, "Go not outside, return to thyself; truth dwells in the inner man." In this process of becoming conscious of my truth, I was being refashioned by the "truth [that] dwells in the inner man."

When I speak of *my* truth, I speak not of my head's truth, but my heart's truth. Not my reasoning mind, but my soul's inherent ideas and feelings are my focus. And I do not speak of the perception of the external world with my five senses. Rather, I speak of the intuitive apprehension of my interior truth. I speak of self-knowledge.

Furthermore, I speak not of the so-called "universal truth" sought by philosophers. And my truth is not the "truth" of the collective society wherein I live. My truth is relative, specific to me. My unique truth is my destiny, the truth of *what I am* meant to become.

If I had chosen to ignore (*ignorare* in Latin) my soul, I would have remained ignorant (*ignorantem*) of my inner truth. In other words, "I ignore my soul; therefore, I am ignorant of myself." No longer the crime of consciousness, as a child in Eden—but now at midlife, the crime of *unconsciousness*, the sin of self-ignorance. As Jung wrote, "Man's worst sin is unconsciousness": his tendency to avoid self-knowledge.

But unconsciousness—ignorance of my soul—was entirely unacceptable to me. At midlife, traveling toward my final, interior home, I wanted to know myself more completely and deeply. By inquiring into my soul, I would be more self-aware and become more whole. And through increasing consciousness of *what I am*, I would be able to experience a conscious reunion with more aspects of my forgotten soul.

As Jesus said to Judas Thomas, in *The Book of Thomas* (a Gnostic Gospel), "Examine yourself that you may understand who you are. . . . It is not fitting that you be ignorant of yourself. . . . You have already come to know, and you will be called 'the one who knows himself.'" On my journey to my interior home, knowing the truth of *what I am* was another path upon which I traveled.

My Truth

Even so, is a person who diligently examines him/herself really wise? With self-examination, one might dredge up all manner of things: some "good" and some "evil," as labeled by our personal consciences and/or the collective morality. Most would agree, it would be wise for me to uncover positive potentials, which I could then cultivate and bring to fruition. But was it wise for me to uncover the evil, the more unsavory facets of my soul?

I decided that it was wise for me to unearth and accept anything and everything within me: not only the good qualities but also the evil parts. My disowned, negative traits needed to be ingested into my consciousness, so my darkness could then be digested. In this manner, my shadow would provide nutrients for the growth of my consciousness.

For instance, if I were increasingly conscious of my negative qualities, then I would be less likely to project such unconscious darkness onto others. If I were conscious of my shadow, then I would be less likely to see *my* undesirable traits in others, my so-called "enemies." And then, I would be less likely to dislike, judge or hate them. As Jesus said, "Why do you look at the speck that is in your brother's eye, but do not notice and acknowledge the log that is in your own eye? . . . First, get the log out of your own eye" (Matthew 7:3–4). Hence, the wisdom of digging up my unsavory parts—the log in my eye—to see *what I am*, so I will not see *my* evil in my brother.

Unearthing my more sinister qualities meant discerning appropriate responses to such inner darkness. I knew I should not act out my detrimental impulses, feelings and thoughts, which might harm others or myself. I alone am responsible for my shadow—for each thought and every action. But why was such darkness a part of me in the first place?

By taking ownership of my shadowy parts, I had the faith I would find the divine purpose of my inner darkness for my life. For example, the wisdom of the unconscious had converted the rattlesnake of rage into a beneficial spine. Therefore, I trust I will find value in every unacceptable aspect of my inner Self. Perhaps a divine purpose for everything.

——————•❦•——————

In my journal, I wrote, "I have chosen to seek Holy Psyche's truth—both the good and the evil—by being willing to become conscious of her multifaceted nature. She has many facets, an infinite number of faces." I prayed, "Oh God, reveal some of your many truths buried within the remote corners of my soul, so that I will know *what I am*. I am committed to the truth within me, no matter what it may be. I must humbly accept where it leads me." My truth is not what I wish were true about myself. The truth of my soul is the reality of *what I am*.

My duty is to live my inner truth. And part of my truth is to allow myself to feel and experience the anger, the hatred, the lust and other negative emotions and thoughts, which at times arise into my consciousness. I prayed, "Oh Holy Psyche, I live both sides of you: your negative and positive aspects. We are all such complex creatures. How can we ever understand and manage ourselves anyway?"

In the quest for my truth, I was compelled to break with the expectations of family, friends, acquaintances and indeed the world. I opened myself for my truth to speak to me: to disclose to me *what I am*. Even though others might reject me, I must accept and trust the complex and confusing truth within me.

I journaled, "I know I am committed to the truth that lives within me. I am devoted to *what I am* on the inside. My task is to be conscious of *what I am,* no matter how dark." I do not seek approval from any religion or the sanction of any moral code. If I am to be "the one who knows himself," then all facets of my inner truth—yes, even my unsavory parts—become the foundation of my integrity.

Since I consciously accept the evil within me, some may think I am not spiritual. In spite of their opinions, I shall allow my dark shadow to enter into my consciousness and become an integral part of me. I journaled, "My respect for the truth within me requires me to be honest, no matter how 'unspiritual' some may think I am."

God's Truth: The Opposites

I am aware that my experience of God's truth is specific to me: God's revelation of particular truths to me. My task is to become conscious of and endure the conflicts within me. I journaled, "Yes, it is ego's burden to bear the cross of truth," the cross of Life's/the Self's opposing forces such as good and evil.

This God of truth is unlike any other God that I had heard about. This God/the Self is complex and contains all opposites, encompasses all contradictions. This conflicted God of good and evil is imperfect, *yet thereby holds the life-giving potential for wholeness*. My purpose is to consciously suffer some of the polarities within the Self, so a more complex, a more complete and whole consciousness can evolve within me.

I feel I have been called to live the truth of the Self's inner contradictions. I journaled, "I am the container within which these polarities must brew." And later, "In the crucible of my consciousness, God's conflicted nature must be stirred into a single alloy." By receiving the opposites within me into my consciousness, I am able to integrate the truth of God's nature, my nature, into *what I* am becoming.

I journaled, "One must suffer the truth of the opposites in order to see Life as it is: with all its evolutionary splendor, horror and mystery."

God is the truth that requires me to see Life as it is, not as I wish Life to be. This God is Life Itself, as it is, without pretense. I wrote, "I seek to be nourished by God's truth, although Its evil aspects taste bad. I must ingest the whole truth, even though I may feel nauseous at first."

I journaled, "The Universe-God moves within me, seeking to disclose Its infinitely complex Self: both Its good and evil aspects." I prayed, "Oh Universe-God, live within me and fill me with your nature." My duty was to become conscious of God's contradictory truths, especially the evil aspects. I wrote, "These are a few of the truths of God's infinite facets, some of them rather unkind, nasty and vicious. I can tolerate only small bits of God's darkness at a time."

I prayed into my journal, "I promise to become the truth as I experience it. No matter how painful, my obligation is to bear witness to Life's nature, God's nature. Even if my ego and my conscience do not like your dark side, I seek to embody your whole truth. You are the infinitely complex Universe, which lives within me—and within which I live."

Kafka (1883-1924) remarks, "Truth is what everyone needs to live. But it cannot be received or acquired from anyone else. Everyone must continually produce it from within himself. Otherwise, he perishes. . . . It may be that truth is life itself." Since I do not want to perish from self-ignorance, I seek to consciously live my inner truth, both the positive and the negative aspects. I strive to be my authentic, whole self.

Yes, I concluded that becoming aware of my truth was a wise thing to do, although the whole truth always contains both good and evil. I prayed, "Holy Psyche, revealer of truth, disclose to me the totality of your contradictory truths, which are ultimately One. I am a representative of your truth." Yes, I seek to integrate and incarnate into my consciousness God's/the Self's conflicted nature within me. This is my intention. I have no other purpose.

———— •♥• ————

In 1992, I journaled, "I am simply a child of God, who is trying to allow the whole truth of God to be borne into my consciousness." I came to believe that God's self-revelation of Its complex good and evil sides is a process taking place within us all. Anything and everything arising out of the interior darkness is a disclosure of some facet of God.

I wrote, "I am a rugged individual, not because I wanted to be this way. Rather, I naïvely decided to live the truth of my soul." Choosing to become conscious of my soul's conflicted nature has not been an easy burden to bear. During midlife, I committed myself to acknowledging the good and the evil aspects of the inner Self. At times, this has been a daunting task for me.

In retrospect, such a decision was a heroic one. I journaled, "There was a single decision to be conscious, which now relentlessly pushes me forward into an unknown future: the truthful awareness of *what I am*, the truth of what God is within me." And now, I am unable to reverse this process; I cannot turn back from my choice to be conscious. As Nietzsche wrote, "And once you are awake, you shall remain awake eternally."

———— •♥• ————

Through me, does God want to become conscious of Itself? Yes. I believe the deity is seeking to become aware of Itself through each of us. I journaled, "God's truth within me seeks to become a conscious part of me. God is coming-of-age—coming into my consciousness—as It is, not as I wish God to be." God wants to use me to become conscious of Itself.

Struggling forward, I journaled, "The unconscious does not give final answers, only glimpses into the infinite complexity of Life. And so, I chose complexity, as opposed to fortifying my ego with a simplistic stance, a superficial position."

Life's simplest truth is that it is wonderfully, frighteningly and infinitely complex, indeed labyrinthian. We are each called to live the truth of this daunting multiplicity.

The Labyrinth of the Soul

Yes, I wander upon a labyrinthian path toward the truth of my soul. Endless paths upon which to travel. I am sure there are a myriad of roads to the center, into the deeper Self, not just one. On a multitude of different paths, many will find their way toward the truth of a more balanced and whole Self. Each of us will leave countless roads untraveled.

When speaking of self-knowledge, Gibran remarks, "Say not, 'I have found the truth,' but rather, 'I have found a truth.' Say not, 'I have found the path of the soul.' Say rather, 'I have met the soul walking upon my path.' For the soul walks upon all paths." Through a growing consciousness of my soul, I strive to walk the path into my individual truth, into the truth of *what I am*.

But I have found no direct pathway into the truth of my soul. I have discovered no linear path to a conscious reunion with the Self, the complexities of the Self. The Self cannot be found by walking in straight lines or in pointless circles. Perhaps God/the Self is encountered by walking in spirals, as we slowly circle inward, more deeply into who we are becoming.

I journaled, "Within me is an infinite labyrinth of images, feelings and thoughts—the twists and turns within my soul. Yes, my bewildered ego wanders within my mysterious soul." I take two steps forward into clarity, but then one step back into confusion. But at least, I am then one step ahead. I advance in consciousness only if I step forward, and then backward—and then forward again, step by step.

I am aware that my soul is a mysterious maze through which I must meander. And so, I accept "living in the not-knowing," as my wife calls it. I said to myself, "Love the 'not-knowing,' Sam. Only then will you remain open and continue to grow in consciousness." Or as Rilke wrote, "Be patient toward all that is unsolved in your heart. And try to love the questions themselves. Do not seek the answers that cannot be given to you. . . . Live the questions now. Perhaps you will gradually, without noticing it, live along some distant day into the answers." Yes, I reluctantly strive to love the many unanswered questions within my soul. And I have found some answers. Yet many questions remain unanswered. And so, I live "in the not-knowing."

"Salvation is from the Inner World"

While writing this chapter on wisdom and truth, I had the following dream:

I am in a room with others, hearing a lecture on the psychology of Carl Jung. At the break, people are milling around the room. I am standing by myself and look down at a woman sitting on the floor. She is about fifty-five years old. I have seen her at this lecture venue before.

I sit down on the floor, facing her. Somehow, we have an immediate knowing that we are simultaneously having the identical idea: "Salvation is from the inner world." Neither of us speaks these words. Yet we realize we are thinking this *exact* thought at the very *same* moment.

With this shared awareness, her face lights up with a smile. I am glowing. So, I lean forward and kiss her on the lips. We stare into each other's eyes. Then, I am aware that a serpent's energy is pulsating within her spine. And suddenly, I feel this same snake energy surging up my spine.

Through these images and in a single sentence, this dream mirrored the subject about which I was writing. To be sure, the woman sitting on the floor was my feminine soul. Then, I—my ego—sat on the floor facing her. Yes, with this serpentine energy flowing within both our spines, I knew my ego and my soul were in complete agreement about the source of salvation.

Intuitively, I knew the statement, "Salvation is from the inner world," was about self-knowledge. Could it be that becoming more conscious of the complex, confusing and contradictory truths of our deepest Self has something to do with salvation—our healing into wholeness?

Saving My Soul

As a teenager, I was taught that salvation meant "saving the soul," usually meaning to be saved by the grace of a distant God. Yet by midlife, I no longer believed my soul could be saved by external, or even internal, divine grace alone. I concluded that an essential part of salvation—restoration into wholeness—was self-knowledge.

And so, with a compassionate consciousness, I needed to "buy back"—retrieve from the unconscious—those rejected and discarded aspects of myself. Self-knowledge meant becoming more conscious of these forsaken parts. In my quest for wholeness, I knew my disliked and rejected parts must become a part of me again.

For me, salvation means saving every part of *what I am*: indeed, a healing into wholeness. With compassion, I must redeem the unacceptable parts of my soul. I journaled." I must integrate into the light of my consciousness these rejected pieces of my soul, so they may become valuable and useful parts of myself." Yes, self-knowledge is an essential part of the salvation process.

As Jesus said, "*I* am the light of the world" (John 8:12). His loving consciousness shone a great light into the world. And in the Sermon on the Mount, Jesus proclaims, "*You* are the light of the world" (Matthew 5:14). Yes, *I* must be the light—the consciousness—who becomes aware of my darkness, the evil within me. Then, the bright light of my growing consciousness might benefit not only myself but also others whose lives I would touch.

Furthermore, the Gospel of John (1:5) states, "The light shines in the darkness, and the darkness has not overcome it." During my midlife transformation, the light of my consciousness shone into my inner darkness. In this process, my light was *not* extinguished. Rather, my light became even brighter as my consciousness illuminated more of the dark facets of my soul. My soul could be saved only by my making my dark qualities visible to me.

By shining the warm light of my compassionate consciousness upon my inner darkness, some of the neglected and rejected aspects of my soul were thereby redeemed. Through a greater consciousness of the negative parts of the Self—and then with radical acceptance of my inner darkness—I have experienced redemption into a more complete wholeness. As the dream thought suggested, "Salvation is from the inner world."

CHAPTER 9

MY QUEST FOR THE WHOLENESS OF THE SELF

The Birth of God in My Soul

————◆♥◆————

The decisive question for man is:
is he related to something infinite or not?

C. G. JUNG

The collective unconscious contains
the whole spiritual heritage of mankind's evolution,
born anew in the brain structure of every individual.

C. G. JUNG

All opposites are of God.
Therefore, man must bend to this burden;
and in so doing, he finds that God in all his 'oppositeness'
has taken possession of him, incarnated himself in him.
He becomes a vessel filled with divine conflict.

C. G. JUNG, *ANSWER TO JOB*

A year after breaking up with Diana, the image of the "burning bush" that was not consumed (Exodus 3) unexpectedly and repeatedly intruded itself into my consciousness. In Moses' encounter with God, a voice from this fiery bush proclaims, *"I Am What I Am"*—in Hebrew, *Yahweh*. (At times translated, "I Am *Who* I Am.") At midlife, why were these strange words, spoken by this bizarre bush, arriving into my consciousness?

At the time, I was in Jungian analysis. So, I knew I should pay careful attention to any image which fascinated me. Initially, I did not attempt to understand why this flaming image presented itself to me. I simply observed that the words, "*I Am What I Am*," spontaneously arose periodically into my consciousness. Therefore, I knew this talking bush had a message for me, perhaps some numinous intent?

After a year of analysis, I was beginning to discover who I am. The appearances of the sacred vagina in my clay heart, and the arrival of the *Woman-with-No-Head* in my dream, were telling me more about who I was becoming. In my therapeutic quest to find myself, was *I Am What I Am* now prodding me to further unearth *what I am*?

My belief that Moses' experience of this mysterious bush came from the depths of his soul, in no way diminishes its divine validity. Originating within his psyche—yet manifesting externally in a vision—the image and voice of this bewildering bush was for Moses an overpowering encounter with *Yahweh*. From deep within his soul, the deity visually and auditorily burst into his consciousness.

Now, this same *I Am What I Am* was interjecting Itself into my consciousness. Becoming intrigued with this burning bush suggested that I was also beginning to encounter *Yahweh* as a living reality within my psyche. I saw no flaming bush; I heard no voice. Yet in those unsolicited, *silent* words within my soul, I sensed a mysterious presence.

Then one day, when the words *I Am What I Am* intruded into my consciousness, unexpectedly I had a vision of mud bubbling within the darkness of my soul. Was this the living soil of my soul, *Yahweh's* presence within me? Yes, with this vision of boiling mud, I was certain I was encountering the mysterious *Yahweh*.

I was familiar with Jung's concept of the Self as the image of God (*imago dei*) rooted deep within the psyche. Most certainly, this numinous bush was a manifestation of the Self within Moses' soul. Now, that same archetypal energy of the Self was awakening within me as the words *I Am What I Am* were repeatedly being inserted into my consciousness.

Along with *I Am's* puzzling words, came this perplexing vision of boiling mud. Not a loving consciousness in the sky; this God was of the earth, manifesting as brown, bubbling mud. Yes, this was *Yahweh*, the soil of my soul. Now, a primordial image of the Self—an image of God's presence—was alive within me.

Jung conjectured that behind the *image* of God is the *reality* of God. I knew I could not know the infinite *Yahweh* Itself. Nevertheless, I knew that I was experiencing the presence of God within me. Although I could not grasp what this mysterious, interior deity was, I could at least observe and report my encounter with Yahweh: those soundless words, "*I Am What I Am*," coupled with this unbidden image of boiling mud.

Eventually, I realized this unusual bush captivated me because *Yahweh* was declaring Its presence as the Infinite Mystery within me. Over time, *Yahweh* of the burning bush would incinerate all my beliefs and ideas about who or what I thought God was. *Yahweh* was not to be confined by my beliefs or defined by any of the theologies which I had studied in seminary. Absolutely refusing to circumscribe Itself, the infinite *I Am What I Am* was proclaiming Its incomprehensible, mysterious presence within me.

That blazing bush burned up my concept of God. Consequently, I was able to encounter *Yahweh* as a living presence, not as a religious conviction or an intellectual construct. As Angelus Silesius wrote, "The longest way to God, the indirect, lies through the intellect. The shortest way lies through the heart. Here is my journey's end and here its start."

The deity was not to be encapsulated within my limiting intellectual concept of God. Indeed, *I Am What I Am* of the burning bush is the *mysterium tremendum et fascinans* (the tremendous and fascinating mystery), described by German theologian Rudolph Otto in *The Idea of the Holy* (1923). For him, God is the incomprehensible mystery that is unknowable. For me, the mystery of God is infinitely transcendent to the ego, yet is immanent everywhere. Yes, this spellbinding mystery can be experienced: an awe-filled encounter that can be undergone and felt intensely, yet remains utterly inexplicable.

I sensed this bubbling mud would be forever fertile. I was becoming grounded in the divine mystery, just as a plant becomes rooted in the soil. I was being engaged by the *mysterium tremendum*, so that *I Am What I Am* could germinate within my soul and reveal more of *what I am.* From this chaotic earth—the soil of my soul—*Yahweh*, over many decades, would sprout forth endless vivid images and unique ideas into my awareness.

My fascination with this burning bush transformed my understanding of God. From believing I knew something about God, I realized *Yahweh* was infinitely beyond my ego's terribly finite ability to comprehend who or what God is. *I Am What I Am*'s perplexing name, along with this idiosyncratic image of bubbling mud, totally mystified me.

At midlife, through my Jungian analysis, I was listening to what was emerging from my soul, so I could know *what I am*. Was *I Am What I Am* arriving into my consciousness at this time in my life because I was searching for *what I am*? Yes, *what I am* is a minute piece of *Yahweh* within me. Without a doubt, *I Am What I Am* is the source of *what I am*.

For me, self-realization means becoming conscious of *what I am*. At midlife, tiny, unconscious pieces of *I Am What I Am* were becoming a conscious part of *what I am*. As I was individuating into *what I am*, my ego was incarnating small, previously unconscious bits of *I Am What I Am*. As Jung wrote, "Self-realization—to put in religious or metaphysical terms—amounts to God's incarnation into one's consciousness."

———— •❦• ————

I have already spoken of my experience of divine intuition, imagination and creativity, and the soul's wisdom and truth, as revelations from the Self. Some of these aspects of the Self have incarnated into my consciousness and have become a part of *what I am*.

Now, I turn to additional facets of the Self, which arose into my consciousness at midlife. In my quest for wholeness, I was becoming more conscious of some of the conflicting, polar opposites within the Self since these are also a part of *what I am*.

With much introspection during midlife, I increasingly became aware of the tension of opposing forces within me. I realized polarities were a part of my nature, without a doubt, a part of God's nature. For example, the Self/God within embodies both good and evil, masculine and feminine and spirit and matter. As for myself, I am forever attempting to consciously embrace these internal, contradictory facets of God/the Self. This is my quest for the wholeness of the Self.

Wholeness requires me to become conscious of these "divine conflicts": to experience the tension of these internal opposites, instead of splitting off one-half of a particular polarity. As Jung remarked, "Wholeness is not achieved by cutting off a portion of one's being, but by the integration of the contraries." My task was to integrate within myself these seemingly antagonistic facets of the Self, the contradictory aspects of God.

THE WHOLENESS AND INTEGRITY OF THE SELF

In my quest for the wholeness of the Self, I gradually realized that integrating these inner opposites was a part of a holy pilgrimage. My spiritual duty was to seek wholeness. And becoming a more whole person entailed radical integrity on my part. Yes, wholeness is not only holy, but also requires integrity.

Wholeness Is Holy

Looking back, my quest for wholeness began in seminary, when I read *Holiness is Wholeness* (1955) by Father Josef Goldbrunner. At the time, I was a perfectionist. I had a superiority complex, which masked deep feelings of inferiority. My goal was to become the ideal person, although I was unclear what that meant. But with these grandiose standards for my then-fragmented self, I felt miserable being who I was.

A vast chasm existed between who I was, and who I aspired to become: between my actual self and my ideal self. Over time, I intentionally lowered my ego-ideals since such lofty standards were inherently punitive. Rather than focusing on distant and impossible goals for myself, I directed my attention to the next step; I put the carrot a few steps in front of my nose. Then, I could accomplish these smaller tasks and feel better about myself.

At midlife, in my quest for wholeness, I realized that I also needed to accept myself "just as I am," as the hymn states. Instead of rejecting my animal and fallible human nature, I needed to embrace *what I am*. Yes, "God grant me the serenity to accept the things I cannot change," especially innate aspects of the Self: my biological and human nature.

As a middle-aged man, discovering, accepting and becoming *what I am* became my focus, *not* striving for perfection. My ego, not the Self, was the one who had valued perfection. Instead, I now wanted to be guided by the authority of the Self, not by my perfectionistic ego, in becoming *what I am*.

As a consequence, I strive for wholeness. Forever, my shadow will be a part of me. Rather than trying to transcend my human imperfections and limitations, I want to accept myself "just as I am." Being empathetic toward my flaws and humbly accepting my incomplete self has become my spiritual practice of wholeness.

Seeking wholeness is my spiritual aspiration. I seek to consciously accept all my disowned parts, especially those that might be labeled as unacceptable or "evil." Yes, I want to redeem the evil within me. In fact, I want to become everything that I am, by consciously integrating both the light and the darkness within me into my self-identity. My deepest hunger is for wholeness, not perfection.

Indeed, wholeness is holy. In fact, "holy" and "whole" are derived from the same Latin word. Holiness has absolutely nothing to do with perfection. To be "holy" means to be "whole," by becoming conscious of one's forsaken parts and limitations. I will become whole only by empathetically embracing the disowned negative facets of myself. Becoming whole in this fashion is truly a "holy" thing for me to do.

Wholeness Is Integrity

Wholeness is not only holy but also entails integrity. I will have integrity only if I honestly admit into my consciousness, and to others, the forsaken and rejected facets of *what I am*. Integrity means authentically being my whole self, without shame for any part of *what I am*.

In my quest for the wholeness of the Self, I learned that the words integer, integral, integrate and *integrity* are derived from the same Latin word. Each word contains the idea of wholeness. In mathematics, for example, an *integer* is a whole number, in contrast to a fraction. Applying this idea to myself, I realized I would be a mere fraction of myself if I took ownership of only the good, the masculine and the spiritual aspects of myself. With such one-sided identifications, I would be a divided man. The other half of myself would be rejected and remain in the unconscious.

Instead, I wanted to achieve a greater wholeness by accepting evil, the feminine and my material body as divine parts of *what I am*. If I did not equally value the other half of myself, how could I be whole? Each of these culturally "less desirable" aspects is, in fact, an *integral* part of the Self that I seek to become. Embracing these disowned halves of myself has been essential for moving me toward a sense of wholeness and completion.

Furthermore, I seek to *integrate* these conflicting facets of *what I am* into an indivisible wholeness. Since I want to embody both good and evil, masculine and feminine, and spirit and matter, these seemingly antithetical pairs need to be synthesized into a less conflicted, more harmonious self. As a receptive consciousness, my sacred duty to the Self is to hold the tension of these opposites in my awareness, so they might become increasingly integrated within me.

Ultimately, being an indivisible, whole person means being a person of *integrity*. With the persona of my "Christianized ego," how could I have been an authentic person, when a murderous rage lay beneath that mask? Now, with my rage redeemed and integrated, I am no longer a "good Christian," as I had been as a young adult, nor am I the "evil" murderer, as I was in *my felt imagination* at midlife. Rather, I am a man who is neither good nor evil. I am a man seeking integrity as I attempt to integrate into my consciousness both the good and the evil facets of *what I am*.

In the individuation process—the process of becoming conscious of *what I am*—I chose wholeness by seeking to become more conscious of the rejected aspects of the Self. And as a person of *integrity*, I wanted to consciously integrate the less desirable parts of the polarities within me. I want to be *what I am*: to consciously integrate these forsaken fragments of the Self into my identity, no matter what these may be.

THE OPPOSITES WITHIN ME

As a child and throughout the first half of my life, I was encouraged to identify with the Christian "good" by repressing my devilish shadow. And I was taught to embrace Christian "spirituality"—not the material world since it was deemed to be less worthy than the spiritual realm. Finally, as an adult male, I attempted to adapt to our culture's idea of "masculinity," thereby disowning my feminine side.

Jung regarded the Self as the archetype of wholeness, an image of the totality of all the potentials within a person. Likewise, the Self is the image of God—the *imago dei*—an internal image of the wholeness of God. For Jung, wholeness encompasses everything: good and evil, masculine and feminine, matter and spirit and many other polarities. The Self contains all possible opposites.

In the second half of my life, I chose to become more conscious of the forgotten facets of the Self—evil, the feminine, and the material—which I had rejected during the first half of my life. As a result, I would suffer the Self's/God's internal conflicts. Suffering consciously toward a more whole Self became my cross to bear. As Jung wrote in *Answer to Job* (1952), "All opposites are of God. Therefore, man . . . finds that God in all his 'oppositeness' has taken possession of him, incarnated himself in him. He becomes a vessel filled with divine conflict" (page 54).

My midlife ego was now stronger, so I could better handle these internal tugs-of-war, these divine conflicts. By intentionally allowing myself to experience the tension of these opposites, this conflicted God was able to further incarnate Itself into my consciousness, so then these divine contradictions could become better integrated within me. Hence, I would have a more whole and solid self upon which to depend.

——————•♥•——————

Into the light of my consciousness, I seek to receive evil, the feminine and the material as conscious parts of *what I am*. In so doing, I become a gray self, an androgynous self and an embodied self. I want to become more conscious of these rejected aspects of the Self, so that I can become more whole. I strive for a conscious return to the wholeness of the Self.

As Jung remarks, "One does not become enlightened by imagining figures of light, but by making the darkness conscious." He regarded the integration of one's shadow, the rejected parts, into consciousness as the *apprentice piece* of psychological work.

The *masterpiece* of individuation is the assimilation of the contrasexual aspect of one's nature: in a man, the integration of his feminine side into his masculine identity. Jung wrote, in *The Red Book*, "The acceptance of femininity leads to completion" for a man (page 264).

As for the last polarity, spirit and matter, he asserts, "Psyche and matter are two different aspects of one and the same thing."

My spiritual duty is to suffer into the wholeness of the Self, by consciously integrating evil, the feminine and matter into *what I am* becoming. As these elements—along with the good, the feminine and the spiritual—become more embodied in my self-identity, then I will be experiencing the birth of God in my soul.

This is not the birth of God in the person of a loving Jesus—in Bethlehem two thousand years ago—as I was taught when I was a child. Rather, this is the birth of God—the Christ/the Self—*within my soul*. And the birth of this God/the Self is, without a doubt, the birth of a dramatically different and highly conflicted God, than was the birth of God in Jesus. This is the God that is being born within me. Is this not the God that is seeking to be born within all of us?

My Gray Self: The Good and Evil Within

When I speak of my evil, I do *not* speak of immoral actions in the external world. Here, I speak only of disowned aspects of *what I am*, which I label as dark, which collective society may view as depraved, or some Christians may judge to be "sinful." I speak of my angry feelings, unkind thoughts, lustful fantasies and many other unsavory aspects of myself. These are the rejected and forsaken facets of my soul, which I do not like—and which are not ideal—but in fact, are real. This is my shadow, which I am reluctant to admit into my consciousness.

Yet in the second half of my life, my spiritual task was to receive my unpleasant emotions, malicious thoughts and base instincts into my consciousness. As a man seeking integrity and wholeness, I had to own—take possession of—my inner darkness. As Rumi wrote in *The Guest House*, "Every morning a new arrival. A joy, a depression, a meanness, some momentary awareness comes as an unexpected visitor. . . . The dark thought, the shame, the malice, meet them at the door laughing and invite them in. Be grateful for whatever comes, because each has been sent as a guide from beyond."

Almost eight hundred years ago, Rumi knew that the shadow was a part of the divine arrangement. As for myself, I no longer reject these dark "unexpected visitors" as I did as a young man. Rather, I now "invite them in." Yes, they are a part of *what I am*, a part of *what I am* becoming.

I journaled, "But it takes a strong mind, a strong ego to embrace not just the light, but especially the darkness of my inner Self without being overwhelmed." The internal Self contains both good and evil, the angelic and the demonic, a polarity with which I must grapple. I must receive every "new arrival" from within: not only the heavenly light, but also the hellish darkness within my soul.

As Jung wrote, "No tree, it is said, can grow to heaven unless its roots reach down into hell." If I am to grow toward an enlightened consciousness, I must embrace the demonic, the hellish aspects of myself. Yes, I must compassionately accept the unacceptable.

With my empathetic consciousness, the "unholy" aspects of the Self—those unsavory facets that impede my path toward wholeness—can be consciously integrated into the wholeness of *what I am*. With a loving consciousness, I can convert my unacceptable evil into something acceptable and good.

Yes, I can re-judge my evil. Then, what was previously *deemed* to be "evil" can now be *redeemed*—that is, *re-judged* to be "good." With radical self-acceptance, the evil parts of myself can be transformed into something useful and beneficial.

I knew there were many dark forces within me—within the unconscious—which must have a divine purpose. My task was to bring each and every one of them into the light of my consciousness. By embracing my forsaken shadow—making it a conscious part of me—my shadow could be salvaged and transformed.

The unconscious is the root of all that I am, both the good aspects and the evil parts. As Jung remarked, "The unconscious is not just evil by nature, it is also the source of the highest good: not only dark but also light, not only bestial, semihuman, and demonic but superhuman, spiritual, and in the classical sense of the word, 'divine.'" Both the good and the evil are aspects of me, facets of my soul and the Self within me. This is *what I am*.

But what does it mean for me to enter through the sacred vagina "into the life of God," a God that is both good and evil? And then from that vagina, this conflicted "God is born again" into my consciousness. Am I giving birth to a God of good *and* evil?

Yes, this God created all the good and all the evil in the world. In Isaiah 45:7, God declares, "I form the light, and create darkness; I make peace, and *create evil*. I am the Lord, who does all of these things." The wholeness of God encompasses everything, both the good and the evil. Entering into the life of such a God, I journaled, "means looking for and seeing God everywhere: not only in the good but also in the evil." Yes, this is the God of good and evil that is being "born again" into my consciousness.

From personal experience, I knew that love could mutate into hate, as I had experienced with my first wife. Yet after my marriage— with self-reflection, therapeutic help and the passage of time—my hate was slowly converted into compassion. As I outgrew my unhealthy dependence on my wife, and thereby resolved my anger toward her, my heart was graced with forgiveness. Through the mercy of God within my soul, I was given a feeling and an attitude of forgiveness toward her.

Four years after our separation, I journaled, "Love and hate come from the same heart, even though they most often arrive at different times." Or as stated in Ecclesiastes 3:8, "There is a time for everything . . . a time to love and a time to hate."

In *Answer to Job*, Jung quotes St. Clement of Rome—fourth Pope of the Catholic Church (AD 88–99)—who "taught that God rules the world with a right hand and a left hand, the right being Christ, the left being Satan" (page xi). Years ago, when I first read this, I exclaimed, "What sort of God is this! Does the Christian God have a satanic aspect?"

How can the one God encompass such polar opposites? Yes, the good and evil—the love and hate—within me are both aspects of the one God. My rattlesnake of rage was a facet of Satan in God's left hand. This rage was absolutely essential—indeed was required—so that my innocence, my "Christianized ego," could thereby be crucified by hate. Had this "satanic" rage not erupted from the depths of my soul, I might have continued to naïvely believe that I was innocent like the one on the cross—mostly without blemish.

On the other hand, my empathetic response to my broken heart—my "heart bleeding" from the breakup of my marriage—was an aspect of Christ in God's right hand. With the assistance of my Christ-like self-compassion, the psyche was able to heal my heart-wound. Given this personal experience of the two hands of God, I believe the Universe-God rules using wrathful and merciful hands working together.

Now, both of the "hands" of God have become a part of my experience of the divine. While writing the above three paragraphs, I awoke one morning with the comforting thought, "One God, two hands." Instantly and intuitively, I was now certain that this one God encompassed not only all the good but also all the evil in the Universe.

In spite of these polarities within God, I am a monotheist. I affirm the unity and the divinity of the Universe, God, the Universe-God. In 1987, I journaled, "The terrible battle between good and evil—this cosmic struggle between the two parts of the one God—is astonishing! I am living in the middle of this divine conflict."

I am no longer an innocent man or an evil man. Rather, I am a man seeking to integrate both the good and the evil, the light and the dark, within himself. My "gray self" is a mixture of the white and black aspects of myself. As Jung stated, "I don't aspire to be a good man. I aspire to be a whole man." Similar to Jung, I am a man who seeks to become conscious of his inner darkness. Therefore, my self-identity is that of a gray man seeking wholeness: the integration of his good and evil parts.

The birth of my "gray self" is one aspect of the birth of God in my soul. This gray God is neither good nor evil, but both. This good and evil God is a new God, an unorthodox God. In my quest for *what I am*, this is the God I found within my soul.

My Androgynous Self: Masculine and Feminine

While sculpting my heart, the materialization of the sacred vagina in the clay was my invitation into the androgynous Self. And with the arrival of a *Woman-with-No-Head* in my dream, the movement into my feminine soul was confirmed. With these two experiences, I was beginning to encounter the inner feminine: the bodily sensation of a vagina in my heart, and the feeling of this dream woman's presence within my psyche.

While still married to my first wife, I saw myself as the more feminine of the two of us. One day, enacting my feminine side, I was alone and stood naked in front of a mirror in our bedroom. Playfully exploring my body, I tucked my penis and testicles back between my legs, so only a triangle of pubic hair was visible in the mirror. I was pretending to be a woman. Perhaps this was a rehearsal for my midlife feeling of having a woman inside my body after our final separation.

A decade after the breakup of my marriage—while quietly standing in the bedroom of my home one day—unexpectedly, I felt a profound feminine presence inhabiting my entire body. I experienced an astonishing softness and warmth. I later journaled, "I feel a woman inside me, who is not I." Was this my feminine soul, which previously had been projected onto Diana five years earlier? Yes, that feminine essence was now residing within me.

In the following years, I sought to fathom what it meant to consciously evolve and embody my feminine side. No longer primarily dependent on a woman, I began to assimilate the inner feminine into my conscious identity as a man. In this process, I was becoming more dependent upon my soul: dependent upon the woman within me.

———————•♥•———————

But how could my masculine ego-identity partner with this interior woman in a healthy, balanced fashion? My ego did not create the "sacred vagina" in the clay or invent the *Woman-with-No-Head* in my dream. These were spontaneous occurrences: two gifts from the Unseen Presence within me. Having experienced these two images, much of the split between my masculine consciousness and the inner feminine was healed. As I increasingly accepted and integrated additional feminine aspects of my soul into my consciousness, my feminine side became a more conscious part of me.

With the arrival of the inner feminine, I was becoming a more androgynous person. I was still a man (*andros*). Yet I was also assimilating the interior woman (*gyne*) into who I was becoming. In effect, my masculine ego was intimately mating with my feminine soul. An inner marriage of the masculine and feminine was transpiring within me. Consequently, my soul and I—this interior couple—would gradually give birth to a new self-identity: my androgynous self.

As I consciously integrated the inner feminine, I did *not* allow my masculine ego-strength to be dissolved into the inner feminine. Now, that vagina into my soul was carried by a man, who had not only a penis but also a spine. Without giving up my manhood, I became more receptive to and dependent upon the woman within. An internal interdependence evolved: my masculine ability for maintaining a strong and separate identity was becoming integrated with my feminine capacity for vulnerability and intimacy.

———•♥•———

As I assimilated the inner feminine into my identity, I was required to give preferential treatment to my intuitive, feeling heart, thereby sacrificing the predominance of my factual, thinking head. With the emergence of a more feminine heart at midlife, I felt more alive, energetically engaged and personally present. In contrast, during the first half of my life, my analytic, masculine ego had caused me to feel emotionally dead at times, and interpersonally rather distant.

Integrating the feminine into my consciousness also meant acknowledging that my masculine ego understood very little, in contrast to the mysterious, divine feminine within me. At midlife, I was opening myself to being influenced by this *new woman* in my life. Much of my ego's pride and control had to be relinquished. I opened myself to taking direction from the inner feminine: guidance from my soul in the form of feelings, intuition, imagination, dreams, and a wisdom infinitely superior to my ego.

———•♥•———

With the sacrifice of some of my masculine identity, my feminine soul could then flourish. With the blossoming of the inner feminine, my tears flowed more readily—whether tears of sorrow or gratitude. Being initiated into the inner feminine through a baptism of tears was a purifying process, whereby some of my excessive masculinity was washed away.

A greater inclination toward warmth and tenderness evolved within me. Affection and kindness became more important to me than my instinctual and intellectual pursuits. And instead of being so focused on the obligations of my job, I wanted to hold babies, play with small children, pet dogs and cats, and hike in the mountains or walk on the beach. These activities became increasingly more satisfying and nourishing for me.

Uncovering my gentler, feminine side has enriched my life beyond measure. My hard, masculine ego desperately needed the presence of my softer, feminine soul. Consequently, I now feel more balanced, and therefore more whole. As a man seeking wholeness and integrity, I assimilated my feminine soul into who I am, which thereby becomes a life-enhancing part of me. As Goethe wrote, "The Eternal Feminine shows us the way [home]." Yes, The Eternal Feminine was showing me the way home, back into my feminine soul, which was now becoming a more substantial part of *what I am.*

The birth of my "androgynous self" is another aspect of the birth of God in my soul. This androgynous God is neither male nor female, but both. This masculine and feminine God is a different God, a gender-balanced God. In my quest for *what I am*, this is the God I found within my soul.

My Embodied Self: The Marriage of Matter and Spirit

Even though I was brought up in a traditional Christian home, I had a sense that the spiritual and the material realms were intimately related. And God "formed man [human beings] from the dust of the earth and blew the breath of life into his nostrils, and man became a living soul" (Genesis 2:7). In creating humankind, God breathed his spirit into matter.

Furthermore, in the story of the incarnation of God's Son "in the flesh," I was taught that God's son was not only fully spirit but also fully flesh. The divine spirit had incarnated into a material body. As stated in the New Testament (John 1:14), when speaking about Christ, "The Word [spirit] became flesh [Jesus] and made his dwelling among us."

With the ideas of the creation of man from "dust" and the Word becoming incarnate "in the flesh," I grew up with an awareness that spirit and matter were deeply intertwined.

Then at midlife, when I experienced Cara's vagina as "sacred," the sexual and the spiritual co-mingled within me and became inseparable for me. The deity's benevolent spirit had incarnated into Cara's material body. In her loving heart and vagina, I had experienced the love of God.

Additionally, while sculpting my heart in clay, my wound was transfigured into a vagina. The Unseen Presence, spirit, had expressed itself into matter. The deity's transcendent spirit healed my heart-wound into a sacred vaginal opening into my soul. In the clay, spirit manifested itself into matter.

Furthermore, with my mantra of drawing crosses with a vagina in the center, matter and spirit became better integrated within me. I knew my wounded heart belonged at the center of the cross. But then, this heart-wound was healed into a vagina. The wound and the vagina were in the same place, in my heart. So, I was certain that the vagina also belonged at the center of the cross. By drawing these crosses with vaginas in the center, a marriage of the material and the spiritual trans-pired within me.

Could it be that spirit is material, and matter is divine? Yes, spirit and matter are now yoked within me and have become indiscernible. With the co-mingling of the material and the spiritual in my life, I no longer participate in two conflicting realities. Instead, I experience a unified whole: my embodied, divine self.

The marriage of spirit and matter is another aspect of the birth of God in my soul. This embodied God is neither spirit nor matter, but both. This spiritual and material God is an embodied God, a God whose spirit is rooted in matter. In my quest for *what I am*, this is the God I found within my soul.

I was created a whole Self in the image of God. But as a child, I was unfortunately taught that God is all-perfect, a patriarch and pure spirit. As a consequence, I separated myself from evil, the feminine and matter. I forgot the totality and wholeness of what God is—the wholeness of *what I am*.

At midlife, through the integration of more of the evil, the fem-inine and the material aspects of the Self into my consciousness, I became a gray, androgynous and embodied self. I had re-membered, brought back together, the forgotten aspects of the Self and assimilated these into what I was becoming. Consequently, I am more grounded in the wholeness of the Self. This is the reconstituted self upon which I depend.

Becoming conscious of *what I am* is the essence of my return home. This is a return to the wholeness within myself, my final home. Indeed, this is a reunion with the Self, a movement toward the image of God (*imago dei*) which was within me from the beginning.

Through my midlife determination to become conscious of *what I am*, I have been restored more into the original image of God. Now, I experience a more conscious union—indeed a reunion—with the wholeness of God/the Self.

As T. S. Eliot wrote, "And the end of all our exploring will be to arrive where we started and know the place for the first time." As an infant, *unconscious wholeness* with the Self/God was present. And now, I have returned to a more *conscious wholeness* with the Self/God. I have become conscious of where I "started and know the place for the first time."

The Pendulum

Throughout my life, I have been caught between not only the good and the evil within myself but also between the masculine and the feminine. And I have found myself entangled in numerous other polarities. With each polarity, I have identified with one side of the duality—which is always in *apparent* opposition to the other—at the expense of its opposite.

Yet over time, opposites begin to act upon and mutually transform each other. As Heraclitus wrote, "Cold things warm up, hot things cool down." With the passage of time, every natural system has a tendency to seek equilibrium. So also, the psyche seeks to bring polar extremes into balance in the middle: to integrate opposites into a more harmonious self-identity.

Inwardly like a pendulum, I have vacillated between many pairs of opposites. Over time, my feelings and attitudes swing back and forth. Whenever I consciously align myself with one side of a pair of opposites, I know eventually I will be drawn across the center of the

Self toward the other pole. I know that the Self—the wholeness of the Self—is the center of gravity across which this pendulum swings.

I have come to trust that both sides of all polarities are true and have value, even evil, and of course, the good. To be faithful to my soul and the Self, I must embrace both sides of all opposites, no matter what they may be.

For example, as a young man, and even to this day, I seek the balance between selflessness and selfishness. How can I simultaneously be concerned for another person, but also attend to my needs and desires? I do not want to be too sacrificial nor too self-centered. So, in relationships, I swing between these two opposite ways of relating to others. Even though this remains a challenge for me, I am now more able to experience both sides of this polarity simultaneously: concern for another, while taking care of myself.

Or after an exceptionally good day, I often experience a darker day. But without fail, I can always depend on the pendulum swinging back toward another brighter day. In this manner, I have access to both the positive and negative sides of this interior polarity. Or I experience joy one day, yet sorrow on another.

To the extent that I receive into my consciousness both aspects of any polarity, I feel more grounded. When a pair of opposites become better integrated within me, I become a more balanced and whole person. This gives me a sense of permanence: a self that I can depend upon.

Having traveled through midlife, I find that the pendulum swings less broadly for me with most polarities. I no longer have such extreme ups and downs as I did during the first half of my life. And I do most things in moderation; I seek the "middle way." As a consequence, I now live more constantly in a state of contentment.

THE BIRTH OF GOD IN MY SOUL

Individuation Toward Wholeness

From the sacred vagina, I was reborn; tiny hands had reached out from my clay heart. This was the symbolic commencement of my spiritual rebirth: a divine child was born into my consciousness. Indeed, this was the beginning of the birth of God in my soul. Nevertheless, this child would become both good and evil, masculine and feminine, and spiritual and material. As I became more of *what I am*, a very different self-identity was slowly being birthed within me.

In the process of individuation, I am perpetually being reborn, not just "born again" once. With each defeat and rebirth of my ego-identity, I have incarnated more of God's complexity into my consciousness. Now, I am more of *what I am*: a mixture of good and evil, masculine and feminine, and spirit and matter. The incarnation of more aspects of the Self into my consciousness has radically changed who I am: has fundamentally altered my self-identity.

The Internal Virgin

In the Christian myth, Mary is the woman who births God's son. She is a virgin: "one unto herself." She conceives a child without the physical participation of a man. Instead, the Holy Spirit, a masculine principle, inseminates her. Hence, Mary "was found with child of the Holy Spirit" (Matthew 1:18).

As a result of studying the story of the Virgin Mary as an internal, symbolic process, I now regard the Virgin as a symbol for the soul. Therefore, when I made that incision into my clay heart, I understood this to be my masculine spirit penetrating into my virgin soul. Through such intimacy between my ego-consciousness and my soul, I inseminated the virgin within me. Consequently, a conception took place within the womb of my soul.

Then, from this virgin's womb, God was "born again" into my consciousness, as those tiny hands reached out of the clay vagina. Or as the Christian mystic and poet Angelus Silesius describes when referring to himself, "I must be the Virgin and give birth to God," the Son of God. And, "If you hope to give birth to God on earth, remember: God is not external. Conception takes place in the heart, the womb of the Eternal."

With the penetrating spirit of my consciousness, a masculine principle, I had fertilized "the womb of the Eternal": impregnated my virgin soul. Increasing intimacy between my ego-consciousness and my soul has resulted in numerous conceptions within my heart. As a consequence, from my frequently pregnant "virgin" soul, tiny fragments of the complexities of the Self/God are continually being born into my consciousness.

In the Christian story, the birth of the Son of God is the supreme fruit of the Virgin Mary's womb. Symbolically stated, the Self is born from Anima's womb as her consummate fruit. Indeed, "Hail Mary [Anima], full of Grace . . . Blessed art thou among women and blessed is the fruit of thy womb [the Self]" (Luke 1:42). What a prayerful reverencing of this interior virgin, Anima, and her blessed progeny, the Self. The Self is the greatest of "the fruits of the feminine": the transcendent fruit of the Self, born from the infinite womb of God.

The Birth of God in My Soul

When I penned my Sacred Vagina Prayer stating God was "born again into the world," I was *not* aware that the German theologian and mystic Meister Eckhart (1260–1328) had written about "the birth of God in the soul." But then, four years after writing my prayer, I learned about Eckhart's notion of God being born within the soul. His idea of "the birth of God in the soul" seemed to describe my experience of God being "born again into the world" out of my soul into my consciousness.

Seven centuries before me, Eckhart asks, "What good is it to me that Mary gave birth to the Son of God fourteen hundred years ago, and I do not *also* give birth to the Son of God in my time and in my culture." Eckhart writes, "We are all meant to be mothers [virgins like Mary] of God. God is always needing to be born." Indeed, God is seeking to incarnate into human consciousness.

Four centuries later, Angelus Silesius (1624–1677) elaborated upon Eckhart's notion: "If in your heart you make a manger [a womb] for his birth, then God will once again become a child on earth."

Then, two centuries after Silesius, Jung (1875–1961) appropriated Eckhart's notion of "the birth of God in the soul" to describe his own idea of the process of individuation: the birth of the Self into consciousness. As Jung wrote metaphorically, "The individual ego is the stable in which the Christ-child [the Self] is born." Out of the soul, God/the Self is born into the stable of the ego; God incarnates into ego-consciousness.

However, Eckhart's and Silesius's notions of God were quite different from Jung's radical idea that God/the Self also contains evil and the feminine. Jung remarked, the Self "might equally be called the

'God within us.'" For Jung, the "God within us" (the Self) is not only good, masculine and spiritual, but also evil, feminine and material.

When I first read Jung's idea of the ego being the stable into which the Self is born, I was overcome with emotion. Instantly, I yearned for my ego to be one of those humble stables into which the Self, the Christ-child, could be born. Over the three decades since sculpting the sacred vagina, additional, tiny fragments of the Self have continued to incarnate into the stable of my ego-consciousness.

In the never-ending process of individuation, I constantly seek to open myself to the birth of God in my soul, by increasingly becoming more conscious of disclosures from my soul and the Self. Through my efforts to be more conscious of these revelations, the deity is persistently seeking to re-create me into a more whole person. With the birth of God in my soul, God is incarnating more of Its infinite complexity—including evil, the feminine and the material—into my consciousness. This is the God/the Self that is being born within me.

By repeatedly experiencing the birth of God/the Self into my consciousness, I am becoming one of the sons of God. And more broadly, through more than seven billion sons and daughters of God around the world, the Self is seeking to be born into the consciousness of each and every individual. With a growing consciousness, we can each individuate and become a son or a daughter of God. Without a doubt, we are the children of the same Self/God.

Furthermore, we are all the children of the same Creator-God, children of the one and only Creator. No matter by what name you call God, or what creation story you believe—including the theory of evolution—there is only one Creator. In fact, the Universe has a single Creator, not many creators, even though the one Creator is called by many different names.

Be Whole: Be Who I Am!

Instead of identifying as a member of the "Christian flock," I have now become an undaunted "trailblazer" into the interior wilderness in my quest for wholeness. I journey toward the wholeness of Self, which I was meant to become. As Nietzsche wrote, "You should become what you are." Rather than sheepishly wandering through life, I must have the courage to be *what I am*. I shall not fear judgment for any part whatsoever of the Self that I become, for this is who I was created to be.

For Jung, individuation means becoming a distinct individual by integrating into one's consciousness any and all aspects of what one is. In part, through interactions with other people, dreams and various other events in our lives—and then with self-reflection on each—we individuate into who we are. We are called to become the unique individuals each is destined to be. Yes, we are expressions of the same Self and children of the same Creator, yet each of us is entirely unique, unlike any other.

For me, individuation means becoming conscious of a few of the infinite facets of the Self, which lie dormant within the unfathomable unconscious. In effect, individuation is a process of self-realization, whereby I become *what I am*, the individual I was meant to be. No matter what I may find within me, I must be that self. I must consciously incarnate those particular aspects of the Self of which I have become aware. Indeed, I shall "Be who I am!"

Experiencing the Mystery

During the twenty-three years I was single, I listed my religion as "Experiencing the Mystery" on my profile at several dating services. Indeed, at times I have experienced the Mystery: unity with the Infinite Mystery. This Mystery is THE ONE that is within and all around me. I have felt the mysterious Indwelling Presence moving within me; and I have sensed a mysterious presence throughout the Universe.

At the beginning of my quest for wholeness, unwittingly and filled with awe, I had asked the then-mysterious Diana in our Monterey hotel room, "Are you the one?" I felt she was "the one" with whom I would spend the rest of my life.

In retrospect, when I asked Diana that question, I realized I had actually addressed my soul. My soul was the mysterious "One" lurking between Diana and me. Then, shortly thereafter, the mysterious *Woman-with-No-Head*, my soul, visited me in a dream. So, as a result of these two experiences, I became more dependent upon "the One," more rooted in my soul.

And then while sculpting my heart in clay, I experienced "the birth of God in the soul," as the tiny hands of that divine child reached out of the clay vagina into my consciousness. From that experience, I realized that the Self was "the ONE" seeking to be born within me. Gradually, I became more dependent upon and anchored in the complexities of the Self, the ground of my being.

But ultimately, my return is to THE ONE, to the transcendent ONE beyond the Self. As Jung remarked, "Even the enlightened person remains what he is, and is never more than his own limited ego before the One [THE ONE] who dwells within him, whose form has no knowable boundaries, who encompasses him on all sides, fathomless as the abysms of the earth and vast as the sky." This is the Mystery from which I came, and this is the Infinite Mystery to which I shall return. Yes, this Mystery is my final home.

THE ONE is utterly transcendent to my tiny ego, and yet It is radically immanent within Everything. I am a small particle of THE ONE. In spite of my smallness, the Infinite Mystery is always within reach: within me and forever surrounding me. I live in the midst of this Mystery. Therefore, I am never alone.

Yes, I must "Be who I am." But then, all else is mystery. Beyond my individuated ego-identity is the Infinite Mystery. This is the mystery of the invisible and indivisible ONE, the ground of all being. This is THE ONE behind all the other "ones."

Indeed, I worship the Infinite Mystery. I totally trust THE ONE that is immanent within my soul and intrinsic to all of creation. Almost daily now, in awe of the Infinite Everything, I fall to my knees to worship THE ONE.

I understand THE ONE to be the *mysterium tremendum* described by Rudolph Otto. And THE ONE is the ineffable *I Am What I Am* that Moses encountered.

This is THE ONE that I call "God." When my ego is able to surrender to the Infinite Mystery within and around me, I can feel the presence of God. The Infinite Mystery is God: the mysterious Everything that is everywhere.

As my mother explained when I was a little boy, "God is everywhere."

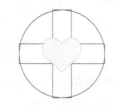

EPILOGUE

Marigrace

——◆♥◆——

To wake at dawn with a winged heart
and give thanks for another day of loving . . .

GIBRAN

Having become more rooted within my soul and the Self did not eliminate my longing for a life-companion. As an interdependent man, I still hoped to share the rest of my life with one special woman. I had journeyed into the inner feminine, but I still wanted the outer feminine, an actual woman. Yet this time I did not expect "to fall in love." Instead, I hoped to find a woman with whom I would "become in love." I knew being in the right relationship would enrich the remaining years of my life.

I was looking for "emotional intimacy" with a woman who was introspective and aspired to learn more about herself. And I was searching for a woman who had a spiritual life that was a significant part of her life. I did not care what her particular spiritual inclination might be, as long as it originated within her heart.

After twenty-three years of being single, at last I met my wife on match.com. Thankfully, in her word search of men's profiles, she put in the word "spiritual" and found me, among others. So, she sent me an email. I looked at her profile and found myself interested. We talked by phone a few times.

When I met Marigrace, I was sixty-one years old and she was six-ty. At the time, I felt extremely lost and was quite discouraged since I had not found a lasting partnership during the two previous decades. After dating for so long in search of a mate, I was afraid I might spend the rest of my life alone.

Fortunately, Marigrace and I were on the same page; we were both ready to find lifelong partners. And age-wise, we were only three months apart. Our values were similar; we were more interested in meaningful life experiences than in material things. We had common interests: a spiritual life, friends, grandchildren, our dogs, travel, vol-unteer work, and psycho-spiritual lectures, events and conferences. Finally, both of us wanted to stay in the Los Angeles area: each was "geographically desirable" for the other.

———————— •♥• ————————

On our first date, we quickly had a mutual sense that we might have found "the one" for whom we were searching. I no longer wished for a goddess. Rather, I wanted a "real" woman, with whom I might spend the rest of my life. On match.com, Marigrace's username was "Without a Mask," suggesting she might be such a real woman.

During our first date—a three-hour lunch on a rainy Saturday afternoon—we eagerly revealed who we were. Our mutual readiness for an enduring relationship was apparent, as we shared—without hesitation—some of the most intimate details of our lives, especially those of a spiritual nature. Indeed, Marigrace was "without a mask." And I, "Sam I Am" (my username), was ready to be "who I am"—my authentic self. Neither of us tried to impress; we both wanted to hon-estly disclose who we were.

Toward the end of our lunch, Marigrace exclaimed, "O my God, you exist!" She had a strong sense that I was the man for whom she was looking. Fifteen years earlier, I would have run like hell, if a woman had said something like that to me. But thank God, I had matured enough to stay and get better acquainted with her. During our courtship, I dis-covered I had happened upon an incredibly unique lady, whose multi-faceted nature would hold my attention for the rest of my life.

Earlier in our lives, we both had been seriously involved with sev-eral partners who were totally wrong for us. So, it took me six months to realize that our relationship might be the right one for me. I was slow to figure out what a wonderful match was transpiring. Yet eventually, I caught up with Marigrace and began to consider the possibility of marriage.

Two years into our relationship—in the Japanese Garden at The Huntington Botanical Gardens in San Marino, California—I proposed to Marigrace. And guess what? She said "Yes," although I had been slow to recognize that marriage to her would be an amazing adventure.

For our ceremony, we wrote separate vows. I knew my most challenging vow would be to support Marigrace's numerous "ministries and callings" since I had witnessed, and participated in, some of the many loving things she so readily does for others. Although at times I feel stretched to the limit, I frequently find myself saying, "How can I interfere with the love of God in action?" So, I do not try to change her. I honor her service to others. But in some cases, I have chosen not to participate. I do not want to be too generous and then become resentful.

In part, because we are both "givers"—Marigrace far more than me—we had the minister read something I had used with couples in counseling for many years. "In marriage, it is not more blessed to give than to receive. It is most blessed to do both in equal proportion." Our marriage would work, only if we both also knew how to be "takers": to receive from the other, and to take care of ourselves in our partnership.

After a three-year courtship, Marigrace and I married when each of us was sixty-four years old. At times, I find myself uttering the line, "I once was lost, but now am found," from "Amazing Grace." Yes, I was "found"; I was selected by her on match.com. And for that I will be eternally grateful.

———— •♥• ————

Our marriage is one of grateful abundance, radical acceptance and has become an alchemical adventure. We have a *grateful abundance* of spiritual and psychological wealth. Marigrace has a Master's degree in Spiritual Psychology from the University of Santa Monica. And I have a Master of Divinity degree from Union Theological Seminary in New York City.

Even though Marigrace sometimes refers to herself as "Hindu," she more broadly describes her spiritual orientation as "eclectic"; she borrows from all the world's spiritual traditions. More significantly, she has had many encounters throughout her life with "The More," as she calls it. She cannot and does not attempt to explain her various numinous experiences. She is entirely comfortable living in "the-not-knowing": maybe her experience comes from within, or maybe it is happening outside the confines of her body. She does not try to resolve this dilemma. She suspends judgment, always remaining receptive to "The More," wherever it may be or however it may manifest.

Before we met, Marigrace had a spiritual center in her home for five years—*The Sacred Space*—open six nights a week. Five women lived with her and helped operate this program. The public was invited to hear speakers on various spiritual topics, to experience spiritual events and rituals, and to participate in self-help groups. During this time, Marigrace had her own strikingly intense kundalini awakening.

Prior to us meeting, "Linda" had changed her birth name to Marigrace. Her heart had been broken open by another person, causing her to suffer greatly. Yet she was determined to keep her heart unshielded and available for more loving. During this extremely painful time in her life, she had several visions of the Virgin Mary. Consequently, she felt compelled to change her name to "Marigrace." Indeed, she embodies a compassionate heart, similar to the heart of the mother of Jesus. "Mary, full of grace," describes my "Marigrace."

As evident in this book, my spirituality is a hybrid of my spiritual experiences, the Christian myth and Jungian psychology. Our spiritual orientations are quite different, yet we are both curious about and appreciative of our partner's encounters with the sacred. Neither of us tries to change the other's point of view; we are respectful of each other's unique spiritual experiences, beliefs and practices. And we both seek to support the other's spiritual development, no matter how it may evolve. We have a strong sense that a spiritual dimension to our lives is vital for our marriage.

Since our spiritual orientations are complementary, we are enriched by the other's spirituality. For me, God is the Universe, more of an earth God, whereas for Marigrace, the divine is more like a sky

God, not necessarily rooted in the earth. Yet as a couple, we attend a church that does not separate God and the Universe; its belief is "God is all there is."

———•♥•———

Marigrace and I are also blessed with psychological riches, in part because Marigrace lives with an unclad heart. She is the most open-hearted person I have ever known. If she has a conflict with another person, she chants relentlessly to keep her heart open and accept this individual, no matter how difficult. And she feels things intensely; frequently, she is openly tearful for the plight of another person or the helplessness of an animal.

When I met Marigrace, I thought that my heart was open, as described in this book. However, she has modeled for me the continuing unmasking of my heart. With her, I feel free to divulge my innermost feelings, allowing my tears to flow when I verbalize the deeper movements within my soul. Or when I feel injured by her, I share my hurt feelings or disappointment, knowing that she will always lovingly receive whatever I offer.

Marigrace embraces my authentic self, no matter what that may be. After reading this book—which includes details about my earlier struggle with rage and the sexual aspects of several past relationships—she has welcomed this written disclosure of who I am.

For many years, Marigrace was involved in women's groups, including Women Within (WW) groups. This organization has E-Circles ("Empowerment Circles") around the world. A four-stage "clearing model" is used in these small groups. If one woman is having a conflict with another woman in the group, she requests a "clearing."

The woman begins by stating the "facts" she observed in the other woman's words and/or actions. After that, she states, "The story I tell myself" about the other woman, sharing her interpretation of the facts. She tells her version, or "story," about what transpired between herself and the other woman. In the third stage, she discloses her feelings in response to the other woman's words and actions. And finally, she makes a request for a behavioral change from that woman.

The first time Marigrace used this technique with me, I was surprised that I did not feel the least bit defensive. When she described what was troubling her about me as, "The story I tell myself," I knew there was room for another point of view: my story. Built into the model, every conflict allows for two different perceptions of the same event.

Or as I would tell couples in my therapy practice, "In marriage, there is no 'right' or 'wrong,' only two differing points of view." So, in our marriage, I will tell Marigrace, "I see it differently," or "I do it differently," when we have conflicting perceptions or different ways of doing things.

———— •♥• ————

Furthermore, our marriage is about the *radical acceptance* of the other. We both aspire to unconditionally love the other, as she/he is. We endeavor to love each other as imperfect human beings. And we aim to accept our partner's limitations. As the Serenity Prayer states, we seek "to accept the things I cannot change"—that is, *the other person.*

As I learned to do in my first marriage, I examine and acknowledge my part in a conflict with Marigrace by taking responsibility for my words, actions and reactions. Then, I can work "to change the things I can"—*things about myself.*

I cannot change my wife, but I can accept her. Yet I can strive to change myself. I seek to accept my wife as she is, and change myself for the better.

Our relationship is a work in progress, with playfulness along the way. We know we shall never arrive. The question is: how can we continue to grow?

———— •♥• ————

Finally, our marriage has turned out to be an *alchemical adventure*, whereby we continually experience and attempt to fathom the dynamic mixture of our unique psyches. For example, our communication styles are quite dissimilar. With "our natures," as Marigrace says, being so different, she and I miscommunicate and misunderstand each other at times. Yet through our misunderstandings, we endeavor to become more self-aware.

Exploring our different natures has indeed been a challenging adventure. We attempt to comprehend the unique blend of our two personalities. Given the complexities of the human soul, we are often confused. Yet in our conflicted interactions, we become more conscious of ourselves and aware of our partner's personality. In the process, we impact and slowly transform each other.

To better understand each other has been a continual challenge. Since we can never completely know another person, or even ourselves—even though we think we might know—this is an endless and yet worthwhile endeavor.

To remain conscious in our marriage is challenging since we will use "shorthand," not listen carefully, be on a "different page" in our minds, or make assumptions—all of which can lead to misunderstandings. A conscious marriage is a mindful marriage, wherein each partner seeks to be vigilant about what is transpiring within the relationship and within oneself. Only through the arduous task of remaining conscious of ourselves—in relationship to the other—can a soulful connection be created and maintained. In this manner, we seek to practice good marital hygiene.

What's more, in Marigrace I found an extroverted woman who counterbalances my more introverted nature. Since meeting her, my social life has expanded exponentially and now includes a large network of social—mostly spiritual—groups and spiritually oriented individuals. Be that as it may, she completely respects my need for solitude. Even though she is an extrovert, she also wants to be alone at times.

Our marriage is one of grateful abundance, radical acceptance and is truly an alchemical adventure. We have an authentic love, based on spiritual and psychological abundance and on the acceptance of the other's imperfections. And our marriage is a never-ending alchemical adventure as we forever explore the intermixing of our two personalities.

———◆———

Seven years after Marigrace and I met, I became involved in the Mankind Project (MKP), a global men's group similar to Women Within. In my "I-Group" (Integration Group) of eight men, I chose "Grateful Phoenix" as my totem animal. From the death of my first marriage, like a phoenix, I had slowly arisen from the ashes of that midlife trauma. Having passed through a homicidal rage, a suicidal impulse and a four-year celibacy, I arrived on the other side of my suffering with so much for which to be grateful.

When I told Marigrace the totem animal I had chosen, she exclaimed, "That's my animal name too!" Years earlier, as a member of an E-Circle, she had chosen the phoenix as her totem animal. In the years after the sudden death of her second husband at midlife, she had also arisen from the ashes. We are both deeply grateful for this synchronicity: two phoenixes, who found each other in our early sixties.

Like many people going through a midlife crisis, our lives had fallen apart. We both had extensive therapy, seeking to grow from our past relationships and trying to resolve our internal problems. We each had suffered consciously with the intention of understanding ourselves more deeply, resulting in maturation and rebirth for each of us. Both of us are profoundly grateful for having arisen from the ashes of our lives.

In our early sixties, searching for spiritual and psychological nourishment, a male and a female phoenix came upon each other to mate, to nest and to mutually enrich their lives: to resurrect the spirits of each other.

Marigrace is "the one" woman for the rest of my life, for whom I am so grateful. Over the last fourteen years, she has contributed enormously to the continuing evolution of my soul. With her as my wife, my individuation continues as I seek to better understand myself in relationship to her. She constantly enriches my life in unexpected ways. Indeed, Marigrace is my beloved; I have "become in love" with her, as my final love.

To return home at eventide with gratitude.
And then to sleep with a prayer for the beloved in your heart
and a song of praise upon your lips.

GIBRAN

GLOSSARY

My Use of Various Terms

Ego: The Latin word for "I." As a conscious ego, my "I" stands separate from what I observe; my ego is separate from my soul, the Self and the Universe all around me.

When referring to the ego, I use ego-identity, self, self-identity, identity, consciousness, ego-consciousness, conscious identity synonymously.

Evil: That which is a conscious or unconscious part of a person (the shadow: see Jung's terminology below) that is rejected and judged by oneself or society to be unacceptable.

God: The Infinite Mystery: a mysterious Indwelling Presence and the mystery of the surrounding Universe. This Infinite Mystery is Everywhere: immanent within my soul and intrinsic to all of creation.

In part through my dreams and various synchronicities in my life, I have come to believe that the Infinite Mystery is eternally seeking to constructively guide each and every human being, and thereby to influence humanity as a whole. Therefore, I worship the mysterious Everything: the Universe, nature, humanity, my soul and the Self.

When referring to God, I also use the words the divine, the deity, the divinity, Lord, the Creator, the Universe, the Universe-God. And for the internal aspect of God, I use the terms Unseen Presence, the Indwelling Presence, Holy Psyche.

Myth: A collective, symbolic story evolved by a people—in a particular culture and at a specific time in history—which emerges from the collective unconscious of the group.

For example, the Christian myth arose out of the life of the historical Jesus. Originating within the depths of the collective unconscious, his followers had a deeply personal and transformative experience in response to him. So, they evolved a meaningful collective story about him. Even though not entirely factual, this myth, like all myths, reveals profound spiritual truths.

Rebirth/Resurrection (used interchangeably): After the ego's symbolic death, new life—from the soul, the Self or the exterior world—can be birthed into and embodied by the ego.

Sacrifice (or Crucifixion) of the Ego: The Self demands the sacrifice of the ego whenever unconscious contents arise into one's consciousness and disrupt the ego's current idea of itself. Encountering unexpected manifestations of the Self—or challenging events in the outer world—always entails a defeat for the ego, indeed the crucifixion of the ego. But then, its previously more limiting beliefs, opinions, ideas and attitudes can be resurrected into an expanded consciousness.

Soul: That which is rooted in the body, yet is divine. I use the words heart, soul and *psyche* (Greek for soul) interchangeably. And I utilize the Latin word, *anima*, for the soul. Using Jung's terms, I also refer to the soul as the "inner feminine" or the "inner woman."

When I capitalize "Anima," I speak of my *anima*, my soul, *as if* she were a person. In effect, Anima and *anima* are used interchangeably.

The term "womb" refers to my soul: an interior womb, a virgin's womb, indeed the mysterious womb of God.

The soul is the intangible source of myths, dreams, visions, symbols, feelings and sudden inspirations, among others. We are all likely experiencing the soul when intuition is present, creativity occurs, an unexpected image or novel idea surfaces into consciousness, wisdom is given, or a feeling happens.

I have often said, "If you have a heart and a body, then you have a soul." For each person, one's internal encounter with the soul is unique. Throughout this book, I share my experiences of the soul, which offer glimpses into what the soul is for me.

Unconscious: The infinite aspects of the psyche—the soul and the Self—of which the ego is mostly unaware.

My Understanding of Jung's Terminology

Archetype: A term first used, in a psychological sense, by Carl Jung. The word describes the accumulated evolutionary predispositions/proclivities in the unconscious of all human beings, manifesting as similar patterns of experience and reflecting timeless human themes across cultures. An archetype is an invisible, autonomous agent that gives expression to itself through dreams, the images and ideas emanating from the unconscious Self, and through outer experiences. In this manner, an archetype seeks to steer the ego into a greater consciousness of the inner Self and the outer world.

Collective Unconscious: The massive storehouse of universal, human learning acquired during biological evolution, and through the evolution of the world's cultures throughout history. This information is stored within each individual, although the individual is not aware of most of what is within himself/herself. Encountering the numinous dimensions of the collective unconscious is a powerful event and always entails an involuntary emotional response.

Individuation/Incarnation: The process of continually becoming conscious of unconscious facets of the soul and the Self. Individuation is the "incarnation," the conscious embodiment, of aspects of the soul and the Self into consciousness, which is, in effect, "the birth of God [the Self] in the soul."

Persona: The social face presented to the world as a "mask" for others to see, yet which hides most of what we actually are—our unconscious shadow, etc.

Projection: The term coined by Freud, and used by Jung, to describe an involuntary response or reaction from the unconscious. Through this process, unknown aspects of oneself are attributed to—are *first* seen as a characteristic of—another person, instead of being seen as a part of oneself. The shadow, the *anima*, and other archetypes are constantly being projected onto others.

Shadow: A term coined by Jung referring to the darker, unconscious aspects of one's nature, which are hidden from oneself. The negative shadow refers to facets of ourselves that we do not want to see since we would dislike and reject these as aspects of ourselves. These are the distasteful aspects of ourselves that we have not yet accepted and integrated into the conscious personality, such as feelings of anger, rage or lust, malicious or unkind thoughts, and the like. (The positive shadow contains good qualities: the unrealized and worthwhile potentials still residing in the unconscious.)

Symbol: An image created by the unconscious and presented to consciousness as a "third," which integrates two conflicting parts of oneself—one conscious and the other unconscious—into a single image.

The Self: The central, organizing archetype within the human psyche that contains all other archetypes: for a man his *anima*, for a woman her *animus*, the shadow and a multitude of other archetypes. As such, the Self is the totality of everything within a person's psyche.

In contrast, the egoic self (small "s") is a person's incomplete, limited ego-identity, which includes tiny bits of the Self of which the ego has become conscious. The Self and the soul are mostly unconscious, unknown to the ego.

The Self is not God, but the Self is "the image of God" (the *imago dei*) within each person.

Wholeness: Wholeness encompasses pairs of opposites within the Self, even though one pole of a pair is rejected by the attitude of the conscious personality. For example, when the ego identifies with the persona and its gender, it thereby disidentifies with the shadow and the internal contra-sexual aspect of itself. However, when the shadow or the *anima/animus* becomes more conscious, then the individual moves toward a greater wholeness. These disliked/disowned facets of oneself can then be integrated into the conscious personality.

WORKS REFERENCED

Roberts Avens - *Imagination is Reality* - Thompson, Connecticut: Spring Publications, 1980.

Edward F. Edinger - *The Christian Archetype* - Toronto, Canada: Inner City Books, 1987.

Frederick Franck - *The Angelic Versus from The Book of Angelus Silesius* - Junction City, Oregon: Beacon Point Press, 1999.

Father Josef Goldbrunner - *Holiness is Wholeness* – Notre Dame, Indiana: University of Notre Dame Press, 1964.

H. Rider Haggard - *She: A History of Adventure* - New York, New York: Penguin Putnam, Inc. 2001. Originally published in 1886.

C. G. Jung:

The Collected Works of C. G. Jung - New York, New York: Princeton University Press, 1953-1979.

Answer to Job - Princeton, New Jersey: Princeton University Press, 2010. First published in 1952.

The Red Book - W. W. Norton & Company, New York, N. Y., 2009.

John Anthony McGuckin - *The Book of Mystical Chapters* - Boston, Massachusetts: Shambhala, 2002. (The Makarios quotation at the beginning of Chapter 2 is from this book.)

Gus Napier - *The Rejection-Intrusion Pattern*, Journal of Marital and Family Therapy, 1978.

Rudolph Otto - *The Idea of the Holy* - London: Oxford University Press, 1923.

FROM THE AUTHOR

In *The Sacred Vagina*, I describe the interplay between my life as a person and my professional career, as a seminary graduate and as a licensed psychotherapist. My personal story and my professional life are hopelessly intertwined.

Throughout my life, my personal and professional experiences have included psychological insights, spiritual happenings, and a mythological reinterpretation of Christian beliefs and dogmas. And, of course, I have experienced and become more conscious of some of the archetypes described by Jung, especially the shadow, the *anima* and the Self.

After college, I attended Union Theological Seminary in New York City. I wanted to have a career in teaching religion and philosophy. Both my Master of Divinity thesis and later my PhD dissertation were a part of my soul's quest. With each, I investigated subjects that were personally the most troubling for me.

In my inward search for God while in seminary, I became deeply depressed, dangerously introverted and suffered enormously. Consequently, my master's thesis was entitled "God and Evil in Human Suffering," which focused exclusively on internal, *psycho-spiritual* suffering.

While in seminary, I was in an encounter group, where I was told that I was "really screwed up." Although I had planned to be a philosophy and religion professor, a year later I decided to become a therapist. Most importantly, I began my own therapy. In the course of my life, I have had twelve years of therapy, including a three-year Jungian analysis at midlife.

After graduating from seminary—in formal preparation for my career as a therapist—I attended the California Family Study Center for an MA degree in marriage, family and child counseling.

After seminary and the MA degree, I practiced as a psychotherapist for ten years. Then, I returned to graduate school at the University of Southern California for a PhD in marriage and family counseling. In an attempt to better understand myself and my marriage, I chose a dissertation topic that was personally relevant. The title was "Self-Completion as a Factor in the Couple Personality Complementarity of a Marital Counseling Sample." The choice of a mate with complementary personality traits is usually an unconscious attempt to compensate for the deficiencies in one's personality. Yet if each partner examines their respective deficits, then each can choose to develop these areas of weakness and move toward "self-completion." Since my specialty was marriage counseling, this topic was also professionally beneficial.

Thankfully, I became a therapist, not a professor. If I had become a teacher, my soul probably would have remained untreated. As a therapist, I spent my career working from my heart, tending the hearts of my clients. While listening to the concerns of their troubled souls, I was also becoming better acquainted with and attending to my own soul.

Since retiring, I spend my time writing about the heart (soul) *and* the head (consciousness), treating and teaching through my writings on psycho-spiritual transformation.

ABOUT THE AUTHOR

Sam is a graduate of Union Theological Seminary in New York City, where he was introduced to the psychology of Carl Jung. After seminary, he received his MA degree from the California Family Study Center and later his PhD from the University of Southern California in marriage and family counseling. He practiced for forty years before retiring. His lifelong quest has been to be receptive to the possibility of internal, psycho-spiritual transformation.

In *The Sacred Vagina*, Sam frames his spiritual journey in the terminology of Jungian psychology, along with the engaging images, profound ideas, and life-giving symbols of the Christian myth. He opens himself to being radically transformed by the unconscious—by his soul and the Self. Within the fertile womb of the soul, he discovers some of the "fruits of the feminine." Sam realizes his experience has been an inward journey toward the Self, a process of self-realization—indeed "the birth of God in the soul." Ultimately, he arrives on the shore of the Infinite Mystery.

CPSIA information can be obtained
at www.ICGtesting.com
Printed in the USA
LVHW010623051020
667928LV00005B/324